The
Reference
Shelf

Representative American Speeches 1998–1999

Editors

Calvin M. Logue
Josiah Meigs Professor of Speech
University of Georgia

and

Jean DeHart
Assistant Professor of Communication Arts
Appalachian State University

The Reference Shelf
Volume 71 • Number 6

The H.W. Wilson Company
New York • Dublin
2000

The Reference Shelf

The books in this series contain reprints of articles, excerpts from books, addresses on current issues, and studies of social trends in the United States and other countries. There are six separately bound numbers in each volume, all of which are usually published in the same calendar year. Numbers one through five are each devoted to a single subject, providing background information and discussion from various points of view and concluding with a subject index and comprehensive bibliography that lists books, pamphlets, and abstracts of additional articles on the subject. The final number of each volume is a collection of recent speeches, and it contains a cumulative speaker index. Books in the series may be purchased individually or on subscription.

Visit H.W. Wilson's Web site: www.hwwilson.com

Library of Congress has cataloged this serial title as follows:

Representative American speeches. 1937 / 38–
    New York, H. W. Wilson Co.
        v. 21 cm.—The Reference Shelf
Annual
Indexes:
      Author index: 1937/38–1959/60, with 1959/60;
      1960/61–1969/70, with 1969/70; 1970/71–1979/80,
      with 1979/80; 1980/81–1989/90, 1990.
      Editors: 1937/38–1958/59, A. C. Baird.—1959/60–1969/70, L. Thonssen.—1970/71–
1979/80, W. W. Braden.—1980/81–1994/95, O. Peterson.—1995/96–, C. M. Logue and J. DeHart.
      ISSN 0197-6923 Representative American speeches.
      1. Speeches, addresses, etc., American. 2. Speeches, addresses, etc.
      I. Baird, Albert Craig, 1883–1979 ed II. Thonssen, Lester, 1904–
      III. Braden, Waldo Warder, 1911–1991 ed.
      IV. Peterson, Owen, 1924– ed. V. Logue, Calvin McLeod, 1935–
      and DeHart, Jean. eds. VI. Series.
PS668.B3   815.5082   38-27962
                                        MARC-S
Library of Congress [8503r85] rev4

Cover: Jesse Jackson

Printed in the United States of America

Contents

092004

Preface

As the world enters the new millennium, both prominent leaders and ordinary citizens of the United States are carefully examining the direction in which the country is headed. In this collection of speeches, an attempt is made to look at some of the more noteworthy public statements made about key American issues from 1998–1999. These speeches hail from a diverse assembly of individuals, and they present a sample of the questions and struggles that Americans face in the ensuing years.

The first section looks at the various ways in which democracy can be preserved in the next century and the feats that the country must overcome in order to thrive in the future. Focusing on the strong history of the nation and how its citizens must strive to return to the ideals and values held by its founders, these speeches urge a move toward a more active and inclusive America. A call for higher goals and a renewed sense of democracy in all aspects of American life is evident in these speeches and is exemplified in the words of Jesse Jackson, who predicted, "we can lift this nation to new heights if we think big enough, work hard enough, and act boldly enough."

The second section examines how the U.S. relates to other nations and highlights the steps needed to keep international policies running smoothly. In particular, these speeches explore American policy toward areas of the world that have dominated headlines in recent years, namely Bosnia, Kosovo, Iraq, and China.

In the third section, the issue of human rights is explored, including the related subject of what has become known as "hate crimes," violent actions committed against individuals on the basis of their race, ethnicity, religion, national origin, disability, or sexual orientation. As host to a diverse community of citizens, the U.S. has always faced intense debate over rights for minorities and women, and the statements and remarks in this collection probe some of the toughest questions being asked about individual rights in this country today.

For the fourth section, a more abstract topic is investigated, that of human morals. Here are three speeches that seek to scrutinize not only the current state of values in America, but also the areas of these values that need improvement if the country is to go forward as an ethically sound entity.

The fifth section looks at religious faith, another highly controversial subject in America. Specifically, the speeches present views on the Christian, Catholic, and Muslim faiths, and also provide a general analysis of spirituality. In addition, the issue of religious freedom in other countries is explored, along with the actions that the U.S. must take to ensure that such freedoms are honored internationally as well as domestically.

Finally, in section six, the matter of communication, education, and the arts in America is examined. This assemblage of speeches takes on a variety of themes, including emerging communication technology, ethics in the media, the evolution of schools, preserving the arts, and striving for excellence in education.

Special thanks to Gray Young, Beth Levy, Hilary Claggett, Denise M. Bonilla, Jacquelene Latif, Sara Yoo, and Lynn Messina for their assistance with this book.

I. Democracy at the Start of a New Millennium

America at the Millennium— A Vision for the Future[1]

Richard A. Gephardt

U. S. House Democratic Leader, 1994–; born St. Louis, MO, Jan. 31, 1941–; B.S., 1962, Northwestern University; J.D., University of Michigan, 1965; House Ways and Means Committee, 1979–1984; House Budget Committee, 1979–1984; Chairman of the House Democratic Caucus, 1984–1988; House Majority Leader, 1988–1994.

Editors' introduction: Richard Gephardt gave this address to the Chicago Council on Foreign Relations on June 1, 1999. In it, he calls for "a progressive internationalism to meet the changing world economy."

Richard Gephardt's speech: Thank you for inviting me here tonight to speak to you about my new book and my thoughts on America's role in the world as we enter the next century.

My book concentrates on what we need to do to make America a better place for the future. I believe that our democracy is imperiled as a result of the apathy and disengagement that has taken hold of the electorate, and because of the politics of personal destruction which have taken hold of the debate in our country.

The decline of civility throughout everyday life, not just in our politics, has shown me that there are fault lines in our country that need to be healed if we are to make it through yet another century. It provoked me to write a book about what we need to do to get America back on the right track— and to come here to share some of my thoughts with all of you.

We need a new citizenship—one that demands more of all of us. We must consciously foster a rebirth of civic activism and mutual tolerance and respect among all of our citizens.

Ultimately, it's up to every man and woman in the nation to sustain our democracy. We need a revival of citizenship in America to light a fire under the politicians—that is the essential prerequisite of real political change. And we need a revival in every aspect of American life—not just in our poli-

> *We must consciously foster a rebirth of civic activism and mutual tolerance and respect among all of our citizens.*

---

1. Delivered in Chicago, Illinois, on June 1, 1999. Reprinted with the permission of Richard A. Gephardt.

tics. We've made continual attempts at top-down reform, but that alone can't adequately address our challenges.

All of us must reassume the full mantle of citizenship. We must once again become active participants, supporters, reformers, and creators, not just of our government, but of all our schools, our workplaces, and our neighborhoods—institutions throughout our society. Only through the initiative and involvement of all our citizens can we create an even better place.

At the same time we try and renew democracy at home, we must actively engage with the rest of the world. Americans must engage in an increasingly interdependent world, acting as global citizens, and projecting our values.

Across the political spectrum, there is an unfortunate tendency to give foreign policy short shrift when compared to domestic priorities. Many assume that the only way we can summon the energy and the resources to address the pressing issues that face us at home is to withdraw from our participation in the world.

We must once again become active participants, supporters, reformers, and creators, not just of our government, but of all our schools, our workplaces, and our neighborhoods—institutions throughout our society.

Today, most of that clamor comes from the right, not the left. There is a strong drumbeat among many conservatives in Congress that says: America should not and cannot continue to fulfill its international obligations as it did in the past.

I don't want to spend any time tonight trying to analyze why this neo-isolationism is taking hold in the party of Presidents George Bush and Ronald Reagan. But this sudden shift away from internationalism is dangerous and must be resisted at every turn.

We have a choice. As I write in my book, we can retreat from the world, fail to engage, and follow the worst isolationist impulses. Or we can embrace the challenges of the evolving world.

I have repeatedly called for a new path—a progressive internationalism to meet the changing world economy. We need to update and reform the multilateral international institutions that were founded in the post-World War II era for a new century. While some isolationists in Congress advocate U.S. withdrawal from, or abolition of the World Trade Organization, the International Monetary Fund, the World Bank, and the United Nations, I advocate their strengthening and their reform.

I supported fast track in 1991. I pushed the World Trade Organization (WTO) implementing bill through Congress in 1994. And I fought hard last year to get $18 billion in IMF replenishment passed. I am supportive of these institutions, but think that their continuing vitality requires they must be substantially reformed to meet our new challenges. These institutions must do a better job of promoting human rights, worker rights, and sustainable development, so global living standards are enhanced and regional conflict diminished.

As all of you here tonight know, in the new global economy, we don't have much of a choice. It is critically important that we continue to engage with the world. Our own economy depends on American leadership and American values taking a prime position on the world stage.

Our future at home depends on the continued movement towards economic liberalization and democratic reform from Chile to China. Foreign policy is not an abstraction among the elites—it is something that is vitally important to everyone who participates in the American economy—from commodity traders who move billions of dollars on the floor of the Chicago Mercantile Exchange to the farmers who till millions of acres across our heartland.

The international economic system which has evolved over the last several decades is a complex and interrelated web of relationships. Each country that is part of this web affects the entire global economy. One only has to recall the contagion effect of the last year's financial crisis in Asia to understand this reality. We all know that sometimes foreign capital is as fast to leave as it is to arrive. In order to build a stable economy, developing nations need to adhere to the rule of law. We need to work harder to make sure the universal values of democracy and adherence to the rule of law take root in China, in Burma, in Indonesia. Not because we want to impose our will on these nations. But because we are meeting the deepest and most basic aspirations of all people.

Basic human rights are universal aspirations—they aren't particular to our country or Western civilization. Contrary to the theories of the Chinese leaders, human rights are universal rights. Lincoln embraced this basic belief—that the Declaration of Independence "gave liberty not alone to the people of the country, but hope to all the world, for all future time."

The blooming of democracy over the past ten years proves he was right. Just ask Nelson Mandela, Aung San Suu Kyi, or Wei Jingsheng—the yearning for freedom and democracy is not a matter of cultural imperialism—it is a matter which touches the souls of all human beings the world over.

Friday, June 4th is the tenth anniversary of the Tiananmen Square massacre. The students who perished simply hoped for a more democratic China. They wanted something that is universal—and timeless. We must not forget their basic goals, and must dedicate ourselves to furthering their cause as an eternal memorial to their sacrifice.

I believe that there is a moral obligation on every generation of Americans to fulfill the ideals of Jefferson and of Lincoln—to help propagate and nourish the growth of democracy everywhere. But even if you reject this moral argument, there is a cold argument based on self-interest which should cause everyone to embrace a bolder engagement.

Lincoln embraced this basic belief— that the Declaration of Independence "gave liberty not alone to the people of the country, but hope to all the world, for all future time."

As the Asian economic crisis has pointed out, booming economies can quickly collapse into smoldering rubble. We need transparency and a strong legal system in these developing market economies, not only so their people can be treated with the respect they deserve as their birthright, but also for a much more fundamental reason—to ensure the stability of this integrated world economy.

These developing economies need to be founded on both capitalism and democracy. Capitalism and authoritarianism just don't mix in the long run. We just can't afford to have countries become part of a world financial and trade system unless we get assurances that they will root out corruption and move towards establishing a strong and independent legal system that guarantees individual rights.

A government that is willing to ignore individual rights will ignore property and commercial rights when it serves its purposes. They go hand in hand and point out why the need to bring developing nations into international norms on human rights will strengthen the hand of American businesses that want to profit from the incredible opportunity that exists in these growing markets.

Capitalism and authoritarianism just don't mix in the long run.

A government that does not respect legal rights of individuals—to be free from arbitrary detention—or the right to peaceably assemble—or to practice one's religion freely—generally has the same attitude towards property rights. International commerce can only be truly stable and mutually beneficial when the legal system of each participant is based on rules—rules that are consistent and enforceable.

I strongly feel that those who argue that China needs to respect human rights and those interested in patent and intellectual property protection have a lot more in common than they might think. And that's why I believe that the fight over human rights not only benefits our ideals, but our economic interests.

For countries to become full partners in the new economy, we need to insist on strong conditions of admission. It does no one any good in the longterm to admit countries that will be more of a liability than an asset to the international economy.

So our challenge is to increase the move towards integration in the global economy while making sure that these moves are in the long-term interest of our national economy. That is why I look favorably on accession of China to the WTO. A good deal with strong enforcement can lead to significant changes in China, bringing them along the road to adherence to the rule of law.

It is in the interest of the United States for China and its $3.4 trillion economy to join the WTO. I commend the Clinton Administration for the progress made in the China WTO accession negotiations thus far. However, China must join under the right terms and our government must be poised to enforce those terms, given China's lack of full implementation of trade agreements in the past.

In addition, the review of Chinese human rights practices by the Congress must continue. We must not abandon our interest in promoting adherence to basic human and legal rights; we must continue to address the broad range of problematic issues, including worker rights, religious persecution, and repression of the Tibetan people and other minorities.

I believe the WTO accession agreement done right will earn the support of a bipartisan majority of the Congress. That agreement would be built upon the document negotiated by President Clinton and Premier Zhu in April. I view that agreement as a floor of what is necessary to promote our interests.

In 1999, the U. S. trade deficit with China may top $70 billion. That's why the accession agreement for China to the WTO must be ironclad. If the agreement allows the U. S. to continue to treat China as the nonmarket economy that it is and requires China to implement it with minimal phase-in periods, I believe that this massive trade deficit will go down. That means more American exports to China. Then U.S. jobs and our industrial base will be enhanced. The real risk to the WTO doesn't come from anti-free trade forces, or from those who advocate human rights. These issues can, I believe, be satisfactorily addressed in Congress. The greatest risk comes from those in Congress who detect a hot political issue.

The debate about the WTO is at risk of falling prey to the aftermath of the Select Committee Report released last week. Congressional Republicans have a knee-jerk need to politicize nearly everything these days. There is plenty of bipartisan blame to go around in this report—Chinese espionage took place on the watches of Presidents Carter, Reagan, Bush, and Clinton.

But the WTO shouldn't be held hostage to the desire by many Republicans in Congress to embarrass the President politically. The American economy will be around long after Bill Clinton has left office; it's up to Congress to separate this debate and do what is in the long-term interest of American investors and workers, not what's in their short-term political interest. We must debate issues on their merits and not let them become prey to what I call the politics of personal destruction, an issue I address in my book.

Unfortunately, this kind of opportunistic isolationism has reared its head far too often in this Congress. The Republicans in Congress often sound a lot more like the party of Buchanan than the party of Bush and Reagan. The recent debate on Kosovo is a good example of the dangerous direction Congress has headed.

The situation in Kosovo is one of the great humanitarian catastrophes of the late 20th century. We have all seen the pictures of families ripped out of their homes by paramilitary

We must continue to address the broad range of problematic issues, including worker rights, religious persecution, and repression of the Tibetan people and other minorities.

forces. And we have seen satellite pictures of mass graves where possibly thousands of men have been executed.

We euphemistically call what has been happening "ethnic cleansing." But make no mistake: the reality is much harsher. Systematic rape as a military weapon. Torture. Mass detention. Mass murder. And potentially attempted genocide.

It is important to remember the facts of the tragedy of Kosovo: 1.5 million ethnic Albanians forced from their homes. There have been mass executions in 67 towns and villages. 100,000 military-aged men are missing and unaccounted for. 300 villages have been burned to the ground. And refugees have been used as human shields.

Last week, the International War Crimes Tribunal in The Hague indicted Slobodan Milosevic on charges of war crimes. This puts what has gone on in Kosovo in proper relief, and dictates a continuation of strong military action against his regime. The neo-isolationists would like us to wash our hands of this problem. They want us to bury our heads in the sand and walk away from the crisis in the Balkans. They seem to forget that the United States is a member of NATO. And the crisis in the Balkans poses a direct threat to the stability of NATO countries. We do have a responsibility in Kosovo, unless one takes the position that the United States should no longer participate in a defense compact that has maintained stability in Europe for fifty years.

And allowing Slobodan Milosevic to get away, unscathed, with this kind of behavior would give carte blanche to countless leaders in various countries to engage in ethnic warfare with no fear of international repercussions. It would hearten every dangerous militarist—and give them a well-founded belief that the United States doesn't have the will to stand up against the most egregious behavior since the Khmer Rouge ravaged Cambodia.

I strongly support the President's recent decision to send more forces to the region to bolster the NATO air campaign and to prepare for an international security presence in Kosovo. These troops, I trust, will reinforce to Milosevic that we are firmly committed to ending his oppression.

In this regard, we should recall the steps taken by President Bush in 1990 as Saddam Hussein's forces invaded Kuwait and terrorized its people. Over several weeks, President Bush deployed over 500,000 U.S. troops to Saudi Arabia to deter further aggression by Iraq. While many in Congress expressed concern about these actions, we deferred to the President's judgment that such a presence was needed to demonstrate our resolve.

President Clinton's decision to strengthen our military presence in the Balkans can serve a similar purpose today. I believe it will accelerate diplomatic efforts, expedite the insertion of a peacekeeping force into Kosovo at the appropriate time, and send a signal that we are prepared to expel Serbian troops from Kosovo by force if necessary.

King Abdullah of Jordan told the Congressional leadership last month that the rogue nations of the Middle East are watching the NATO operation in Kosovo very closely. He said that, if we remain resolute and achieve our objectives, those nations will be deterred from defying the international community.

However, if we falter in Kosovo, those nations will be emboldened to cause additional problems for us and our allies. We don't have unlimited resources; we cannot always project American military force every time there is a crisis. But this is the place we must stand our ground, and stand together against Milosevic's aggression.

Republicans led the charge against a resolution supporting the air war. And last week, they attempted to add an amendment to the military funding bill that would cut off the military operation at the end of this fiscal year. But this isn't the Clinton–Gore war, as many Republicans are fond of calling it. This is a NATO military action which has the support of all 19 countries that make up this alliance. We need to show the same kind of unity at home in order to ensure that this action is finished quickly and successfully.

This crisis is about our fundamental values. It's about the future of NATO. About the stability of Europe. And about sending a message to every militaristic demagogue that they can't saber rattle their way out of domestic crises. It is time for bipartisan leadership to meet our challenges abroad. We must work together, as Democrats and Republicans, to remind the American people that our international responsibilities are in our long-term self-interest, and are in our moral interest.

We once thought that the end of the Cold War would usher in an era of peace and stability. We wouldn't trade what we have now for what we had before glasnost and the velvet revolution. But we are faced with a set of international responsibilities that are no lighter or easier to bear than our obligations during the Cold War.

The dangers of the post-Cold War world are nearly as great. We don't have a superpower to rail against to mobilize the American people; we are dealing with many countries that present serious challenges to American leadership, our military power, and our values.

Now is not the time to walk away. Now is the time to build upon our history of internationalism which has a rich tradition in the parties of Harry Truman and Ronald Reagan. Now is the time to reject a politically convenient isolationism that is based more on partisanship than principle.

President Lincoln's words over one hundred years ago still echo in our ears. America was and still is the last, best hope of mankind. We must fulfill our responsibilities as citizens of

Now is the time to build upon our history of internationalism which has a rich tradition in the parties of Harry Truman and Ronald Reagan.

our own country, and of the world, if we are to keep that idea alive for yet another century.

We can't do it as Democrats or as Republicans alone. We can only do it together, as citizens. I hope our nation can join together to make sure that our bedrock values continue to serve as a shining light for all humanity.

Law Day Remarks[2]

Stephen Breyer

Associate Justice of the United States Supreme Court, 1994–; born San Francisco, CA, 1938; graduate of Stanford University, Oxford University (Magdalen College), and Harvard Law School; law clerk to Justice Arthur J. Goldberg, 1964 term; Special Assistant to the head of the Justice Department's Antitrust Division, 1965–67; professor of law, Harvard University and Harvard Kennedy School of Government, 1967–80; Assistant Watergate Special Prosecutor, 1973; Special Counsel to the U.S. Senate Judiciary Committee, 1975; Senate Judiciary Committee's Chief Counsel, 1979–80; appointed Judge of the U.S. Court of Appeals for the First Circuit, 1980, and Chief Judge of that Circuit, 1990; Member of the Judicial Conference of the U.S., and of the U.S. Sentencing Commission; authored books and articles on administrative law and government regulation.

Editors' introduction: Associate Justice Stephen Breyer delivered this address to 400 persons attending a Law Day Luncheon sponsored by the Tulsa County Bar Association. Insisting that "our democratic system of government cannot work without the understanding, active support, and participation of millions of ordinary Americans," Breyer was troubled by citizens' "indifference towards public life." The speech was carried by C-SPAN.

Stephen Breyer's speech: In 1951 Justice William O. Douglas spoke here in Oklahoma at a Law Day Commemoration. That was seven years before President Eisenhower issued a formal proclamation officially creating a special, national Law Day. Oklahoma was ahead of its time.

Speaking soon after the Iron Curtain's descent, Justice Douglas stressed the differences between a democratic society based upon human liberty protected by law and a totalitarian society oblivious to freedom, based upon personal will. "We must," he said, "be true apostles of the democratic faith."

Today, almost a half century later, that "democratic faith" has swept the world. The Iron Curtain has lifted. Former Eastern Bloc nations, like so many others, have reached conclusions similar to those that this Nation accepted more than 200 years ago. They have embodied in written constitutions guarantees of democratic political institutions and protection for basic human liberties. They have entrusted to judges a

---

2. Delivered in Tulsa, Oklahoma, on May 4, 1999. Reprinted with the permission of The Honorable Stephen Breyer.

portion of the task of protecting those guarantees in practice. And they have tried to make their judiciaries independent, so that the judges can enforce those guarantees without fear of retaliation.

This year's Law Day theme, "Celebrate Your Freedom," reflects this near worldwide success. But the Tulsa Bar has added a cautionary note. "With freedom," it says, "comes responsibility." That cautionary note is important. I shall speak about that responsibility.

Almost five years ago I became a member of the United States Supreme Court. I confess to a few butterflies in my stomach the first year or two. Indeed, I kept thinking of a New Yorker cartoon that Andy Coats once told me about. A circus dog is about to set out, very gingerly, upon a tightrope, while a clown below unfolds a scroll. It says, "All Rex could think when he stepped out upon the high wire was that he was a very old dog and this was a brand new trick." Five years, however, has worked changes. It has made me less anxious. It has given me more experience interpreting the Constitution. It has enabled me to try to develop consistent approaches to its various parts and begin better to understand the document as an integrated whole.

One thing, however, has not changed, and it will never change. That is my sense of awe as I watch the parade of Americans who appear before our Court. They include every race, every religion, every kind of ethnic origin, every possible point of view. They present the most contentious issues imaginable. My awe reflects the fact that so many differences among so many different people, which in other nations might have been settled in the streets with fists or guns, are settled in America in courts of law. That is the national treasure that this day celebrates.

Several years ago, a Russian paratroop general, visiting our Court, asked me to explain why that is so. How do we maintain our legal system—a system that guarantees freedom under law? "What is your secret?" he asked, "A written constitution? Independent courts? Your organized Bar? The U. S. Marshals Service?" I replied that I know of no secret, but I am certain a set of written documents is not sufficient—not even documents so well written as the United States Constitution. I told him about the case of *Cooper v. Aaron*—the case in which nine Justices of the Supreme Court told the Governor of Arkansas that he had to let black school children enter a white school. I did so because I wanted to stress the fact that judges by themselves could not have enforced that decision. Rather, President Eisenhower sent federal paratroopers to Arkansas to force the governor to withdraw the state police and let the children in. The President's decision to send troops made the difference. And that Presidential decision, like the judicial decision that prompted it, grew out of two hundred years of American history, a history that

My awe reflects the fact that so many differences among so many different people, which in other nations might have been settled in the streets with fists or guns, are settled in America in courts of law.

included a civil war and racial segregation that denied to black citizens the very equality that the Constitution itself had promised.

My point was that our constitutional system consists not simply of legal writings; it consists of habits, customs, expectations, settled modes of behavior engaged in by lawyers, by judges, and by the general public, all developed gradually over time. It is that system, as actually practiced by millions of Americans, that protects our liberty. And it is our responsibility, particularly as lawyers, to preserve the traditions, habits, and expectations of behavior that underlie that system, that create the freedom we enjoy, not just on paper, but in reality. As John Marshall said, "The people made the Constitution and the people can unmake it. It is the creature of their own will, and lives only by their will."

How then do we preserve those crucial traditions? We all know some of the answers. When I speak to lawyers and judges from other nations, I often say that strong free legal institutions require judicial independence (including adequate judicial resources and insulation, through protected tenure and pay, from political influence). They require a press free to discover and expose corruption. And they require an independent bar, a bar whose lawyers will not hesitate to look a judge in the eye and say, politely of course, "Judge, I am afraid you're wrong." That is our system, and as lawyers we work to preserve it.

We do so in part by avoiding pat answers to difficult questions. I learned very early as a judge to avoid labels—they often make the hard question too easy. (Justice Cardozo once received a letter that read, "Dear Justice Cardozo: I hear you're a liberal judge. Can you give me $10?") It is not the answers to the questions that make our system special; it is the way we find those answers. And we work to preserve our traditions every time we enter a courtroom, advise a client, or open a law book.

But that is not enough. Contrary to popular myth, ours is not a system of, by, or for judges and lawyers. It is of, by, and for "We the People." Our democratic system of government cannot work without the understanding, active support, and participation of millions of ordinary Americans. And here there is cause for concern.

There is cause in the indifference towards public life revealed in the rather familiar quasi-comic statistics. It does not bother me when I read that the public is less aware of the names of Supreme Court Justices than of the Three Stooges. But it does bother me when I read that more teenagers can name the Three Stooges than can name the three branches of the federal government; or that three times as many know that "90210" stands for Beverly Hills than that "the birthplace of the Constitution" stands for Philadelphia. More worrying are the statistics that show whether the public has

Contrary to popular myth, ours is not a system of, by, or for judges and lawyers. It is of, by, and for "We the People."

confidence in Government, whether it trusts the Government all or most of the time. Those statistics, despite swings, have headed rather consistently downward since 1964—with close to 80% of the public trusting the government then, compared with about 35% today. And it bothers me when I too easily detect in the media or in conversation a cynical note, an edge that appears more often than it used to. I listen for the word "just," as in "it's just politics," or similar words that put the speaker above the fray, avoiding the need to address the merits of an argument. The merits matter. Will Rogers liked to ask, "If I don't see things your way, well, why should I?" That's a question that asks for answers, not a "put down."

I worry about indifference and cynicism because indifference means non-participation, and cynicism means a withdrawal of trust. I worry because our system of government, our way of life, depends upon both trust and participation. Let me add one more reason why this is so: the Constitution, however marvelous a document, does *not* dictate the substantive decisions that make up the content of our communal life. It is an *enabling* document. It creates democratic governmental institutions; it avoids concentration of governmental authority through separation and division of power; it provides certain guarantees of equal treatment; and it protects basic human liberty. In a word, it provides a framework for democratic decision-making. It sets a few basic limits, related to freedom and to fairness. But within that framework and those limits, it says nothing about the content of the decisions that "We the People" will produce. It creates a method for making decisions; it then leaves decision-making to the democracy that it creates. For this reason too, the Constitution not only foresees participation by the public, it demands that participation, for without trust and participation the Constitution cannot work.

What then can we lawyers do to build and to maintain the necessary trust, to encourage the necessary participation? For one thing, as I need not tell you who are here today, we can participate ourselves, for example, in the work of bar associations. Bob Meserve, a former ABA president, once told me lawyers love meetings. And Libby Hall, a professor at the Law School where I taught, told me long ago, "Go to ABA meetings." I do. And I enjoy them. Why do I enjoy professional associations, like the ABA, with its 400,000 members and 600,000 committees? Not because all those meetings are fascinating. But because it is through those meetings that we change, improve, reform the law and our legal institutions. Legal reform in America is not dictated by judges or even by legislatures. It arises, more often than not, from a consensus of the Bar and the public whom the Bar serves. Those meetings help create that consensus, by identifying where change is needed, by discussing proposals, by identifying and overcoming problems and disagreements. They are a critical element of helping the law work better for the public it is meant to serve.

We can participate broadly within our communities. Roscoe Pound described an indispensable element of our profession as "a spirit of public service." As we grow older we more fully understand that personal and professional satisfaction lie not solely in what we obtain from our profession, whether bank account or title, but, perhaps more importantly, in what that profession helps us to contribute to the lives of others. This element is embodied in your decision this week to support, for example, the Blood Bank, the Food Bank, the Cancer Society, and most importantly, to help provide legal services for those who need but cannot afford them. How can we possibly build confidence in our legal system if barriers created by costs, delay, or complexity stop millions of Americans from using it? In London's High Court on the Strand, I noticed an office called "Citizens Advice Bureau." In that office anyone can ask about a problem. He cannot expect to receive full legal advice, but he will find out where to go next, how to get started. The need to provide legal service is great; the ways of doing so are many.

Perhaps most importantly, we can teach what we have learned—about our institutions and about the need for participation—to others. There are many ways to do so. A decade ago one of my former law clerks, Michael Brown, began a volunteer organization seeking to teach inner city youth, and, by doing so, to bring them into the broader community's life. Today, that organization, City Year, has programs in ten cities. This very week, your own Association sent lawyers into the classrooms of Tulsa to lead discussions with students about the law. Students can return the visit, abolishing the rigid distinction between courtroom and classroom. We have more teaching tools today than ever before. But, to return to those troubling statistics, although almost 70% of the new, technologically adept generation can tell you that the first three letters following "http:" are "www," only half as many know that the first three words of the Constitution are "We the People." We hear a lot about a "generation gap"—perhaps we can try to close the "civics gap."

Still, the best way to teach is through example. Every time we represent a client, we argue in a courtroom, we participate in a professional or public meeting, we take on pro bono work, we set an example. And every time we fail to act in response to an opportunity, we also set an example. With every action, and inaction, we send a message to our peers, and, more importantly, to the next generation. That message can say, it should say, that standards matter, that law matters, that civic life matters, that participation matters.

May I close by quoting a memorial to Tulsa's founder, J.M. Hall: "It is our duty," says the memorial, "to pass on what

> *How can we possibly build confidence in our legal system if barriers created by costs, delay, or complexity stop millions of Americans from using it?*

we have received, not only unimpaired, but enlarged and enriched by our handling." This Law Day, we celebrate the free democratic institutions that we have inherited. More importantly, we acknowledge our responsibility to pass on those institutions, intact at the least, improved if possible.

Rebuilding the House: The Fourth Movement of the Freedom Symphony[3]

Jesse L. Jackson

President, PUSH (People United to Save Humanity), 1971–; born October 8, 1941, Greenville, SC; North Carolina Agricultural and Technical College, B.A., 1964; National Director of SCLC Operation Breadbasket, 1967; founded National Rainbow Coalition, 1986.

Editors' Introduction: In this speech, Jesse Jackson states that it is time to "embark on the fourth stage of our struggle to make this a more complete union." He introduced the speech by proclaiming, "We will expand the private finance culture and make the government work for all Americans. Dr. King said our mission was to save the soul of America. This is our sacred task that we assume boldly and completely. Whether Sierre Leone, Liberia, Ethiopia, Eritrea, Congo, Puerto Rico, Yugoslavia, China, Cuba, Mexico, Libya, Syria or Iraq, we will hold fast to the dream of an inclusive World Order."

Jesse Jackson's speech: Majority dreams; shared economic security; inclusion; leave no one behind. "And there we saw the giants, the sons of Anak, which come of the giants, and we were in our own sight as grasshoppers, and so we were in their sight." (Numbers 13:33)

Justice is not a minority vision; it is a universal goal.

Big and Little.

We can't be big and little at the same time. If we see others as giants and ourselves as grasshoppers, so others shall see us. You can't get majority answers asking minority questions. You can't get major blessings praying minor prayers. Big ideas, big dreams, big expectations, and big victories are beyond those with minority complexes. We must see ourselves through a big door, and not just through a tiny keyhole. Without vision, the Bible says, the people perish. A grasshopper's vision is limited; its horizons are small. We must see ourselves as giants, with vision enough for an entire nation, not just part of it. Justice is not a minority vision; it is a universal goal. Equal opportunity is not a minority agenda; it serves the entire society. Freedom is not a minority value; it is the unalienable right of every man and woman.

---

3. Delivered at the NAACP 90th Annual Convention on July 14, 1999. Reprinted from http://www.rainbowpush.org.

Dr. King was a black minister in the segregated South. But his vision and his courage made him a world leader. They sing "We Shall Overcome" in China, Poland, Indonesia, Africa, and Nicaragua. Dr. King is honored by freedom lovers everywhere. His words, his dream incite passion across the globe.

The Bible says we shall be transformed by the renewal of our minds. We are not grasshoppers; we are giants—if we allow ourselves to aim high enough, look far enough, work hard enough, and transform ourselves and the world. Our destiny and that of our nation are in our hands.

This week, we gather in the wake of a remarkable triumph for those who fight for justice in this land. We just witnessed the entire nation celebrate a great victory for civil rights. We see the principle of affirmative action embraced warmly in every corner of the country.

I refer, of course, to the victory of the American women in the World Cup soccer tournament. Their victory—made possible by Title IX that leveled the playing field between boys and girls, men and women—is the ultimate testament to the power of affirmative action. And America's embrace of these women is a testament to the political appeal of affirmative action. But only if we overcome our own minority complex and are big enough to see a majority answer.

We are winning.

With conservatives controlling the Congress, with conservatives proclaiming their takeover of the Democratic Party, with affirmative action still under assault, with poor mothers forced into insecure, low paying jobs without health care or day care, it is easy to lose sight of how far we have come.

Yes, we have a long way to go. But we have come so far. We are winning. We have changed the course of the nation, together. We have not won every skirmish, we've suffered setbacks. The road has been hard. But we are winning. We are on the right side of history.

As this century ends, we can look back on the past hundred years with a sense of hope and a sense of accomplishment.

America entered this century in a condition of shame. A country locked in apartheid. Only a generation away from legal slavery. Voting restricted to white males. Segregation the law of the land.

A hundred years later, much has changed. Much has changed. We leave this century with a century of freedom's progress. Our dreams were stronger than the chains of our captors. And today our dreams are the dreams of all America.

We appealed to the better angels of our natures. We were willing to struggle. We were willing to suffer in the cause of justice. And we have prevailed. Women have the right to vote. Segregation is against the law. The Voting Rights Act

We leave this century with a century of freedom's progress. Our dreams were stronger than the chains of our captors. And today our dreams are the dreams of all America.

extended the power of the ballot to those who had been locked out. Affirmative action opened locked doors, lifted glass ceilings that constricted the dreams of the vast majority.

Freedom Symphony

If I were to write a Civil Rights Symphony, a Freedom Symphony if you will, I know what the first three movements would be, for their strains already resound through the land. The first was the struggle to end slavery, the clash of ideas, of vision, of arms, the drumbeat of armies. The second was the struggle to end legal segregation, the trumpets of freedom's struggle, the drumroll of Dr. King's call to sacrifice. The third was the struggle to give all Americans the right to vote, the firm beat of marching feet.

The fourth movement remains to be written. It is the climax, the hardest one to compose, the one for which the others were the prelude. It is the movement begun by Dr. King just before his death.

This is the struggle to provide shared economic security and justice in the land. To lift up the least of these—all of underserved America, black, white, brown, and red. It is the struggle to insure a healthy start for all of God's children.

The struggle for equal access to education, for investment in the promise of the young. It is the struggle for health care for every American, of whatever color or creed. it is the struggle for shared access to capital, for greenlining the regions that have been redlined—from the Southside of Chicago to southern Ohio, from the Mississippi Delta to the Appalachian hills.

This fourth movement represents a shift in how we think and how we act. A shift from the race gap to the resource gap, the access-to-capital gap. From the horizontal struggle for equal rights to the vertical struggle for economic justice, to bridge the digital divide.

This is the unfinished movement of Dr. King. He knew that a multi-ethnic, multi-cultural campaign for economic justice had to be the final movement for the civil rights struggle.

He knew that we had to move beyond voting rights and public accommodations to build a majority movement with a majority vision, one that challenged not only our public institutions, but our private institutions—the corporate boardrooms, the suites of investment bankers, the offices of pension fund managers. We had to move from Edmund Pettis Bridge to Wall Street, LaSalle Street, and Silicon Valley.

But Dr. King's campaign was derailed. He was assassinated marching with sanitation workers organizing for a union in Memphis. Then the War on Poverty was lost to the war in Vietnam. To Watergate. And then torpedoed by Ronald Reagan. By the Cold War. By a quarter century of conservative reaction. By raging deficits. Deferred, disdained, derailed—until today.

All the changes of this century that made America great—women's right to vote, workers' right to organize, desegregation of the military, ending legal apartheid in 1954, the integration of baseball, football, basketball, and soccer, the Supreme Court—labor laws, OSHA, EEOC, OFCCPR, the 1964 Public Accommodations Bill, the 1965 Voting Rights Act, Title VII, Title IX—none of these changes came from the White House down. They came from your house and my house up.

We must not sit around waiting for some candidate to deliver us. We, the people, have the power in a democracy. We determine humane priorities; we must project division, build a coalition, and outwork forces of resistance . . . .

The Turning

The old excuses are over. The lid on our imagination has been lifted. The time has come to fulfill the legacy that Dr. King left for us.

Today we stand at an historic turning. The Cold War is over. Deficits have become surpluses. The conservative reaction is spent and in disarray. The old excuses are over. The lid on our imagination has been lifted. The time has come to fulfill the legacy that Dr. King left for us.

We have changed the room. Now it is time to change the house. And, to do that, we have to change the House, and the Senate too.

We changed the room. We unlocked locked doors. We got a seat at the table. Affirmative action helps to put the majority in the room—women, blacks, browns, Asian Americans, Native Americans. Equal treatment may still be slighted; but its value is beyond argument.

We have changed the way the majority of Americans think about race. And not just race. Civil rights, women's rights, environmental protection—these are mainstream values now, as conservatives found out to their astonishment. California Governor Pete Wilson thought he could pave a road to the White House by running against affirmative action, immigrants, unions, and choice. Instead, he earned himself a well-deserved rest and made himself irrelevant to the nation's future.

We have lifted the burden of race. Yes, racial conflict is still with us. Racism still abides. Discrimination is not erased. But we can say with confidence and some pride, we have changed the room. We have lifted the legal obstacles to race. We have lightened the burden of race. That was the necessary first step. But it is not the last step.

Now that we've changed the room, it is time to change the house. Now we have to redress the growing divide between upstairs and downstairs, between two nations—one affluent, one struggling; one locked in gated communities, one locked in no exit neighborhoods.

We must wage a campaign that encompasses the hopes of all Americans, the promise of positive change of all races and faiths. We must change the entire house.

We must shift our focus from the race gap to the resource gap, the structural gap, the divide between upstairs and downstairs. The resource gap affects the white folks who live in Appalachia just as surely as it affects the black folks who live on the west side of Chicago. They affect the white folks who struggle in rural towns of the nation's heartland as well as they impact the brown folks who live in Corpus Christi, Texas, or East Los Angeles.

We must close the North South divide.

Forty-six million Americans without health insurance, just one serious illness away from financial ruin. This is not right.

Fourteen million American children—one out of four—growing up in poverty, struggling for adequate food and shelter in the world's wealthiest nation. That is not right.

Fifteen hundred Americans die every day from cancer. We possess the resources to boost research and end cancer as we know it; yet we fail to do so. That is not right.

We are a nation of first-class jails and second-class schools. The-jail-for-profit industry is a source of shame and international disgrace. Two million Americans in jail (500,000 more than in China). Ninety percent are high-school dropouts; ninety-two percent are functionally illiterate. Three out of four who are released will be locked up again. Our public housing money goes mostly to build stadiums and prisons. Mass incarceration is not an answer. It is a social and human catastrophe.

Income and wealth inequality in America is at new records. Wages are only beginning to make up some lost ground, while CEO salaries soar through the roof. The average CEO now makes over 400 times what the average worker makes. The poorest workers do the hardest toil. They take the early bus. They work the night shift. Yet a worker on a minimum wage can work full-time year round and still not be able to lift his or her family out of poverty. That is not right.

And as severe as the gaps between rich and poor within the United States may appear, they pale in comparison to the gaps that exist between the rich and poor nations of the world.

The Challenge and the Change

How do we build and lead a multiracial coalition for change? We must focus not on that which divides us, but on that which unites us. The ties that bind us together are strong and many.

The need for comprehensive, affordable health care from birth to death, the need for investment in public education, from preschool to college, the need for good jobs, with good

We are a nation of first-class jails and second-class schools.

wages and benefits, the need to preserve a secure base for retirements, a commitment to guarantee all children a healthy start, to make equal opportunity a reality not a promise, a commitment to affordable housing and a decent environment, a renewed emphasis on building strong families, strong communities, on valuing what we are rather than what we have, a commitment to spreading capital around—as Jim Hightower says, capital is like manure: if it is all in one pile, it doesn't do much except smell. Spread it around and it makes the crops grow.

We can move forward on this common ground. We have the strength. We have the vision. We must join with our brothers and sisters in Appalachia and in Watts, on the west side of Chicago, and the south side of Texas. We must march together because it is in our common interest to do so.

We must heal the breach. It is precisely because we have changed the room that we can now renovate the house. We can challenge Wall Street on its own terms.

Rural and urban America have what investors seek: underserved markets, underutilized talent, and untapped capital. We have markets, money, talent, location, ability, will to work, and a patriot's claim.

The combined market of America's minority population consists of some 60 million people.

It commands more than $600 billion in annual earnings. Compared to the world's economies, it would rank fifteenth, ahead of Mexico, Switzerland, Indonesia, and India. It is more accessible than these, more stable, closer to airports and highways. It is growing in economic prowess every year. It is time to open up these untapped markets. To bring capital to the areas that have been redlined. And already we have made progress.

Our work on the Wall Street Project has been turned into a presidential initiative. I was proud to accompany President Clinton on his tour across America for the New Markets Initiative which people in this room did so much to define. Building a bridge from Wall Street to Appalachia, from Wall Street to the Delta, from Wall Street to Harlem—that is part of our new journey. But it is only a part.

Just as we must build the bridge to Wall Street and engage private capital, we must change our public priorities to invest public capital. In education and health care. In Head Start and child care. In affordable housing, and clean water, and clean air. We need a government that stands for labor rights and environmental protections across the world so that this new global marketplace works to lift people up, not drive them down in a race to the bottom. Private capital is necessary; public investment is vital.

The Clear Choice

And that is why we must change not just the house but the House and the Senate as well.

By virtue of our hard work, by God's grace, by luck and pluck, we have an amazing opportunity to make America better. The Cold War is gone. The deficits are gone. Now if the economy stays strong, we see surpluses of some $2.6 trillion dollars over the next decade alone. We have the opportunity to change the house, to redress the growing divide between upstairs and downstairs. But to do so, we will have to change the House and the Senate.

This week, the Republican majority in the House and Senate decided what to do with those surpluses. They passed tax bills that they proclaim represent the "defining difference" between Republicans and Democrats. House Speaker Dennis Hastert twisted arms to enforce party unity in order to pass the bill that he said defined the Republican Congress, who they are, what values they represent.

What does this House bill do? It is extraordinarily revealing for it is one of the most shameful, reckless, dishonest, and corrupt pieces of legislation that I have witnessed in my lifetime. It is shameless because it gives to the rich what it takes from the poor. According to the Treasury Department, one third of the 800 billion dollar ten-year tax cut goes to the wealthiest one percent of Americans. Less than one percent goes to the poorest 20 percent. The wealthiest people—those with incomes over $300,000 who already control about 50 percent of the nation's wealth—get a tax break when all is said and done projected at over $37,000 a year. The poorest Americans—those with incomes under $13,000, whose wages have been losing ground over the last decades—get about $15.

Where does the money come from? Republicans say from the "on-budget surplus." But virtually all of that surplus comes from enforcing harsh cuts on all federal spending, except Social Security and Medicare, which are funded separately, cuts of 20 percent or more over the next few years. But Republicans pledged to raise spending on the military, which consumes half of that. They will increase spending on roads and bridges. They won't cut spending on Veterans. That means that the rest of the government—programs in education, Head Start, early childhood health care, housing—the programs for the most vulnerable Americans—will face cuts of 40 to 50 percent. This is an utterly shameless, morally offensive proposition. Reverse Robin Hood. At a time when inequality is at record heights, Republicans propose to take from the most vulnerable to give to the wealthiest. That is not right. It is dishonest, because in fact Republicans know they won't make cuts that deep. Yes, they will cut housing, as they did this year. They are prepared to cut education and throw kids out of Head Start. But they aren't going to cut the FBI by 50 percent. They aren't going to cut the environment by 50 percent. They aren't cutting farm supports in half. What will they do? Look at what they are doing right now on next year's budget. They are grabbing every dodge and deceit, every budget trick they can find. They call the census "emergency funding." They fund the veterans hospitals out of a budget gimmick. They are considering making farm price supports an emergency appropriation. Where does that money come from? It comes from the fake "lock box" they set up to use Social Security taxes to pay down the national debt. That's right, they promise to protect Social Security and Medicare on one hand and raid it on the other. It is reckless because the tax cut goes to the wealthiest Americans when the stock market is already in a bubble and the economy is already humming. Federal Reserve Chair Alan Greenspan says a tax cut is a bad idea and makes it clear that the Fed might well raise interest rates, threatening economic growth, if the tax cut is passed. It is corrupt because, while it promises all Americans tax relief, it delivers only to the wealthy and various special interest industries. The people who pay for the Republican Party.

We must have corporate campaign finance reform to protect the integrity of the one-vote principle.

One hundred billion dollars in special interest, corporate tax breaks. A return of the three-martini lunch. Tax write-offs for big oil, insurance companies, banks, nuclear power. Not surprisingly, George Bush, the Republican heir apparent, has raked in massive contributions from the heads of the very industry associations whose interests have been served. That is not right.

Republicans call this the defining piece of legislation for their Congress. George Bush, the compassionate conservative, endorses this tax cut. Apparently his compassion is reserved for the victims of his conservatism.

I think this is an insult. An insult to our intelligence. An insult to the nation's morality. Indeed, an insult to the decency of the very wealthy people that Republicans are pandering to.

President Clinton's program is better. He'd use part of the surplus to pay down the debt. Part to protect and expand Medicare. Part as a tax break for low-income workers, giving them help in saving for retirement. And part to limit the cuts in education and children's programs. We must have corporate campaign finance reform to protect the integrity of the one-vote principle. Often, the very wealthy circumvent the vote with dollars by leveraging both parties as opposed to the democratic political order informing the economic order in the interests of shared economic security.

Too few people control too much media. With unlimited amounts of money they now seek to pressure and privatize the White House. America deserves better. But we must lift our sights. We can and should do better. We have an historic opportunity to make the investments vital to keep this economy strong—in educating the young, in research and development in the green technologies of the future, in health care for all Americans. We have the resources to lift up those who have been left out—to insure that every child gets a healthy start, that every worker gets a living wage, to insure that every working person can find affordable housing, to end hunger in this rich nation. We know what a mother would do if a family burdened with debt, with all the children contributing, suddenly found itself with enough income to pay all its bills and still have some money left over. She'd use the money wisely. She'd pay down the mortgage and put some away for a rainy day. She'd repair the roof and patch the plumbing. She'd make certain that all her children had health care. She'd insure that the youngest had enough food, and a healthy start. She'd help the older children afford a good education.

But she certainly wouldn't give the money back to her most successful children already living in luxury, even if they had contributed the most when times were hard. She would thank them for their commitment, praise them for their success and their hard work. And show them that the money was being spent wisely and prudently. Americans are better than Republicans think. They are not dying for a tax cut. The wealthy are not in revolt for more money. Most would rather spend the extra money wisely on securing Social Security, extending Medicare, investing in education and the environment. Many are moved by the plight of poor children in a wealthy land. We are a better people than Republicans think. We deserve a better leadership. The latest attempt was to get 80 percent of the budget surplus to the top 20 percent, with even more to the top one percent; they say a tax cut, but they really mean public education cut, benefits cut, exploiting foreign labor to undercut organized labor. Beware of wolves in sheep's clothing. We must be reminded to measure character by how you treat the least of these.

We must not dream small dreams. We must not settle for little changes. The struggle will be long, but we shall keep on, keeping on.

Change the House

And so we must leave this meeting with our minds made up. It is time to lift our sights. To revive our spirits. And to begin to compose the fourth movement in the Freedom Symphony, to finish Dr. King's unfinished work. We need to raise a moral challenge to this nation. We need to make an economic challenge to Wall Street. We need to march, and educate, and inspire. And we have to organize to change the House and the Senate. This is a campaign we can win, a movement we can write, fitting of the movements that came before. We must not dream small dreams. We must not settle for little changes. The struggle will be long, but we shall keep on, keeping on. We stand tall for foreign policy principles but not foreign to our values: (1) a commitment to international law; (2) human rights; (3) self-determination; (4) economic justice; and (5) one set of rules, whether China or

Cuba, Kosovo or Sierra Leone. We will stand for the right for the American dream under one big tent under which all of us find security, and none will be left in the margins. There are five basic principles: (1) equal protection under the law; (2) equal opportunity; (3) equal access; (4) fair share; and (5) a concern for the least of these. As I look over the course of this past century, I see the scars, the battles, the horrible obstacles. But most of all I see the progress wrought, the victories won. We are a better nation one hundred years later. Where hate abounded, love has abounded more. Where injustice resided, justice has raised the call. I look to the next century with unbounded hope, high expectations, great optimism. The road is long and hard. But I am willing to work and I ain't no ways tired. We can lift this nation to new heights, if we think big enough, work hard enough, and act boldly enough. This central biblical assertion continues to rain down throughout the years. Is anything too hard for God? It is a rhetorical question. Nothing is too hard for God. Tyrants, tyranny, oppressors come and go, but our God and those who have faith in Him prevail. For nothing is too hard for God. No! And there is nothing too good for the faithful. We need not test our God—just trust and acknowledge Him in all our ways. It's healing time. The biblical writer said it best. If my people, who are called by my name, will humble themselves and pray, and seek my face, and turn from their wicked ways, then God will forgive their sins and will hear from heaven, and God will heal their land.

Winning the Cultural War[4]

Charlton Heston

Actor; president of the National Rifle Association; born Evanston, IL, 1924; attended New Trier High School, Wilmette, IL.; majored in theater, Northwestern University; Staff Sergeant, Army Air Corps, World War II; co-director, Thomas Wolfe Memorial Theater, Asheville, NC; starred in nearly 60 feature films, including The Greatest Show on Earth, Planet of the Apes, Julius Caesar, *and* Peer Gynt; *numerous theater productions, including* Antony and Cleopatra; *and television productions, including* Studio One *and* The Colbys; *Academy Award for Best Actor in* Ben-Hur, *1959; authored* The Actor's Life: Journals, 1956–1976; Beijing Diary; In the Arena; *and* Charlton Heston's Hollywood.

Editors' introduction: Using a TelePrompTer, Mr. Charlton Heston spoke to some 300 students, faculty, media representatives, and community citizens in the Ames Courtroom at Harvard University's Law School Forum, an ongoing speaker program. In the speech, after reminding listeners that he "marched for civil rights with Dr. King," Heston contended that forces in society were "telling us what to think" and "what to say." Following the speech, Heston fielded questions for twenty minutes. The speech received wide coverage in the national media.

Charlton Heston's speech: I remember my son when he was five, explaining to his kindergarten class what his father did for a living.

"My Daddy," he said, "pretends to be people."

There have been quite a few of them.

Prophets from the Old and New Testaments, a couple of Christian saints, generals of various nationalities and different centuries, several kings, three American presidents, a French cardinal and two geniuses, including Michelangelo.

If you want the ceiling repainted I'll do my best.

It's just that there always seems to be a lot of different fellows up here. I'm never sure which one of them gets to talk. Right now, I guess I'm the guy.

As I pondered our visit tonight it struck me: if my Creator gave me the gift to connect you with the hearts and minds of those great men, then I want to use that same gift now to reconnect you with your own sense of liberty—your own freedom of thought—your own compass for what is right.

Dedicating the memorial at Gettysburg, Abraham Lincoln said of America, "We are now engaged in a great Civil War, testing whether this nation or any nation so conceived and

---

4. Address to The Harvard Law School Forum on February 16, 1999.

so dedicated can long endure." Those words are true again. I believe that we are again engaged in a great civil war, a cultural war that's about to hijack your birthright to think and say what lives in your heart.

I fear you no longer trust the pulsing lifeblood of liberty inside you—the stuff that made this country rise from wilderness into the miracle that it is.

Let me back up a little. About a year ago I became president of the National Rifle Association, which protects the right to keep and bear arms. I ran for office, I was elected, and now I serve. I serve as a moving target for the media who've called me everything from "ridiculous" and "duped" to a "brain-injured, senile, crazy old man." I know—I'm pretty old—but I sure Lord ain't senile.

As I have stood in the crosshairs of those who target Second Amendment freedoms, I've realized that firearms are not the only issue.

No, it's much, much bigger than that.

I've come to understand that a cultural war is raging across our land, in which, with Orwellian fervor, certain acceptable thoughts and speech are mandated.

I fear you no longer trust the pulsing life-blood of liberty inside you—the stuff that made this country rise from wilderness into the miracle that it is.

For example, I marched for civil rights with Dr. King in 1963—long before Hollywood found it fashionable. But when I told an audience last year that white pride is just as valid as black pride or red pride or anyone else's pride, they called me a racist.

I've worked with brilliantly talented homosexuals all my life. But when I told an audience that gay rights should extend no further than your rights or my rights, I was called a homophobe. I served in World War II against the Axis powers. But during a speech, when I drew an analogy between singling out innocent Jews and singling out innocent gun owners, I was called an anti-Semite.

Everyone I know knows I would never raise a closed fist against my country. But when I asked an audience to oppose this cultural persecution, I was compared to Timothy McVeigh.

From *Time* magazine to friends and colleagues, they're essentially saying, "Chuck, how dare you speak your mind like that? You are using language not authorized for public consumption!"

But I am not afraid. If Americans believed in political correctness, we'd still be King George's boys—subjects bound to the British crown.

In his book *The End of Sanity*, Martin Gross writes that "blatantly irrational behavior is rapidly being established as the norm in almost every area of human endeavor. There seem to be new customs, new rules, new anti-intellectual theories regularly foisted on us from every direction.

"Underneath, the nation is roiling. Americans know something without a name is undermining the country, turning the mind mushy when it comes to separating truth from falsehood and right from wrong. And they don't like it."

Let me read a few examples.

At Antioch College in Ohio, young men seeking intimacy with a coed must get verbal permission at each step of the process from kissing to petting to final copulation—all clearly spelled out in a printed college directive. In New Jersey, despite the death of several patients nationwide who had been infected by dentists who had concealed their AIDS, the State Commissioner announced that health providers who are HIV-positive need not—need not—tell their patients that they are infected.

At William and Mary, students tried to change the name of the school team "The Tribe" because it was supposedly insulting to local Indians, only to learn that authentic Virginia chiefs truly like the name.

In San Francisco, city fathers passed an ordinance protecting the rights of transvestites to cross-dress on the job, and for transsexuals to have separate toilet facilities while undergoing sex change surgery.

In New York City, kids who don't speak a word of Spanish have been placed in bilingual classes to learn their three R's in Spanish solely because their last names sound Hispanic.

At the University of Pennsylvania, in a state where thousands died at Gettysburg opposing slavery, the president of that college officially set up segregated dormitory space for black students.

Yeah, I know—that's out of bounds now. Dr. King said "negroes."

Jimmy Baldwin and most of us on the March said "black." But it's a no no now.

For me, hyphenated identities are awkward—particularly "Native-American." I'm a Native American, for God's sake. I also happen to be a blood-initiated brother of the Miniconjou Sioux.

On my wife's side, my grandson is a thirteenth generation Native American—with the capital letter on "American."

Finally, just last month, David Howard, head of the Washington, D.C., Office of Public Advocate, used the word "niggardly" while talking to colleagues about budgetary matters. Of course, "niggardly" means stingy or scanty. But within days Howard was forced to publicly apologize and resign.

As columnist Tony Snow wrote, "David Howard got fired because some people in public employ were morons who (a) didn't know the meaning of niggardly, (b) didn't know how to use a dictionary to discover the meaning, and (c) actually demanded that he apologize for their ignorance."

What does all this mean? It means that telling us what to think has evolved into telling us what to say, so telling us what to do can't be far behind.

Before you claim to be a champion of free thought, tell me: why did political correctness originate on America's campuses? And why do you continue to tolerate it? Why do you, who're supposed to debate ideas, surrender to their suppression?

Let's be honest. Who here thinks your professors can say what they really believe?

That scares me to death. It should scare you too, that the superstition of political correctness rules the halls of reason.

You are the best and the brightest. You, here in the fertile cradle of American academia, here in the castle of learning on the Charles River, you are the cream. But I submit that you, and your counterparts across the land, are the most socially conformed and politically silenced generation since Concord Bridge.

And as long as you validate that—and abide it—you are—by your grandfathers' standards—cowards.

Here's another example. Right now at more than one major university, Second Amendment scholars and researchers are being told to shut up about their findings or they'll lose their jobs. Why? Because their research findings would undermine big city mayors' pending lawsuits that seek to extort hundreds of millions of dollars from firearm manufacturers.

I don't care what you think about guns. But if you are not shocked at that, I am shocked at you.

Who will guard the raw material of unfettered ideas, if not you?

Democracy is dialogue! Who will defend the core value of academia, if you supposed soldiers of free thought and expression lay down your arms and plead, "Don't shoot me."

If you talk about race, it does not make you a racist.

If you see distinctions between the genders, it does not make you sexist.

If you think critically about a denomination, it does not make you anti-religion.

If you accept but don't celebrate homosexuality, it does not make you a homophobe.

Don't let America's universities continue to serve as incubators for this rampant epidemic of new McCarthyism.

But what can you do?

How can anyone prevail against such pervasive social subjugation?

The answer's been here all along. I learned it 36 years ago, on the steps of the Lincoln Memorial in Washington, D.C., standing with Dr. Martin Luther King and two hundred thousand people.

You simply—disobey.

Peaceably, yes. Respectfully, of course. Nonviolently, absolutely.

Before you claim to be a champion of free thought, tell me: why did political correctness originate on America's campuses? And why do you continue to tolerate it?

But when told how to think or what to say or how to behave, we don't. We disobey social protocol that stifles and stigmatizes personal freedom.

I learned the awesome power of disobedience from Dr. King—who learned it from Gandhi, and Thoreau, and Jesus, and every other great man who led those in the right against those with the might.

Disobedience is in our DNA. We feel innate kinship with that disobedient spirit that tossed tea into Boston Harbor, that sent Thoreau to jail, that refused to sit in the back of the bus, that protested a war in Vietnam.

In that same spirit, I am asking you to disavow cultural correctness with massive disobedience of rogue authority, social directives, and onerous laws that weaken personal freedom.

But be careful—it hurts.

Disobedience demands that you put yourself at risk.

Dr. King stood on lots of balconies.

You must be willing to be humiliated—to endure the modern day equivalent of the police dogs at Montgomery and the water cannons at Selma.

You must be willing to experience discomfort. I'm not complaining, but my own decades of social activism have left their mark on me!

Let me tell you a story.

A few years back I heard about a rapper named Ice-T who was selling a CD called "Cop Killer" celebrating ambushing and murdering police officers. It was being marketed by none other than TimeWarner, the biggest entertainment conglomerate in the world.

Police across the country were outraged. Rightfully so—at least one had been murdered. But TimeWarner was stonewalling because the CD was a cash cow for them, and the media were tiptoeing around it because the rapper was black.

I heard TimeWarner had a stockholders meeting scheduled in Beverly Hills. I owned some shares at the time, so I decided to attend.

What I did there was against the advice of my family and colleagues. I asked for the floor. To a hushed room of a thousand average American stockholders, I simply read the full lyrics of "Cop Killer"—every vicious, vulgar, instructional word.

"I GOT MY 12 GAUGE SAWED OFF I GOT MY HEADLIGHTS TURNED OFF I'M ABOUT TO BUST SOME SHOTS OFF I'M ABOUT TO DUST SOME COPS OFF . . . ." It got worse, a lot worse. I won't read the rest of it to you. But trust me, the room was a sea of shocked, frozen, blanched faces. The TimeWarner executives squirmed in their chairs and stared at their shoes. They hated me for that. Then I delivered another volley of sick lyrics brimming with racist filth,

In that same spirit, I am asking you to disavow cultural correctness with massive disobedience of rogue authority, social directives, and onerous laws that weaken personal freedom.

where Ice-T fantasizes about sodomizing two 12-year-old nieces of Al and Tipper Gore.

"SHE PUSHED HER BUTT AGAINST MY . . . "

Well, I won't do to you here what I did to them. Let's just say I left the room in echoing silence. When I read the lyrics to the waiting press corps, one of them said, "We can't print that." "I know," I replied, "but TimeWarner's selling it."

Two months later, TimeWarner terminated Ice-T's contract. I'll never be offered another film by Warner's, or get a good review from *Time* magazine. But disobedience means you must be willing to act, not just talk.

When a mugger sues his elderly victim for defending herself—jam the switchboard of the district attorney's office.

When your university is pressured to lower standards until 80 percent of the students graduate with honors—choke the halls of the board of regents.

When an 8-year-old boy pecks a girl's cheek on the playground and gets hauled into court for sexual harassment—march on that school and block its doorways.

When someone you elected is seduced by political power and betrays you—petition them, oust them, banish them.

When *Time* magazine's cover portrays millennium nuts as deranged, crazy Christians holding a cross as it did last month—boycott their magazine and the products it advertises. So that this nation may long endure, I urge you to follow in the hallowed footsteps of the great disobediences of history that freed exiles, founded religions, defeated tyrants, and, yes, in the hands of an aroused rabble in arms and a few great men, by God's grace, built this country.

If Dr. King were here, I think he would agree.

Thank you.

Nurturing Culture in America's Democracy[5]

Bill Ivey

Chair, National Endowment for the Arts, 1998– ; born Detroit, MI, 1941; holds degrees from University of Michigan and Indiana University; Director, Country Music Foundation, 1971–1998; folklorist; musician; music preservationist; former senior research fellow, Institute for Studies in American Music, Brooklyn College; former instructor, Blair School of Music, Vanderbilt University; trustee and former chair, National Academy of Recording Arts & Sciences.

Editors' introduction: Bill Ivey gave this speech to the Alliance for the Arts in New York City on October 27, 1998. In it, he states, "Like a Seurat painting, the image of America is formed by many points of color and texture."

Bill Ivey's speech: It is a real pleasure to be here in New York City with the Alliance for the Arts. I'm particularly pleased to see such a broad spectrum of the arts represented in this audience today, and to have this chance to acknowledge the key role each of you plays, not only in the arts here in New York City, but in our nation, as well.

I can think of no other city in the world that boasts the same depth and breadth of cultural offerings and artistic ferment. New York possesses the full spectrum of arts activity that makes up America's cultural sector. From the Metropolitan Opera to the community folk traditions of City Lore, the Endowment is pleased to be a part of this exciting arts scene.

In recent years, I know the attacks on the Endowment have affected the arts communities throughout the country, and certainly that is clear in New York City. As a sometime musician and the former full-time head of a non-profit organization, I've walked down the same path and know how difficult it can be.

For now, the question of our survival appears to be behind us. Our budget was approved just last week—and while we didn't get the increase we had hoped for, we will keep going after it until we get more money. Ninety-eight million just isn't enough!

I am, however, extremely gratified for strong bipartisan support that has come together behind the Endowment and the arts in this country. During our fight for survival, the NEA and its supporters developed a singleness of purpose. A steady momentum built, and now I believe we must main-

5. Remarks by Bill Ivey, Chairman, National Endowment for the Arts Alliance for the Arts, New York City, New York, October 27, 1998.

tain that momentum, harness the energy and sense of urgency, and use it to move our agenda forward.

When I first came to the Endowment, understandably, I found something of a siege mentality. For much too long, the Endowment has been in a reactive mode. But those days are gone. It is time to be proactive and positive. It's time to rebuild, refocus, and plan for the future, and today I want to talk to you about our plans to move forward.

I believe there are two immediate tasks to accomplish. First of all, we must articulate a vision for the arts in America, one that can support a deep, lasting federal commitment to artists, arts organizations, and citizen service. Second, we must connect our vision to those specific goals, strategies, and outcomes that make the best use of our resources. As we enter the new millennium, I believe passionately that Americans must have a clear understanding of the role that the arts play in maintaining our national creativity and in preserving our living cultural heritage.

As we enter the new millennium, I believe passionately that Americans must have a clear understanding of the role that the arts play in maintaining our national creativity and in preserving our living cultural heritage.

If we are so damned important, we better start to talk and act important. We must position ourselves to be judged by what we are—what we mean to our nation—rather than by what we do. And we must never again find ourselves in the situation where one controversial grant threatens to destroy the nation's primary cultural agency.

As a nation, our citizens must also understand our place in history as one of the great civilizations of the world, and our accompanying responsibility to nurture and preserve our heritage and legacy for future generations. Ultimately, our civilization will be judged by the decisions we make—or fail to make—to carry out these responsibilities.

Today, I want to enlist your support and help as I begin a dialogue with American communities about the vital role the arts play in developing and maintaining our national character, creativity, and strength, as well as their importance in our daily lives.

The Arts: Central to our Democracy

Let me begin by offering the outlines of a broad vision vivid enough to justify a significant federal commitment to our nation's creative life.

Many of you know I am a folklorist, and my perspective on life, and on the arts, is colored by my training, education, and abiding interest in folklore. As a folklorist, I see artistic expression as central to the life of both individuals and communities. I see art and life as strands of the same cloth, woven together so tightly that they are inseparable.

Folklore emerged as an academic discipline in the late 19th century. It focused initially on societies that were, back then, identified as *peasant* or *primitive*. In these communities, art was central to intellectual, social, and religious life. In studying tribes and villages, folklorists made one of their great contributions to the understanding of human behavior—that artistic activity is central to community life—and that art can be used as a window into culture.

For the folklorist, the arts present us with ways to communicate, connect, and come together. Societies carry collective memory in music, stories, customs and ceremonies, and use the arts as a vehicle to move values and traditions from generation to generation. Through stories, dance, songs, and images, we communicate our beliefs, hopes, and dreams. This cultural personality that societies craft tells the world who they are, what they believe, and how they see themselves and the world around them.

Now, the arts are especially important in a complex democracy like ours, one that offers equal participation to literally hundreds of cultural traditions. This promise of equality translates into an endless process of negotiation and accommodation—a process which, at times, threatens to tear at the very fabric of our civil society.

But the arts represent a place where our democratic notion of blending, borrowing, and sharing really works. With art, ideas can flow, guilt-free, across cultural barriers. As singer-songwriter Paul Simon wrote in a recent *New York Times* article about George Gershwin, "Music is sometimes the only benign avenue of communication between antagonists." And I believe this holds true for all art forms.

Just look at the American South—a part of the country that was home to me for twenty-five years. Even as this region served as the great testing ground of our democracy and its principles, it was simultaneously the place in which the forced accommodation of black and white traditions gave America jazz, rock and roll, blues, and country music—some of our nation's greatest contributions to world culture.

And in a different kind of cultural accommodation, opera and vaudeville begat musical theater, while American music and ballet combined to produce modern dance. In another kind of accommodation and borrowing, technology and theater gave us American film. The collision of art and technology, the blending of ethnic traditions over real and metaphorical borders: art has been the vehicle for communication, the richest metaphor of our democratic heritage.

And sometimes art *precedes* society. A black fiddler played on a recording session with a white country band in 1928—years . . . decades before the South began to integrate its civil life.

As a people, we have always had trouble coming to grips with the nature, and the importance, of our cultural life. The very concept of American art is difficult to grasp, because American art, like America itself, is not one thing. Like a Seurat painting, the image of America is formed by many points of color and texture.

And unlike some European nations, we don't claim a single national artistic culture. In America, many cultural traditions

With art, ideas can flow, guilt-free, across cultural barriers.

stand side by side in our diverse land. French historian Alexis de Tocqueville said of America that we were too fixated on the frontier, too grounded in the practical, and too suspicious of "great ideas" to ever be a nation defined by arts and letters.

But even though we don't claim a single national culture, we do possess a great national arts process, of borrowing, sharing, and of shaping entirely new art forms from the intersection of communities and ideas. If art is a window into culture, what the world sees in modern dance, musical theater, jazz, blues, and country music is the down-and-dirty work of a great democracy.

Our approach to "making art" in America draws heavily on our deepest democratic principles on which this nation was founded—tolerance, generosity, fairness, openness, opportunity, freedom of expression, and creativity. These values are embedded in the work of artists, and in America's unique arts process.

It is this very democratic artistic process of blending, borrowing, and sharing—taking from here and there, adding this to that—that makes us a creative people. We envision possibilities, embrace ideals, and embody innovation.

It's our creativity as a nation that is possibly our greatest natural resource. And because it is so valuable and so essential to our nation and our people, it must be nurtured and preserved.

It's our creativity as a nation that is possibly our greatest natural resource. And because it is so valuable and so essential to our nation and our people, it must be nurtured and preserved.

Our creativity earned the past hundred years the title "The American Century." Think of all that we have accomplished. We entered this century in horse-drawn carriages, and within sixty years put a man on the moon—and are now looking toward Mars and beyond. We entered this century with the telephone as our most sophisticated technology, and now our voices and images fly instantly around the world with the touch of a button. When we entered this century, thousands died regularly from what we now think of as curable diseases. Today, we can not only transplant human organs, but we can clone human cells.

And as an essential, although sometimes unacknowledged, backdrop to a century of political advancement and scientific progress, our nation gave the world modern dance, rock and roll, abstract expressionism—Gershwin, Leadbelly, Graham, Springsteen, and Cage. We are hands down the most prolific, most innovative nation on the face of the earth, and I believe that is due to the creativity of our people.

Life within our democratic metaphor has made us creative, and our artistic accomplishments sing the praises of our national political experiment. To retain our economic, military, and technological strength as a nation, I believe it is absolutely imperative that we nourish the creative spirit of our people.

And that mission falls squarely within the realm of the National Endowment for the Arts. No other federal agency works in that special place where heritage and tradition touch the hand, mind, and spirit of the living artist.

Now, I have been quoted as saying that the NEA should hold an importance equal to that of the Department of Defense. By that I mean that I envision a nation whose government and citizens fully recognize the importance of our creative life to our nation's future well-being and security. I envision a nation in which a commitment to our "internal" defense—a connection to heritage and creativity for all our citizens—is considered as important as America's commitment to the defense of our political borders.

So, to me, a federal role in nurturing the arts—in heritage and creativity—is not a frill, nor is it optional or secondary or something just for fun. It is an essential act of patriotism.

A Plan for Moving Forward

Now, that is the vision of how the arts work in our democratic nation and why I believe they are so important. But to be effective, the Endowment has recently translated some of these ideas into a plan of action, based on specific and measurable goals. Let me briefly tell you what those goals are:

First, we believe that the American public should have access to a wide range of arts experiences. The Endowment envisions increasing access to the arts for all Americans, everywhere. This includes metropolitan areas, small towns, and rural areas—and our senior citizens, minority communities, and people with disabilities.

We are using technology to extend our audience reach. We recently launched a new Web site to bring more arts information and cultural experiences to a broader audience.

We intend to mirror the concerns of this Administration that federal government agencies exist to serve the American people. And above all, it is the Endowment's mission to support and nurture excellence in *all* artistic traditions.

Second, we believe that artists and organizations should have numerous opportunities to create and present artistic work. And that means we must find ways to get back to the business of nurturing America's creativity by supporting individual artists.

We *can* help one segment of the arts community serve more effectively. The NEA's most recent appropriation legislation included an increase in the ceilings for our museum touring exhibition indemnification programs. We can now indemnify blockbuster exhibits—the lifeblood of so many major museums in America's biggest cities—to the level of 500 million dollars. This will help museums do their work.

Third, we believe the arts play a central role in our nation's education system and in lifelong learning for its citizens. We are committed to putting the arts back into the basic curricu-

To me, a federal role in nurturing the arts—in heritage and creativity—is not a frill, nor is it optional or secondary or something just for fun. It is an essential act of patriotism.

lum of our school systems—beginning with preschool and continuing with required courses for high school graduation—and beyond. If we are to maintain our creativity and nourish our cultural heritage, we must begin by engaging all our children in the arts.

Fourth, we believe it is imperative that our nation's cultural heritage is preserved, documented, and conveyed to future generations. As a nation, we have to decide whether we care enough to make a substantial federal commitment on behalf of our citizens to nurture and preserve our living cultural heritage. And we must begin the process of identifying and preserving our heritage today.

The Endowment has already begun to pursue partnerships with the for-profit arts community, the owners of so much of America's intangible cultural property. It is through such partnerships that music, dance, film, radio, and television will be preserved and made available to young people in the next century.

Fifth, we want to ensure that America's cultural organizations in the 21st century possess organizational strength and financial stability to realize their goals. The Arts Endowment has just embarked upon a year-long study to determine how best to deploy NEA resources to ensure the long-term health of American arts organizations. This study, when combined with the research of private foundations, will provide the NEA with a blueprint for institutional stabilization in the next century.

Sixth, we believe that the arts are central to the realization of community dreams. Not only do the arts anchor communities, grow the economy, and increase jobs—but they give communities identity, a sense of shared pride, and a way to communicate across cultures. When we invest in the arts, we are investing in people.

Working Toward a National Cultural Policy

We must accomplish these goals—and more—if the arts are to remain viable and strong for the next century. Many of you are already hard at work in these areas. And in the next year, the Endowment will be challenging America to bring more of the arts to their communities, and to connect the arts with economic development, community life, and with the well-being of our young people.

We all know that the federal government can only do so much. The real work will be carried out by leaders, like each of you, who are dedicated to ensuring the best and most vibrant arts life for your communities.

But I believe at the federal level we have to take our commitment a step further. Just as the Office of National Drug Control Policy (ONDCP) has developed a strategic plan against drugs, and the Department of Education has established Goals 2000, a strategic plan for education, we must begin to articulate a cultural policy for the arts. We must raise the level of awareness and understanding among our citizens about the importance of the arts to our country, our national creativity, and the heritage we will pass on to future generations.

We already possess a de facto policy today—the result of a centuries-long interplay of commerce, patronage, philanthropy, and government support. That policy must be gathered up, articulated, and honed for the millennium ahead. It must be:

- National and unified in theme, but community-based in execution;
- Broad in its definition of our cultural sector, including the classical traditions of Western Europe, popular art forms, and folk and community-based art;
- Linked to national policy goals in education and international affairs;
- Grounded in an authentic vision of America's diverse cultural heritage;
- Committed to excellence; and
- Dedicated to citizen service and measurable outcomes.

Conclusion

This seems like a propitious time to begin working toward developing a national cultural policy. The NEA is enjoying renewed support, and this year total state funding for the arts will likely reach an all-time high.

And the end of the century and the beginning of a new millennium gives us a reason to sum up our achievements and look to the future. If we did nothing, America's thoughts would inevitably be drawn to issues of heritage and legacy.

In brief, we have reason to be bold—much to gain with little risk. And if we are successful, we can define an ongoing role for the arts in America that will lift America's creative spirit to new heights.

II. International Initiatives

Bosnia: A True Success Story[1]

George Alfred Joulwan

Retired U.S. Army General; senior advisor, Global USA, Inc.; B.S., West Point; M.A., political science, Loyola University; Commander, 1st Infantry Division, U.S. Army, Vietnam, 1966–67; special assistant to the president, 1973–74; Director, Force Requirements, Office of the Deputy Chief of Staff for Operations and Plans, U.S. Army, Washington, D.C., 1985–86; Commander in Chief, U.S. European Command; Supreme Allied Commander, Europe; Commander for NATO-led forces in the Balkans; Silver Star; Legion of Merit; Presidential Service Badge.

Editors' introduction: General George A. Joulwan addressed 300 leading citizens at the Talus Rock Girl Scout Council's annual fund-raising event at the Sunnehanna Country Club. As the architect of NATO's Bosnia strategy, General Joulwan explained that initiative as "a new era in preventive defense."

George Alfred Joulwan's speech: What a great introduction! Thanks. And though I do not need to tell this group, you are indeed fortunate to be represented in Washington by Congressman Jack Murtha. Not only is he devoted to his district in Western Pennsylvania, but he is absolutely dedicated to the security of our nation. In my seven years as a CINC, as commander in chief of U.S. forces in both Central and South America and in Europe, Middle East and Africa, no other member of Congress was more supportive than Jack Murtha. He cares deeply about this country and he cares deeply for the young men and women who wear the uniform of our country. I want to thank him personally for his support—and on behalf of the millions of troops I was privileged to command.

Let me also say a special word about Mrs. Murtha. She, too, cares about both country and community. Her dedication to the Girl Scouts of America here in Johnstown is indicative of her concern for the youth and future leaders of our country. Thank you—for your interest, commitment, and concern. I might add that another reason I am here is that I am the father of three daughters—all three were in the Girl Scouts. And that included Girl Scout troops when we were stationed in Europe. The Girl Scout experience instilled poise, self-esteem, and character into my daughters. It was a

---

1. Talus Rock Girl Scout Council, Sunnehanna Country Club, Johnstown, PA, April 14, 1998.

wonderful foundation on which to build as one matures. All three are graduated from college—Penn State, I might add—and all three are married. And I have two granddaughters who soon also will be Girl Scouts. So it is indeed a pleasure to be here.

I only have three speeches . . . .

So I am pleased to be here with people who truly care about young children and our country. And I thank you for all you are doing. And it is in that spirit that I want to talk to you tonight. As a former Supreme Allied Commander in Europe and as a father and grandfather.

My purpose tonight is to discuss a true success story for the United States and Europe—Bosnia. Bosnia is important to the United States and to NATO and the world because it symbolizes a new era in preventive defense—that is to prevent conflict rather than to fight a war. And that concept is important to you here in Johnstown who suffered more from casualties in the Gulf War than any other district in America. Bosnia is also important because even though American leadership is crucial, Europeans are providing the bulk of the troops—to include Russia. And Bosnia is important because with success in Bosnia a new security arrangement is possible for Europe. A security arrangement for the 21st century built on democratization and free enterprise; on mutual trust and confidence, and on freedom, justice, and liberty. This is what General Marshall envisioned in the Marshall Plan of 1947. Fifty years later we have the opportunity to realize Marshall's dream. That's why we *must get it right* in Bosnia. And the main message I want to leave with you is the absolute need for *clarity* of *mission* and *purpose* by our political authorities any time we commit young American men and women in harm's way. And as we are on the verge of a new phase in Bosnia, my purpose this evening is to share with you my thoughts on the way ahead.

I will do so as one who was closely involved with the Dayton Accords and as one who was overall responsible for the NATO and military operations in Bosnia. As one who strongly believes in the importance of U.S. leadership and involvement in not only fighting and winning our nation's wars but being proactive in preventing deadly conflict. And as one who sees a genuine opportunity for peace, stability, and a better life for all the people of Bosnia. To achieve this stability we along with our NATO allies and partners have taken risks for peace in Bosnia—and continue to do so today.

It is interesting that, as we meet tonight, planners from 36 countries are meeting at my former headquarters in Mons, Belgium, to determine the force structure for the next phase. I started this process nearly three years ago and it works. Indeed, European forces will compromise nearly 80% of the new force for SFOR after June of this year. And U.S. forces

Bosnia is important to the United States and to NATO and the world because it symbolizes a new era in preventive defense—that is to prevent conflict rather than to fight a war.

will drop from 8,500 to about 6,000. But the issue that still needs to be answered is "to do what?"

When the President agreed to keep American troops in Bosnia beyond June of 1998, he did so "in principle" pending clarity on the missions to be assigned to the follow-on force. The President was right to do so. As the vanguard of NATO, U.S. troops are essential to the consolidation of the gains that have been made since Dayton and to the nurturing of peace and stability in the Balkans. It is doubtful whether the peace will hold without the presence of outside military forces. Now the President needs to assure the American people, Congress, and, more important, the troops that the mission and tasks to be performed after June are spelled out when the final decision is made to keep American forces on the ground in Bosnia. Not to do so can result in failure and unwanted casualties.

As one who had the responsibility for providing military advice on the implementation force (IFOR) and the stabilization force (SFOR) to the President as well as the 16 nations of NATO, I suggest that a comprehensive dialogue take place for the next phase of the operation. When I briefed the President and his advisers in the Oval Office in November 1995, I recommended the following conditions be met for the commitment of U.S. troops: *clarity of mission and purpose, unity of command, robust rules of engagement, and timely political decisions.* The President agreed with the comprehensive military plan based on those conditions as did the 16 nations of NATO. As a result, when the NATO-led force deployed to Bosnia in December of 1995 and the U.S. troops crossed the Sava River, we did so with great confidence and determination because the mission was clear and the troops were well trained for the tasks assigned. Despite *dire predictions*, the multinational force was successful in accomplishing all tasks assigned and without, to date, one hostile death casualty. That's 855 days! That's because we did it right. And we need to do it right in the next phase of the operation beyond June 1998.

Given the conditions mentioned above, what then should be the issues for the post-June 1998 commitment of U.S. forces to Bosnia? The key question that must be answered is the specific mission of the follow-on force. In November 1996, when the decision was made to down-size IFOR from 60,000 to an SFOR of 30,000, I had several sessions with NATO and U.S. decision-makers on the missions to be performed. To determine the size of SFOR I asked the 16 ambassadors of NATO's North Atlantic Council three questions. Do you want SFOR to hunt down and arrest indicted war criminals? Do you want SFOR to perform civil police functions? And do you want SFOR to forcibly return refugees to their homes? The answer to all three questions was no. Indeed the written political guidance of 26 November 1996 from the

Council reflected this intent of NATO's political authorities. If the answers were yes then I would have recommended additional troops and training. Those same questions need to be addressed now before a decision is made to extend the mandate beyond June. The answers to these questions must provide clear political instructions so that the senior military leadership can give the best advice to our political authorities on the force required to do the tasks assigned, the resources needed, and the risks involved. Most important, such guidance will provide the framework to *train* the force to the tasks. And it is *training* that is absolutely paramount for our forces in Bosnia—train to mission enhances mission success and minimizes casualties.

Clarity of mission is also needed because SFOR is a multinational operation. Thirty-six nations contribute forces. Over 75% of the SFOR is from nations *other than the United States*. Indeed NATO's Partnership for Peace initiative is bearing fruit in Bosnia. There is a *Russian brigade* conducting joint patrols in the American sector; I had a *Russian general* on my staff as my deputy; *Ukrainian* troops are in Mostar; and Polish soldiers work alongside those from Scandinavian countries. As a result of our success to date in Bosnia, mutual trust and confidence is being developed between former adversaries. An unprecedented number of treaties are being signed between countries that for centuries have been bitter enemies. NATO is now ready to admit three new members—Poland, Czech Republic, and Hungary. *Stability and democracy* are taking root in Eastern and Central Europe. But the path for long-term security in Europe goes through Bosnia.

> *As a result of our success to date in Bosnia, mutual trust and confidence is being developed between former adversaries.*

It is in this larger context that Bosnia is important. NATO's credibility and relevance are on the line in Bosnia. Therefore, the tasks and missions need to be understood and debated now. And we must get it right not only for the military but primarily for civilian implementation as well. Again, let me be more specific.

Under the Dayton Accords the military force provides a *secure environment* for the international police force (IPTF), the UN High Commissioner for Refugees (UNHCR), and other UN and international agencies to operate. It does so by ensuring the military and paramilitary forces of the former warring factions do not engage in hostilities, conducts over a hundred patrols a day, monitors 600 heavy-weapon storage areas, and *within capabilities* provides assistance to civil agencies. On the later task the support has been significant; sixty bridges have been built, 2,500 kilometers of road paved, four airports opened, and significant support provided to the High Representative and international organizations. Three elections held in Bosnia in the past two years were successful in large part due to IFOR and SFOR support. Another question that must be answered, therefore, is to what extent the new military force will support civilian tasks in Bosnia. The military force required to carry out those tasks is significant. While I accept the need for soldiers to provide a secure environment for civilian agencies, it is also important for civilian agencies to have a sense of urgency in meeting the goals set forth in Dayton. There were 11 annexes in the Dayton Agreement—only one applies to the military, the other 10 are the responsibility of civilian agencies. As we enter the next phase *clear milestones* should be established and met by civil agencies and organizations. An *integrated civil-military* plan must be developed for all facets of the Bosnia mission. I say this because the military can create an *absence of war*; but *only* the civilian agencies and the ethnic groups themselves can bring true peace. And one of the critical areas that needs to be addressed now is that of the police.

If the political authorities in Washington and Brussels want the new military force to assume other tasks such as internal police functions, then Washington and the North Atlantic Council need to clearly state that mission. Surely there is a requirement for a robust functioning police force in Bosnia. Crime and corruption are rampant. Custom violations are the norm. Citizens are intimidated and refugees are denied returning to their homes. But is the military force the *right* organization to do police actions? Temporarily seizing radio towers is one thing; arresting citizens and shooting rubber bullets into an unarmed mob is yet another. The President made the point in his December speech when he called for a *"self-sustaining secure environment"* in Bosnia that will allow us to remove our troops." *I agree*. Therefore, a key issue for dicussion before our troops are committed beyond June is what is the future security plan for Bosnia that will meet the President's objective?

Right now a *capability gap* exists between the heavily armed troops of SFOR and the unarmed international police task force (IPTF). In two years the IPTF has never exceeded 2,000 police from over 20 nations and funding has been very difficult to obtain. What the President needs to insist on is a more robust role for the international police and a sense of urgency in establishing a multiethnic police academy that graduates 500–800 professional police every three months. Not to do so only ensures that the military force will slide down the slippery slope and become policemen without adequate training and rules of engagement. And without a long-term security plan, the probability increases that U.S. and NATO forces will remain for a *very long time in Bosnia*. But there is an alternative—an armed international police force.

The armed international police force could come from several of our allies and partners and perform the critical policing functions until sufficient local police trained by the IPTF graduated from the police academy. France, Belgium, Italy, and Germany have highly regarded paramilitary police

Temporarily seizing radio towers is one thing; arresting citizens and shooting rubber bullets into an unarmed mob is yet another.

forces. Organized in battalions, properly armed and equipped, these paramilitary police are exactly what is needed for the next phase in Bosnia. Many of these organizations are now under the ministers of defense in their respective countries and routinely work side by side with the military. The armed international police force should come under the command and control of the military command in Bosnia and thereby preserve the principle of unity of command. An integrated staff would ensure tasks were understood and assigned to the right organization.

With an armed international police force, the capability gap between the unarmed IPTF and the heavily armed NATO armed force is filled. The international police force could operate within the secure environment of the military force and with the local police assist in crowd control, return of refugees, and other police functions. With an armed international police force in place plus a sense of urgency in graduating professional local police from an IPTF-monitored police academy, then it is possible to see an eventual end to a large military presence in Bosnia. Of course, some officials within our own government would prefer to give police tasks to our soldiers—and so would several of our allies. If that is the case—and if the President agrees—then the administration should clearly make known the police-function requirement before the decision is final to extend the force beyond June 1998. *But soldiers generally make poor policemen.* Law and order need to be *institutionalized* with the support of an armed international police force. However, if the president and the alliance want to give the military police functions then let's get the mission clear now and *not back into it after June.*

> *With an armed international police force, the capability gap between the unarmed IPTF and the heavily armed NATO armed force is filled.*

Another issue that requires discussion is the role of the follow-on force in hunting down and arresting indicted war criminals, such as Radovan Karadzic and General Mladic. Certainly these indicted war criminals need to be brought to justice before the International Tribunal at The Hague. Right now the NATO-led force is restricted in what actions it can take in actively conducting operations against those accused of brutal atrocities in this war. *Those restrictions were imposed by the 16 nations of NATO.* Indeed, Dayton places responsibility for bringing war criminals to justice, on the parties who signed the agreement—Presidents Milosevic, Tudjman and Itzebegovic. But SFOR will do all within its mandate to bring indicted war criminals to justice as was done recently in Prejidor and Vitez. However if the political authorities want the military multinational force to hunt down and arrest Karadic and Mladic then that guidance must be given in the written mandate from the North Atlantic Council, of which the United States is a leading member. Given that clarity, the military authorities will generate the force, request the resources, identify the risks, develop actionable intelligence, and when the political decision is made will execute the mission.

As I said, clearly war criminals belong before the International Tribunal in The Hague, Netherlands. And I strongly believe we need to be proactive in doing so. In fact, in November 1996 I presented a plan to the head of the International Tribunal, Judge Goldstone, and his successor Judge Arbor on how NATO could assist in apprehending indicted war criminals and stay within its mandate. The plan called a force of police or military other than SFOR, formed and trained outside Bosnia, and committed to arrest indicted war criminals to include Karadic and Mladic whenever there was actionable intelligence. SFOR would form the outer ring of protection for this apprehension force and coordinate the action. Last March we began planning and training for the first operation under this new plan. The targets were two war criminals identified in sealed indictments—that is, the war criminals did not know they were indicted and subject to apprehension.

Since the two suspected war criminals were in the British sector, the United Kingdom had the lead. We began an intensive intelligence collection effort to locate the two suspects. I spent a great deal of time coordinating with the Secretary General of NATO to ensure that clarity of mission and the political guidance were sufficient. Indeed, I briefed the president of the United States in Madrid in July. I told both that if there was any reaction by the Serbs to attack SFOR I would immediately respond with air strikes. Both agreed. The only deviation from prior guidance I made was that the military would determine the time and place for apprehension. This was to protect the troops and to improve our chances for success with minimum civilian casualties. Once we had good intelligence, the force was formed and trained in June in the UK, deployed to Bosnia on July 9, conducted its mission on July 10, and withdrew on July 11. In this encounter one of the indicted war criminals drew a pistol and fired at the British soldiers, wounding one of them. The British returned fire and killed the indicted war criminal. Thus are the hazards of conflict. If we had listened to the media and other critics who thought you could send two soldiers to a cafe where the indicted criminals were drinking coffee — tap them on the shoulder and arrest them—we would have two dead soldiers. I value our soldiers' lives to risk them so foolishly. We did it right in Prejidor. And subsequently it was done right in Vitez and just last week again in the British sector. If the political authorities want SFOR to do more in the next phase then make it clear in the written guidance. This assures political as well as military accountability. No more Somalias!

The long-range security plan the President has called for also should include the evolution and role of the militaries in Bosnia. National institutions, in addition to entity security

If the political authorities want SFOR to do more in the next phase then make it clear in the written guidance. This assures political as well as military accountability.

structures, need to be developed. A national-level Minister of Defense and joint staff and commanders should be the objective. NATO's *Partnership for Peace* (PfP) initiative could be used to encourage the development of national security institutions. The three ethnic groups have all expressed interest in joining their neighbors in the PfP program. In time, NATO and 27 partner nations could be exercising, conducting seminars, and building trust and confidence with a multiethnic military in Bosnia. With a continuing NATO PfP presence in Bosnia, the need for a large, armed NATO force could be significantly reduced over the long term. Indeed, the Partnership for Peace initiative could be used as an incentive for Sarajevo, Zagreb, and Belgrade to join the rest of Europe in accepting the basic principles of respect for international boundaries, human rights, and democratic norms. This is an effective means by which to transition to what the president called a "self-sustaining secure environment" in Bosnia.

Let me briefly summarize: it is important that the missions and the tasks for the follow-on force in Bosnia be *clear* before the final decision is made. That an armed international police force be formed to work with the NATO force and the IPTF to develop a "self-sustaining security environment in Bosnia." That clear political guidance be given on hunting down war criminals, police functions, and forcibly returning refugees. That the Partnership for Peace initiative be offered as an incentive for Sarajevo, Belgrade, and Zagreb to join their neighbors in Europe in respect for borders, human rights, and democratic principles. To provide this clarity now creates the best conditions for success in Bosnia.

Ladies and gentlemen, much has been accomplished over the past two years in NATO's first operational mission since its inception. *Optimism has replaced pessimism; hope has replaced despair for the people of Bosnia.* The United States and its partners have demonstrated their ability to respond to the new threats that confront the Euro-Atlantic community and the world. Within the framework of NATO, American political and military leadership have been instrumental in providing the resolve and resources to create the conditions for success in Bosnia. This has been done with *candor, compassion, vision, and clarity.* And our troops, along with those of 36 nations to include Russia, have performed superbly for over two years. It truly is *one team with one mission!* A new security framework for *conflict prevention* in Europe will result with the success of this multinational force. But it is important that the U.S. stay engaged—not as the world's policeman, but the world's leader.

The president is right to stay the course in Bosnia. But this important mission requires thoughtful consideration before final approval. It must be based on well considered tasks for all those who continue the tedious and potentially dangerous work of building the foundation for a lasting and truly self-sustaining peace in Bosnia.

Ladies and gentlemen, I was a 2D Lieutenant in Germany when the Berlin Wall was being built and a LTG Corps Commander in the famous Fulda Gap when it was torn down. I saw Germany reunited and Russian troops depart from Central Europe. As Supreme Commander, I witnessed NATO's transition in mission and structure to a new NATO but one built on the rock-solid foundation of the past—shared ideals and values, and mutual respect and confidence. Indeed, these are exciting times! There is unprecedented opportunity for peace, stability, and prosperity in a Europe that has seen two world wars and millions of deaths in this century. We can enter the 21st century with great hope for our children and our grandchildren. It has been my privilege to serve my country for 40 years to create this opportunity for peace and freedom. We must not fail. And with the help of patriotic citizens as we find here in Johnstown, Pennsylvania, I know we will succeed. I urge you to stay involved and interested in world affairs, to commit yourselves to make the world a safer, better place. I know you will. God bless you for your support of our troops and of our great nation. Thanks for what you're doing for the young people of Johnstown. And thank you for keeping Jack Murtha in the Congress of the United States.

On Kosovo[2]

William J. Clinton

President of the United States, 1992– ; born Hope, AR, 1946; B.S., Georgetown University, 1968; Rhodes Scholar, Oxford University, 1968–70; J.D., Yale University, 1973; professor, University of Arkansas Law School, 1973–76; Attorney General, Arkansas, 1976–77; Governor of Arkansas, 1979–81 and 1983–92.

Editors' introduction: On March 24, 1999, to stop the Federal Republic of Yugoslavia's assault upon ethnic Albanians in Kosovo, NATO launched a series of air strikes. As the conflict escalated, thousands of ethnic Albanians were driven from their homes and communities. Many were killed; others escaped to Albania, Macedonia, and adjacent countries. In the speech below, as the air attacks increased and three American soldiers were captured, President William J. Clinton addressed the families of military personnel stationed at Norfolk Naval Station. He asked for continued "determination and resolve."

William J. Clinton's speech: . . . First, I'd like to thank Secretary Cohen and General Shelton for their truly outstanding service in our administration at a difficult time. I'd like to thank Admiral Gehman, Admiral Reason, General Pace, General Keck, and the other leaders of all the forces represented here. I thank Secretary Danzig, National Security Advisor Berger, and others who came with me from the White House. Mayor Oberndorf, thank you for welcoming me to Virginia Beach. I'd like to say a special word of appreciation to the members of Congress who are here—your representatives, Congressmen Scott and Sisisky; Senator Levin, our ranking member of the Armed Services Committee; and a special thanks to my longtime friend, Senator Chuck Robb, who is one of the most courageous members of the United States Congress, and Virginia is very fortunate to be represented by him. Let me say to all of you, I came here today primarily to thank two groups of people—our men and women in uniform, and their families, for the service and sacrifice that makes America strong. I just met a few moments ago with several members of families—spouses and children of members of four different services who are deployed away from here now. They're all over here to my right. And whatever it is you would like to say to me today, I think there's a very good chance they said it. They did a very good job for you, and I'm very proud of them.

---

2. Delivered at Hampton Roads Military Community, Norfolk Naval Station in Norfolk, Virginia, on April 1, 1999, at 1:17 p.m.

I heard about the financial sacrifices and I heard about human sacrifices. I don't think that anyone could say it better than this lady over here with this beautiful baby in the red hat, with the "I miss you, Daddy" sign. I thank you. And this sign, "I love my TR sailor, support our troops."

I wanted to come here today because I want America to know that the sacrifices made by our men and women in uniform are fully mirrored by their families back home, by the opportunities that are missed to be with wives and husbands and children on birthdays and holidays, and just being there for the kids when they're needed at night and in the morning as they go off to school. They are fully felt in terms of the financial sacrifices of the family members left at home to pay the bills and see to the health care and other needs of the children.

And America should know that and should be very, very grateful to all of you. We are grateful and we think all Americans will be grateful as they know what you do.

Let me also say I had a chance to speak just before I came out here with the 510th Fighter Squadron at Aviano Air Base in Italy, part of our Operation Allied Force in Kosovo, to thank them and to hear of their immense pride and determination in their mission.

I know that many, many people here have friends or family members who are working hard in our mission in Kosovo. I know this port is home to 100 ships, not only the powerful battle groups now at sea led by the *Enterprise* and the *Theodore Roosevelt,* but also ships in the Adriatic—guided missile destroyers like the *Gonzalez*; fast-attack submarines like the *Norfolk.* Yes, you can clap for your ships, that's okay.

I can't name every ship or every unit, but I know that all of you are proud of all of them. Again, let me say, too, a special word of thanks to the family members of those who are deployed in the Kosovo operation now.

And let me say to all of you, we spend a lot of time—perhaps more time than you would think—in the White House, and at the Pentagon, talking about our obligations to the families of our service members. We know that we are asking more and more of you as we have downsized the military, and diversified and increased the number of our operations around the world. We know that the more we ask of you, the greater our responsibilities to you.

We know that we owe you the support, the training, the equipment you need to get the job done. We know we owe you fair pay, decent housing, and other support. Our new defense budget contains not only a substantial pay raise, but increased funding to keep our readiness razor-sharp. It is our solemn obligation to those of you who accept the dangers and hardships of our common security.

Since the Cold War ended, we have asked more and more from our Armed Forces—from the Persian Gulf to Korea, to

Central America to Africa—today to stand with our allies in NATO against the unspeakable brutality in Kosovo.

Now, this is not an easy challenge with a simple answer. If it were, it would have been resolved a long time ago. The mission I have asked our Armed Forces to carry out with our NATO allies is a dangerous one, as I have repeatedly said. Danger is something the brave men and women of our country's Armed Forces understand because you live with it every day, even in routine training exercises.

Now, we all know that yesterday three Army infantrymen were seized as they were carrying out a peaceful mission in Macedonia—protecting that country from the violence in neighboring Kosovo. There was absolutely no basis for them to be taken. There is no basis for them to be held. There is certainly no basis for them to be tried. All Americans are concerned about their welfare. President Milosevic should make no mistake: the United States takes care of its own. And President Milosevic should make no mistake: we will hold him and his government responsible for their safety and for their well-being.

But I ask you also to resolve that we will continue to carry out our mission with determination and resolve.

Over the past few weeks I have been talking with the American people about why we're involved with our NATO allies in Kosovo, and the risks of our mission and why they're justified. It's especially important that I speak to you and, through you, to all men and women in uniform about these matters.

The roots of this conflict lie in the policies of Mr. Milosevic, the dictator of Serbia. For more than 10 years now, he has been using ethnic and religious hatred as a path to personal power and a justification for the ethnic cleansing and murder of innocent civilians. That is what he did first in Bosnia and Croatia, where the United States with our allies did so much to end the war. And that is what he is doing in Kosovo today. That is what he will continue to do to his own people and his neighbors unless we and our allies stand in the way.

For months, we tried and tried and tried every conceivable peaceful alternative. We did everything we could through diplomacy to solve this problem. With diplomacy backed by the threat of NATO force, we forged a cease-fire last October that rescued from cold and hunger hundreds of thousands of people in Kosovo whom he had driven from their homes. In February, with our allies and with Russia, we proposed a peace agreement that would have given the people of Kosovo the autonomy they were guaranteed under their constitution before Mr. Milosevic came to power, and ended the fighting for good.

Now, the Kosovar leaders, they signed that agreement—even though it didn't give them the independence they said

they wanted, and that they had been fighting for. But Mr.
Milosevic refused. In fact, while pretending to negotiate for
peace, he massed 40,000 troops and hundreds of tanks in
and around Kosovo, planning a new campaign of destruction
and defiance. He started carrying out that campaign the
moment the peace talks ended.

Now the troops and police of the Serbian dictator are ram-
paging through tiny Kosovo—separating men from their families, executing many of them in cold blood; burning
homes—sometimes, we now hear, with people inside; forc-
ing survivors to leave everything behind, confiscating their
identity papers, destroying their records so their history and
their property is erased forever.

Yesterday, Mr. Milosevic actually said this problem can
only be solved by negotiations. But yesterday, as he said
that, his forces continued to hunt down the very Kosovar
leaders with whom he was supposed to be negotiating. Alto-
gether now, more than half a million Kosovars have been
pushed from their homes since the conflict began. They are
arriving at the borders of the country, shaken by what they
have seen and been through. But they also say—as a delegation of Albanian Americans, many of whom have relatives in
Kosovo, told me personally in the White House yesterday—
that NATO's military action has at least given them some
hope that they have not been completely abandoned in their
suffering. Had we not acted, the Serbian offensive would
have been carried out with impunity. We are determined that
it will carry a very high price, indeed. We also act to prevent
a wider war. If you saw my address to the country the other
night and the maps that I showed, you know that Kosovo is a
very small place. But it sits right at the dividing line of
Europe, Asia, and the Middle East; the dividing line between
Islam and Christianity; close to our Turkish and Greek allies
to the south, our new allies, Hungary, Poland, and the Czech
Republic to the north; surrounded by small and struggling
democracies that easily could be overwhelmed by the flood
of refugees Mr. Milosevic is creating.

Already, Macedonia is so threatened. Already, Serbian
forces have made forays into Albania, which borders Kosovo.
If we were to do nothing, eventually our allies and then the
United States would be drawn into a larger conflict at far
greater risks to our people and far greater costs.

Now, we can't respond to every tragedy in every corner of
the world. But just because we can't do everything for everyone doesn't mean that for the sake of consistency we should
do nothing for no one. Remember now, these atrocities are
happening at the door step of NATO, which has preserved
the security of Europe for 50 years because of the alliance
between the United States and our allies. They are happening in violation of specific commitments Mr. Milosevic gave
to us, to our NATO allies, to other European countries, and to

Had we not acted, the Serbian offensive would have been carried out with impunity. We are determined that it will carry a very high price, indeed.

Russia. They are happening to people who embrace peace and promise to lay down their own arms. They put their trust in us, and we can't let them down.

Our objective is to restore the Kosovars to their homes with security and self-government. Our bombing campaign is designed to exact an unacceptably high price for Mr. Milosevic's present policy of repression and ethnic cleansing, and to seriously diminish his military capacity to maintain that policy.

We've been doing this for seven days now—just seven days. Our pilots have performed bravely and well, in the face of dangerous conditions and often abysmal weather. But we must be determined and patient. Remember, the Serbs had 40,000 troops in and around Kosovo, and nearly 300 tanks, when they began this, before the first NATO plane got in the air. They had a sophisticated air-defense system. They also have a problem which has been festering for a decade, thanks to the efforts of Mr. Milosevic to make people hate each other in the former Yugoslavia because they are Muslims instead of Orthodox Christians or Catholics; because they're Albanians instead of Serbians or Croatians, or Bosnian Muslims, or Macedonians, or you have it—whatever. It is appalling.

For decades, those people lived in peace with one another. For ten years and more, now, a dictator has sought to make himself powerful by convincing the largest group, the Serbs, that the only way they can amount to anything is to uproot, disrupt, destroy, and kill other people who don't have the same means of destruction—no matter what the consequences are to everybody around them; no matter how many innocent children and their parents die; no matter how much it disrupts other countries.

Why? Because they want power, and they want to base it on the kind of ethnic and religious hatred that is bedeviling the whole world today. You can see it in the Middle East, in Northern Ireland. You can see it in the tribal wars in Africa. You can see that it is one of the dominant problems the whole world faces. And this is right in the underbelly of Europe.

Are we, in the last year of the 20th century, going to look the other way as entire peoples in Europe are forced to abandon their homelands or die? Are we going to impose a price on that kind of conduct and seek to end it?

We have to decide whether we are going to take a stand with our NATO allies, and whether we are prepared to pay the price of time to make him pay the price of aggression and murder. Are we, in the last year of the 20th century, going to look the other way as entire peoples in Europe are forced to abandon their homelands or die? Are we going to impose a price on that kind of conduct and seek to end it?

Mr. Milosevic often justifies his behavior by talking about the history of the Serbs going back to the 14th century. Well, I value the history of this country, and I value what happened here in the 18th century. But I don't want to take America back to the 18th century. And he acts like he wants to take Serbia back to the 14th century—to 14th-century values, 14th-century ways of looking at other human beings.

We are on the edge of a new century and a new millennium, where the people in poor countries all over the world, because of technology and the Internet and the spreading of information, will have unprecedented opportunities to share prosperity, and to give their kids an education, and have a decent future, if only they will live in peace with the basic human regard for other people—that is absolutely antithetical to everything that Mr. Milosevic has done.

So I ask you—you say, what has this got to do with America? Remember, we fought two world wars in Europe. Remember that the unity, the freedom, the prosperity, the peace of Europe is important to the future of the children in this room today. That is, in the end, what this is about. We're not doing this on our own. We could not have undertaken it on our own. This is something we're doing with our NATO allies. They're up there in the air, too. If there's a peace agreement, they've agreed to provide 85 percent of the troops on the ground to help to monitor the peace agreement and protect all the ethnic groups, including the Serbs. This is something we are doing to try to avoid in the 21st century the kind of widespread war, large American casualties, and heartbreak that we saw too much of in the century we are about to leave. So this is not just about a small piece of the Balkans.

But let me ask you something. When we are moved by the plight of three servicemen, when we stay up half the night hoping that our rescue teams find that fine pilot who went down when his plane was hit, when we see a sign that says, "I love my TR sailor" or "I miss my Daddy," we remember that all political and military decisions ultimately have a human component that is highly individualized.

Think how you would feel if you were part of the half million people who lived peaceably in a place, just wanted to be let alone to practice your religion and educate your children and do your work—if people came to your house and your village and said, Pack up your belongings and go; we're going to burn your property records, we're going to burn your identity records. And if your husband or your son is of military service age, we might take them out behind the barn and shoot them dead—just because you have a different religion, just because you have a different ethnic background. Is that really what we want the 21st century to be about for our children? Now, that is what is at stake here. We cannot do everything in the world, but we must do what we can. We can never forget the Holocaust, the genocide, the carnage of the 20th century. We don't want the new century to bring us the same nightmares in a different guise.

We also want to say again how proud the United States is that each of NATO's 19 members is supporting the mission in

Remember, we fought two world wars in Europe. Remember that the unity, the freedom, the prosperity, the peace of Europe is important to the future of the children in this room today.

Kosovo in some way—France and Germany, Turkey and Greece, Poland and Hungary, the Czech Republic, Britain, Canada—all the others. And this is also important.

Let me finally say—I'd like to read you something. Near the end of the second world war, President Roosevelt prepared a speech to give at a holiday honoring Virginia's famous son, Thomas Jefferson. He never got to give the speech. But it still speaks to us, his last words. And to those of you who wear the uniform of our nation and to those of you who are part of the families of our uniformed service members, I ask you to heed these words.

After the long war was almost drawing to a close, these were Franklin Roosevelt's last words that he never got to deliver: "We as Americans do not choose to deny our responsibilities. Nor do we intend to abandon our determination that, within the lives of our children and our children's children, there will not be a third world war. We seek peace, enduring peace. More than an end to war, we want an end to the beginnings of all wars."

That is what we are trying to achieve in Kosovo. That is what many of you in this room, perhaps, and your colleagues, did achieve in Bosnia. We want to end a war that has begun in Europe, and prevent a larger war. And we want to alleviate the burdens and the killing of defenseless people. Let us heed President Roosevelt's last words. Let me say again, for those of you who serve and for those of you who serve as family members, and who sacrifice as wives and husbands and children: I thank you for your service and your sacrifice, and America thanks you.

God bless you.

U.S. Policy Toward Iraq[3]

John Hillen

Senior Fellow in Political-Military Studies and special assistant to the president and CEO, Center for Strategic & International Studies. Attended Duke University, King's College, London, and Oxford University. Former Olin Fellow for National Security Studies, Council on Foreign Relations. Former U.S. Army officer and decorated veteran of close combat in the Persian Gulf War. An army paratrooper, he continues to serve as reserve officer in the U.S. Special Operations Command. Contributing editor, National Review. *Author of* Blue Helmets: The Strategy of UN Military Operations *(Brassey's, 1998) and editor of* Future Visions for U.S. Defense Policy *(Council on Foreign Relations, 1998). In 1999 Hillen was appointed a member of the congressionally mandated National Security Study Group chaired by former senators David Boren and Warren Rudman.*

Editors' introduction: As someone who fought in the Persian Gulf War, John Hillen possesses a unique perspective of both Iraqi leader Saddam Hussein and the U.S. policy in regard to Iraq. Here, in a speech given before the Committee on Armed Services of the U.S. House of Representatives, Hillen offered the opinion that the administration has not developed a policy framework that "would prepare Congress, the American people, and our allies for a lasting solution to the problem of Saddam Hussein."

John Hillen's speech: Mr. Chairman, Congressman Skelton, members of the committee; it is an honor to come before you today to offer some thoughts on current U.S. policy towards Iraq. Eight years ago today I was one of the northernmost U.S. soldiers occupying Southern Iraq and we were confronted with a similar set of questions even then.

Current Policy

As the committee is aware, since the end of Operation Desert Fox in December, the United States has undertaken a low-key but active campaign against Iraq—focused almost exclusively on challenges to the no-fly zones from Iraqi planes and anti-aircraft batteries. Public reports state that in over three thousand combat sorties flown in the past ten weeks, the U.S. has attacked over one hundred different targets with almost three hundred precision guided munitions.

---

3. Statement of Dr. John Hillen, Senior Fellow in Political-Military Studies, Center for Strategic & International Studies, before the Committee on Armed Services of the U.S. House of Representatives on March 10, 1999.

The administration seems quite happy with these attacks—indeed happier still with the notion of these attacks as representing the centerpiece of a new U.S. strategy towards Iraq. As one senior military officer quoted in the *Washington Post* remarked, "It's a strategy we fell into. It's not one that was originally planned. But it's working out very, very well for us." Several very high-ranking administration officials with whom I've spoken recently have reinforced this optimism about the success of the new policy.

I would like to offer the committee a different view on this issue. To call any military strategy a success presupposes a coherent measurement of that success. The current set of operations against Iraqi air defenses are deemed successful because, by and large, American and British planes are hitting their targets and slowly degrading Saddam's anti-aircraft capabilities. Of this there is no doubt, and we should all greatly admire the skill and professionalism of the aircrews carrying out these missions. Nonetheless, while these short-term military goals appear definable and achievable, they do not appear to be conclusively linked to an endgame in Iraq. If the U.S. is only in the business of incrementally "plinking" 1970s-era anti-aircraft batteries in Iraq, then the policy is indeed a success. If, on the other hand, those military actions are supposed to be conclusively linked to a larger and more sustainable political objective in Iraq, I'm not so sure. Using the destruction of anti-aircraft batteries in Iraq to measure the success of our policy may be as irrelevant as using body counts to measure the success of American strategy in Vietnam. The daily military actions, in and of themselves, are important tactical victories. But do they add up to a comprehensive policy? The question the President and his policy staff must answer is strategic—"to what end?"

The administration claims that containment is the official strategy and the U.S. wishes only to keep Saddam "in his box" such that he lacks the military capability to threaten his neighbors, develop weapons of mass destruction, or destabilize the Persian Gulf region in some way. American officials have even indicated that if Saddam ceases his challenges to the no-fly zones, then what has been described as a "low-grade war against Iraq" will stop. At the same time, the President and his National Security Advisor have strongly hinted at the need for a change of regime in Iraq and joined Congress in passing the Iraq Liberation Act. There is an inherent tension between these two goals and I would argue that the administration cannot have it both ways. In the first place pursuing two different policies on the cheap greatly reduces the chances of either coming to fruition. Secondly, the administration has not constructed a policy framework for either that would prepare Congress, the American people, and our allies for a lasting solution to the problem of Saddam Hussein. American and British pilots are busy in

If the U.S. is only in the business of incrementally "plinking" 1970s-era anti-aircraft batteries in Iraq, then the policy is indeed a success.

the skies over Iraq, but little work has been done in the White House to plan for either a post-UNSCOM containment strategy or the chance to help force Saddam from power. For his part, Saddam appears to be counting on the fact that an administration with only 22 months left in office will be mostly interested in running out the clock.

Incoherent as it is, the current policy could most optimistically be explained as "playing for a break." Some analysts who agree with my thesis that American actions do not appear to be linked to a larger objective still maintain that bombing is better than nothing. Perhaps—so long as there are no American POW's in the equation. However, when you weigh the considerable danger of a Saddam Hussein with an unfettered and unmonitored weapons-of-mass-destruction program, the current campaign is not much better than nothing. The recent bombings have not been directed towards Saddam's ability to build and deliver weapons of mass destruction or his elite forces—the two instruments with which he maintains control and could threaten the region. There is the possibility that attacking remote anti-air-craft sites may send some indirect signal to the Iraqi military that Saddam is a weak and dangerous leader. I cannot see how this could be a stronger signal than when he lost two thirds of his army in Desert Storm, but that is the line of argument. Even then, if Saddam is weakening and Desert Fox or this current campaign is accelerating his demise, the U.S. is ill positioned to influence or take advantage of the outcome. Our lukewarm approach to a regime change in Iraq has put America in the back of the bus, not the driver's seat.

Playing for a break—where the U.S. applies small amounts of relatively risk-free military pressure in the hopes of something good happening—can work. Some of the architects of President Reagan's policies in Central America have described their approach this way. If we have patience and good fortune in Iraq then this method could be supported. I believe that Saddam is too wily a survivor and his WMD program too dangerous and advanced for America to rely on this strategy. As we used to say in my unit, hope is not a method. More important, I will describe in this testimony two scenarios where the threat posed by Saddam in the future will grow greatly unless the U.S. takes action today. The immediate threat is not imminent, but decisions are.

Containment

A policy of containment, bombing or no bombing, is not sustainable for several reasons. First, it is inconclusive, having not yielded even the glimmer of a solution to the Iraq problem for the past eight years. Second, every indecisive round keeps pressure on Saddam, but also allows him time and breathing space to further develop weapons of mass destruction. This is especially so now that the UN inspections regime, imperfect as it was, has collapsed. Third, the continued sanctions on Iraq give Saddam legitimacy and strengthen his hold on power over the suffering Iraqi people. Fourth, the policy is expensive and demoralizing, costing the U.S. billions every year to rush troops to the Gulf and further taxing the much-stretched American military. Fifth, containment fatigue is setting in, with allies and other powers tiring of the routine and wanting to resume normal (read business) relations with Iraq.

Finally, and most importantly, the current containment policy leaves many parties other than the U.S. in charge. During all these crises, America has reacted with great gusto, but the prime determinant of the outcome has been Saddam. Occasionally, an interlocutor has been involved to give temporary direction—such as Russian Prime Minister Yvgeni Primakov last November and UN Secretary-General Kofi Annan in February of 1998. Given the amount of political and military capital the U.S. is spending to keep Saddam under pressure, retaining the initiative of action should be the foremost element of a strategy for dealing with a dangerous bully.

What is needed is a serious policy review, one that evaluates containment squarely against other options that could guide America's long-term Iraq policy.

Policy Options

What is needed is a serious policy review, one that evaluates containment squarely against other options that could guide America's long-term Iraq policy. Such a policy should match available military capabilities to a recognizable and definable political end-state. For a strategy to be successful, military actions must, in a sense, deliver the political goal (or at least posture the U.S. for success). Three times last year, the U.S. prepared a bombing campaign that was a good military plan, but not a strategy. As one commentator noted, even Desert Fox was "a target list in search of a strategy." One of the reasons the current policy is so inconclusive is that there is little confidence that U.S. military action, while competently undertaken and making Americans feel satisfied, will actually produce the goods. In this case, making Saddam behave as he never has in his almost forty-year reign.

A top-to-bottom policy review would examine options such as containment, but in different form. A broader form of containment might include a more robust inspections plan, tighter restrictions on Iraqi economic sanctions (i.e., closing the large current loopholes), an extension of the "no-fly zone" to a "no-drive" zone, and a clearly articulated policy on when and how military force would be used in response to Iraqi transgressions. A more narrow form of containment might abandon the UN sanctions and focus strictly on key Iraqi military capabilities that the U.S. can monitor through its intelligence networks. The veneer of a UN effort could be dropped in this case, allowing a smaller coalition of the U.S., Britain, Kuwait, and key Gulf States to enforce the policy.

This would allow for considerably greater flexibility in reacting to Saddam's moves.

A bolder departure from current policy might be a deterrence strategy. In this plan, the U.S. would keep a small force in Kuwait and Saudi Arabia, but would basically deter major Iraqi aggression from "over the horizon." This plan explicitly accepts the fact that Saddam will remain in power, but de-emphasizes his conflict with the United States while clearly delineating the conditions under which U.S. power might return in order to strike Iraq. For this policy to be a success, it would have to combine a more laissez-faire approach with an iron resoluteness to use massive force when Iraq has truly stepped over the line, as it did in 1990 when it invaded Kuwait.

As I noted, in November President Clinton tacitly endorsed an even different approach—a policy to undermine the Hussein regime, thus helping those elements in Iraq that might overthrow Saddam. This too is a departure from containment. Congress has allocated $97 million to support the efforts of Iraqi opposition groups, although how useful that money might be is a matter of considerable debate. Having observed the Shiite rebels in action against Saddam in April of 1991, I am not optimistic that any Iraqi opposition group could mount an effective campaign against Saddam without considerable U.S. military help. As the botched Kurdish rebellion of 1996 showed, many dissident groups are more interested in fighting each other than fighting Saddam.

Without significant U.S. help on the ground, I believe that Iraqi opposition groups are just good enough to get themselves into trouble. The U.S., having encouraged them to rebel, should be willing to rescue them in the event of set backs. Should the U.S. choose to pursue this policy, as President Clinton hinted he might, all involved must understand that it is not a free lunch. Although, like most of you here, I wish the Iraqi opposition success and support U.S. aid to these groups, I am skeptical that Saddam can be deposed without a major U.S. political, financial, and military commitment that could involve American ground as well as air support in fighting Saddam.

Removing Saddam Hussein's Regime

Ultimately, if the U.S. is determined to remove Saddam Hussein from power, there is only one sure way of doing so: invade and conquer Iraq. If we want the job done, there is no realistic way to do it on the cheap. Only U.S. Armed Forces have the power to defeat Saddam's military and security services, and only the willingness of the United States to employ whatever force is needed is likely to convince our friends in Europe, Asia, and the Middle East to go along with the plan. Moreover, as so much of this conflict has been about preserving American prestige, it could hardly be

As the botched Kurdish rebellion of 1996 showed, many dissident groups are more interested in fighting each other than fighting Saddam.

expected that the U.S. could cheerfully bankroll, supply, and even provide air cover for an Iraqi rebellion that failed or put another dictator in power. If involved at all in supporting or fomenting an Iraqi rebellion against Saddam, the U.S. would be in it up to the elbows and had better be prepared to commit tens of thousands of ground troops to a prolonged campaign if they were needed. There is no way to swim in this pool without getting wet.

That said, in the absence of a stunning Iraqi provocation, an invasion is the least probable and riskiest course of action the U.S. could currently pursue towards Iraq. A legion of headaches would confront the United States in pursuit of this course and residual problems could plague us for years afterwards. However, there are two scenarios in which an invasion of Iraq would not be our worst course of action—indeed, in one case, it may prove to be our best choice. I do not come here as an advocate for an immediate invasion and occupation of Iraq, but I do advocate thinking seriously about the possibility of such action in the event of these two circumstances.

In the first scenario, the U.S. would reinforce some limited success on the part of an Iraqi opposition movement. I wish, for the sake of our friends in the Iraqi opposition and the American public, that Saddam Hussein could be removed with only a light American touch—air support, logistics, training, intelligence, and the like. I am not sanguine about their chances under these circumstances. Moreover, if the U.S. is not prepared immediately to heavily reinforce an opposition in which we have invested our prestige, America should think carefully about being involved at all. At some point in time, Iraqi opposition groups are likely to need more help than was expected. Needless to say, the more the U.S. is involved on the front end of such efforts, the more it can influence the manner and form in which American troops may be involved further down the road. It will be much easier for the U.S. to ensure success and maintain influence if it is a key player from the beginning, rather than having to come in as a key player on the heels of an imminent disaster or stalled effort. There are many questions contained herein and too many to address today. The main point I can make at this time is that these sorts of issues must be thought through, war-gamed, and planned for. I do not believe the administration is prepared in that sense.

The second scenario centers on the possibility of Saddam Hussein's Iraq being on the verge of developing nuclear weapons. Saddam has every incentive to do so, recognizing, as the Pakistani defense minister said at the time, that the chief lesson of the Gulf War was to not take on the United States unless you had nuclear weapons. Biological and chemical weapons are easier to develop and can be used to devastating effect, but they do not, as a nuclear capability

If the U.S. is not prepared immediately to heavily reinforce an opposition in which we have invested our prestige, America should think carefully about being involved at all.

would, make Iraq a world power overnight. If Saddam were close to realizing this capability, as many analysts think he is, the U.S. would face a threat more serious than that of the Iraqi invasion of Kuwait in 1990, both in terms of U.S. national interests and the stability of the vital Gulf region. It is well worth thinking now about how to handle an Iraq on the brink of developing nuclear weapons. A preemptive invasion of Iraq might then be our least worst course of action.

Strategic preemption on this scale is a difficult decision because the best time to undertake the decision is early—when the threat is not manifest enough to galvanize the various actors involved. Unfortunately, the worst time to preemptively invade Iraq would be when Saddam actually has a nuclear capability or is close enough to shock the world. Then the international community would be motivated to take action, but against a much more formidable opponent. The audio tapes made in the Oval Office during the Cuban missile crisis of 1962 show President Kennedy, faced with the prospect of a nuclear Castro, expressing his regret that he did not use the Bay of Pigs or some earlier opportunity to depose the Cuban leader. Similarly, much of the international community long bemoaned the failure to dispatch Hitler while he was weak, rather than paying the terrible cost to do it when he was strong. It is my fervent hope that we have no similar regrets if facing a nuclear Saddam in the future.

The Cost of Invasion and Occupation

The basic military campaign would be well within American capabilities. Planned as it would be by a cautious military, it would probably entail a worst-case scenario force of roughly 300–400,000 troops and would probably take roughly 2 to 4 months to deploy and prepare the forces, followed by a one-to-three-month war. Under reasonably optimistic assumptions, the United States would probably take only about three to four thousand casualties (of which 1,000 might be killed in action). As in the Persian Gulf War, at least a hundred thousand reservists would need to be mobilized and the National Guard would have to be shipped off to training centers to prepare for certain eventualities.

Under a range of plausible scenarios, however, the cost in U.S. military and Iraqi civilian casualties could increase significantly. If Saddam's loyalists chose to fight to the death rather than surrender and throw themselves on the tender mercies of the Iraqi populace, casualty figures could double or even triple as American troops would be forced to clear Iraq's cities in house-to-house fighting where our advantages in technology, tactics, and air power would be heavily discounted. If Saddam were to employ chemical or biological agents in defense of his regime—and he would have scant incentive to refrain from doing so—U.S. and Iraqi civilian casualties could rise even higher.

Nevertheless, the military costs of an invasion pale beside the political and diplomatic morass the U.S. would encounter. Defeating the Iraqi military is easy. The problem is that of the dog chasing the car—what does he do with it once he's caught it? Once an international coalition dominated by the U.S. military conquered Iraq, we would be stuck with a basket case of a country. After decades of Saddam's totalitarianism, two prior wars, years of crippling sanctions, and a U.S. invasion, Iraq would be devastated. Its economy would be in shambles, its governmental structure gone, its basic human services—the production and distribution of food, medicine, energy, and other basic necessities—would be ruined. Like Germany or Japan after World War II, the United States would have to rebuild a nation that has collapsed.

Every one of Iraq's neighbors and a number of other European and Middle Eastern states would have a tremendous stake in the future Iraq. They would want to control who rules in Baghdad, what the new state looks like, and how it is oriented. Nor are they likely to simply stand on the sidelines and offer advice. Even before the military campaign is completed, they would be maneuvering and manipulating events to try to ensure that the post-war Iraq conformed to their needs. And many of their needs would contradict one another and the likely preferences of the United States.

Turkey would want a strong central government in Iraq that kept a very tight rein on the Kurds and prevented them from exercising anything but the most nominal autonomy. Saudi Arabia would want a strong Iraqi state dominated by the (minority) Sunni population to serve as a bulwark against Iran and prevent the Shiite from enjoying power. The Jordanians would probably want a weak Iraqi state—at least weak enough so that it cannot threaten them—but that was also favorably inclined to continue to provide Jordan with cheap oil. Egypt too would probably prefer a weak Iraq because Baghdad is Cairo's greatest potential challenger for leadership of the Arab world. Both Syria and Iran would actively work for a weak Iraqi state, and may try to ensure the dominance of Iraq's Shiite majority. Russia may want a strong, independent Iraq; one independent enough to renew its former relationship with Moscow and perhaps even purchase Russian military hardware. France may not care whether the Iraqi state is weak or strong, but would certainly want to make sure that French firms were not excluded from their fair share of Iraqi contracts. In short, the United States would be beset on every side by wheedling, cajoling, pleading, subverting, and hindering allies, all intent on seeing their interests satisfied in a future Iraqi state.

The American people would no doubt demand that democracy be established in Iraq. After all, American soldiers would have died to conquer the country and it would be highly unpalatable to the U.S. public for those soldiers, sailors, and airmen to have died simply to replace one dictator with another. This too could arouse the vehement opposition of regional states, most of whom are autocracies of one form or another and who probably would be alarmed at a democratic precedent in their part of the world. They might openly oppose or covertly subvert a democratic Iraqi government. In addition, the Iraqi people may not be ready for pluralism, and a U.S.-installed democracy might collapse into a new autocracy.

Moreover, who is to say the U.S. would be pulling the strings through this political cauldron of an occupation? In order for the occupation to garner local and international political support, the UN or a regional organization such as the Arab League would have to provide some kind of transitional authority that would govern Iraq and provide basic services in between the initial U.S. military occupation and the restoration of some form of Iraqi government. As with the UN operation in Somalia in 1993, the U.S. would be heavily vested, politically and militarily, but not necessarily 100 percent in charge. There is no guarantee that if the rebuilding of Iraq were left to the UN or the Arab League it would turn out democratic, stable, or well-disposed toward the United States.

A Nuclear Saddam

As challenging as this endeavor may seem, it may not be as bad as a future with a nuclear-armed Iraq. Not all proliferation is equally bad. We worry much less about India, Pakistan, or Israel possessing nuclear weapons than North Korea or Libya. Saddam Hussein is arguably the most dangerous man in the world, even without a ready nuclear capability. If Saddam were to acquire nuclear weapons, the world would suddenly become a very dangerous place.

Certain facets of Saddam Hussein's personality make Iraqi possession of nuclear weapons almost uniquely dangerous. In the past, the U.S. has been able to count on nuclear-armed states behaving within certain established parameters. Even when these states were adversaries—such as the USSR or China—this knowledge provided some margin of security. But the world has never had to deal with a nuclear-armed state led by someone like Saddam Hussein before. The entire corpus of arms-control regimes, confidence-building measures, and deterrence logic that underpinned the nuclear age thus far could prove meaningless to Saddam. Like the terrible dictators of our past, he plays by different rules.

This is not to say that Saddam is "undeterrable." On numerous occasions in the past, he has demonstrated that when faced with superior force and a willingness to use that

There is no guarantee that if the rebuilding of Iraq were left to the UN or the Arab League it would turn out democratic, stable, or well-disposed toward the United States.

force, he will back down. Indeed, Saddam refrained from employing biological or chemical agents against either Israel or the forces of the U.S.-led coalition during the Gulf War because he was deterred by the Israeli and American (and French and British) nuclear arsenals. But that card might be removed should Iraq's nuclear program realize its objective.

Deterring Saddam is much more difficult than deterring other leaders. Moreover, what deters Saddam is often difficult for others to discern. Because Saddam has such disregard for lives other than his own, threatening to kill large numbers of his people per se is meaningless to him and therefore inadequate to deter him. It becomes a deterrent only if Saddam believes that so many deaths would prompt some kind of move against him—by the Iraqi military, the Iraqi people, his loyalists, etc.—that would threaten his control over Iraq. However, if Saddam calculates that he runs no such risk, or that he runs a greater risk of being ousted if he backs down, he will not be deterred. A good example of this problem was his decision not to withdraw from Kuwait in the fall of 1990. Saddam recognized that tens of thousands of Iraqis would die in a war with the U.S.-led coalition, but this mattered little to him because he feared that if he were to retreat from Kuwait his supporters would turn on him. Thus, he chose to gamble that he could win the war despite the certainty that Iraq would take heavy losses.

Because Saddam consistently exaggerates his own strength and his adversaries' weaknesses, possession of nuclear weapons is likely to encourage his propensity toward risk-taking. In the past, improvements in Iraqi military power have always emboldened him to take ever more reckless foreign adventures. For instance, in 1975, when Iraq was weak, Saddam backed down in the face of the Shah's U.S.-equipped military. Iraq then went on a massive military modernization and expansion program, so that by 1980, after the Iranian revolution (which also greatly weakened the Iranian military), he gambled on an invasion of Iran. Similarly, Iraq emerged from the Iran-Iraq war with a massive conventional military as well as a large arsenal of BW and CW weapons and ballistic missiles. These new capabilities were critical to Saddam's decision to invade Kuwait and then try to hold it against the U.S.-led coalition.

If Saddam were to acquire nuclear weapons, there can be no doubt that he would attempt to use them to achieve tangible foreign policy gains. As he has done so often in the past, Saddam almost certainly would miscalculate the risks and again embroil Iraq, the Middle East, possibly Europe, and probably the United States in a new war—one in which Saddam had nuclear weapons to add to his side of the balance sheet.

Perhaps the best way to illustrate the danger posed by a nuclear-armed Iraq is to compare it to North Korea. Because we were unable to enforce an Iraq-like set of restrictions on North Korea, Pyongyang was able to develop nuclear weapons despite Western efforts to control proliferation. Today, we live with great unease about how North Korea will behave with its nuclear arsenal and have gone to great lengths to "buy" it from them. Yet North Korea is almost peaceful and cautious when compared to Saddam's Iraq. North Korea has mostly contented itself with limited terrorism and subversion in the 45 years since the end of the Korean War. Moreover, it appears to have no ambitions outside the Korean peninsula—if it still harbors those old designs at all.

By contrast, Iraq has fought four major wars, attacked or threatened to attack seven different nearby states, and provoked countless smaller clashes in the thirty years since Saddam's Ba'athist regime took power. If we are nervous that deterrence alone will not be enough to prevent North Korea from employing its nuclear arsenal, we should be downright terrified of how Saddam would behave with nuclear weapons of his own. Many in the foreign policy community criticized Washington's buyout of North Korea as caving in to international blackmail. Whatever Pyongyang's goals, there can be little doubt that Saddam would try (at the very least) to use his own nuclear arsenal in grand-scale extortion of his neighbors and the U.S. In these circumstances, the United States would be confronted with a variety of bad options. We could learn to live with Saddam's nuclear arsenal and hope that our deterrent was so overwhelming that even Saddam would understand it. Or we could invade Iraq before Saddam has completed development of the weaponry. Doing so would have the advantages of dismantling the Iraqi WMD program once and for all, and removing Saddam from power. Under these conditions, even the litany of problems the U.S. would have to address in an invasion might be a lesser burden than living in a world in which Saddam Hussein possessed nuclear weapons.

An invasion of Iraq would only be warranted under these most extreme circumstances. Unfortunately, the most extreme circumstances are entirely plausible. Invading Iraq would not be another Grenada, Panama, or Desert Storm. It would represent the deepest, most immediate, and most protracted investment of American lives, diplomacy, prestige, and political capital since Vietnam. It could, in these relatively benign strategic times, be the defining moment of one or more American administrations. Faced with the specter of a nuclear Saddam, it is a moment worth contemplating.

Real leadership from an American President can shape the will and ambitions of the international community. President Clinton or his successor should not be tempted into kicking the Iraq can down the road yet again. Instead, the President should invest the political capital necessary to make the case against Saddam and mobilize domestic and international opinion in the direction of removing him. If Hussein is dangerous enough for the world laboriously to keep in a box, he is dangerous enough to expel from Iraq. The campaign to build the case for undermining and overthrowing Iraq will be long, difficult, and accomplished only with much diplomatic sweat, military muscle, and the blood of many involved. Having undertaken some limited military action in the past weeks, perhaps President Clinton answered in his mind the question of whether it was worth fighting for. That same question should be put before Congress. If the answer is yes, the fight should at least accomplish something important.

Altering U.S. Sanctions Policy[4]

Jim Kolbe

U.S. Representative 1984– ; born June 28, 1942, Evanston, Il.; moved to Santa Cruz County, AZ, 1947; page for Senator Barry Goldwater (R-AZ) 1958–60; B.A., Political Science, Northwestern University, 1965; M.B.A., concentration in Economics, Stanford University, 1967; United States Naval Reserve, active duty, Vietnam: 1968–69; Navy commendation medal, "V" for valor; Arizona State Senator, 1976–82: Chairman, Judiciary Committee; majority whip, 1979–80; member of House Appropriations Committee.

Editors' introduction: With tensions high between the U.S. and several key nations this past year, America's foreign economic policies have fallen under heavy scrutiny. Jim Kolbe, a Republican senator speaking to the Center for Strategic and International Studies, advised that the U.S. should be more open to free trade with other nations, and that as an economic superpower at it's highest peak in years, the U.S. must realize that free trade means "opportunity, hope and progress." Kolbe also spoke out against unilateral sanctions, saying they are costly and ineffective in their current use.

Jim Kolbe's speech: Good morning, it's a pleasure to be with you as CSIS convenes this important conference. CSIS has long been a leader in economic policy. That tradition is carried forward today with the release of two new studies on the impact of unilateral economic sanctions. I commend Dr. Weintraub and Doug Johnston for their work and for bringing us together today.

As someone who works within the "hallowed" halls of Congress, I am often struck by the disconnect between members' perception of the U.S. role in international affairs and the reality of the global political and economic environment. Ten years after the fall of the Berlin Wall, the world today remains difficult and dangerous, in many ways more dangerous than during the height of the Cold War. We see growing fundamentalism and terrorism continue to pose a threat to stability, particularly the Middle East. Tribalism still haunts the Balkans, threatening to spill beyond defined borders into a full-blown and uncontrolled regional conflict. Deep poverty persists in many parts of the world. The scourge of disease continues to ravage many parts of Africa, Asia, and Latin America. Despite the progress we've made in defining a new relationship with the former Soviet Union, the threat of nuclear and chemical proliferation is not far from the sur-

Ten years after the fall of the Berlin Wall, the world today remains difficult and dangerous, in many ways more dangerous than during the height of the Cold War.

---

4. Remarks before the Center for Strategic and International Studies, Congressman Jim Kolbe, May 6,1999, 8:30 a.m. to 9:00 a.m.

face. And even though these events take place far from our shores, there is no question that they affect each of us.

But with the public, and in Congress, our perception of the world has changed in a very different way. Many of the most senior and global-oriented legislators have retired. In their place, we have witnessed the rise of a new, younger majority—a majority raised outside the shadow of World War II and even Vietnam. Many of these younger members were elected on a platform that is limited to domestic reform measures. And this has been their primary focus—balancing the budget, cutting taxes, and returning power to the states. And while we have been successful in these objectives, there are some disturbing trends I've noticed over the past several years which I would like to address today. In particular, I want to talk to you about two developments: an increasing retrenchment of foreign policy and the rise of unilateralism. Both are infecting U.S. foreign policy today.

Rise of Economic Entrenchment

America was never as ready to meet the challenges of the global economy as it is today.

Over the past several years I have seen a significant rise in the calls for economic retrenchment, particularly since the passage of NAFTA and the Uruguay Round. Many in Congress fear open trade and international economic competition. When they hear the words "free trade" a whole panoply of fears are unleashed. When discussions turn to new trade agreements, many of them immediately visualize factories being closed and jobs shipped to the third world. Others see international bureaucracies created, bureaucracies enacting new, sovereignty-limiting regulations to govern our lives. Still others see a flood of inferior, dangerous goods pouring into the country. Some equate free trade with open immigration.

I will not belittle these fears. They are real. But in my view, America's leaders have nothing to fear from free trade. America was never as ready to meet the challenges of the global economy as it is today. When we look around the world, we find that the United States continues—unchallenged—as the dominant economic power. As proof, we need only to look at recent economic trends in other industrialized nations. In comparing ourselves to other industrialized countries, it is clear that every single industrialized nation in the world lags behind the United States.

While the United States economy cranks up new jobs while inflation is practically non-existent, double-digit unemployment hovers near postwar record levels in Germany, France, and Italy. In Japan, too much government regulation and a banking system crippled by billions of dollars in bad loans has put a choke hold on growth with no signs of economic recovery.

In part, because of problems elsewhere on the globe, the United States stands as the undisputed economic leader in the world. But we did not get there without pain. The American people earned it through a decade of corporate downsizing, industrial restructuring, and belt-tightening. In Washington, we reduced the federal budget deficit to just a little over one percent of our national output, down from more than 4 percent in 1992. We deregulated a number of our service sectors, an action which has made us the leader by light years in service sectors that rely on the information technology revolution.

The United States now dominates trade in international services, a sector which accounts for more than half of our GDP and that employs half of our workforce.

But what about manufacturing? What about that great *sucking sound* of jobs as our workers try to compete with Mexico and Malaysia, where workers may earn as little as 43 cents an hour? How can American workers ever compete with these nations without "downward pressure" on our wages and standard of living?

It is true—wage rates in the U.S. manufacturing sector are significantly higher than most other countries. But why is that? It is because our manufacturing workers are better educated and better skilled. And because they are backed by more technology and capital investment, they produce more goods faster, and with higher quality, than our competitors. One individual working in manufacturing in Ohio is likely to have more technology at his or her fingertips than entire factories have in the third world. Because of these factors they are worth more. And they will continue to be worth more if we invest in education, worker training, in R&D and technology.

You recall that shrinking manufacturing sector that the protectionist always talks about? It does not exist. America's manufacturing sector as a percentage of GDP is 21%, almost exactly the same as it was in 1967. The difference is that a smaller percentage of our workforce is producing a vastly larger quantity of manufactured goods. In three words, it's improved worker productivity.

The U.S. market also is the most lucrative in the world. Our $6.7 trillion dollar economy creates more wealth and opportunity for the average American than most people can even dream of overseas. The value of the increased production in the United States in just one year is greater than the entire output of Taiwan.

This is not a time for timidity.

Free trade means opportunity, hope, and progress. Opportunity for a better life for the American worker. Hope for future generations. And progress toward a world free from the economic stagnation that leads to civil strife, individual impoverishment, war, and repression.

But at the very time we should be capitalizing on our strengths and advantages to define the new economic paradigm for the 21st century, instead we find ourselves gripped by fear. Rather than pushing the administration to open markets, Congress chides it for not being tough enough on "unfair foreign trade practices." While lecturing ailing economies on the need to open their markets, Congress passes legislation to close our markets.

At the other end of Pennsylvania Avenue, we find a complete lack of leadership. Fast track has not been mentioned since the State of the Union. The administration's proposal for CBI parity came wrapped in protectionism more extreme that any other bill introduced. Meanwhile, the administration spurns an undeniably good WTO deal with China to seek special protections for our own steel and textile industries. When it comes to economic engagement, we seem headed in the wrong direction.

Rise of Unilateralism

There is another, equally disturbing trend we are witnessing in foreign policy. That is the explosive and haphazard growth of unilateral sanctions.

Foreign policy 101 tells us that one-size solutions do not fit all. These are complex issues we are dealing with. They require careful forethought before action, not knee-jerk unilateralism.

In recent years, the U.S. Congress has shown a greater willingness to employ unilateral economic sanctions in a dubious effort to achieve our foreign policy goals. Every year in the House we see any number of measures tacked on to appropriations bills which are designed to influence the conduct of foreign nations. These range from amendments to cut off foreign aid to countries which vote against the U.S. in the United Nations to amendments to eliminate all non-food aid to particular countries.

Now, I am not saying that these are not legitimate foreign policy issues. But I do emphatically question the efficacy of the methods. Foreign policy 101 tells us that one-size solutions do not fit all. These are complex issues we are dealing with. They require careful forethought before action, not knee-jerk unilateralism.

Some will ask—not too many in this room, I trust!— What's wrong with Congress expressing its sense of moral outrage through sanctions? Shouldn't America's representatives stand up for what they believe is morally right?

Unilateral Sanctions Do Not Work

Well, we should continue to speak out for what we believe is right. But the problem with using unilateral sanctions is that in almost all cases, they simply do not work! In today's global economy, foreign rivals can and do quickly and easily replace American imports and companies.

Sanctions Are Costly

Sanctions also have an enormous impact on the U.S. economy, costing between $15 and $19 billion in lost sales since 1995 alone. The costs go far beyond initial lost sales, however. The ripple effects of lost follow-on sales, diminished confidence in the reliability of American suppliers, lost market share—these impacts are often hidden and difficult to quantify.

Now, I am not saying that economic sanctions should never be imposed. They can, in certain circumstances, be an effective tool of foreign policy. This is most particularly true when they are applied selectively and multilaterally. But we must remember that they are just a tool; they are not the ultimate solution. They should be used judiciously with due consideration given to their long-term impact.

In Congress, we frequently tend to legislate ourselves into a box. We create a particular statutory foreign policy procedure to deal with a specific problem, only to find out later the repercussions of our action. Although the circumstances change in a way that calls for a different or more refined approach to a particular country or issue, the statutory mechanism designed to deal with that foreign policy remains. We are locked into an overly mechanistic approach to a complex issue.

A perfect example is China. Because of an old law called Jackson-Vanik, our bilateral relationship grinds to a halt every spring while Congress wrestles with Jackson-Vanik and NTR status. What is Jackson-Vanik? It is a statute that was narrowly designed to sanction a specific country on a very specific issue—the problem of Jewish emigration from the former Soviet Union. Two decades later, the statute is still on the books.

And what has happened during those two decades? Well, the Berlin Wall fell. The Soviet Union collapsed. Communism in Eastern Europe is all but dead and freedom of Jewish immigration is really no longer an issue. The whole rationale behind the Jackson-Vanik statute is gone. Yet its impact remains and it still drives our foreign policy—not towards the former Soviet Union, but towards China!

Because of Jackson-Vanik, the U.S. Congress is forced to reanalyze our relations with China every year. Every year we find ourselves questioning whether we should cut off our economic and political ties. This is patently absurd. Our foreign policy towards the most populous country in the world is being dictated by a decades-old statute which was crafted to address a very different problem than the multiplicity of issues we have with China today.

Our relationship with China is both dynamic and complex. We have legitimate concerns about nuclear proliferation, about our growing trade deficit, and about human rights and religious freedom in China. But there is no way these concerns can be addressed through a legislative procedure such as Jackson-Vanik. It constrains our ability to formulate a coherent, effective, and long-term foreign policy toward China that effectively integrates economic, political, and human rights components.

Our foreign policy towards the most populous country in the world is being dictated by a decades-old statute which was crafted to address a very different problem than the multiplicity of issues we have with China today.

Or take another example—our annual drug certification exercise. Each year, under the Foreign Assistance Act, the President is required to submit a list of drug-producing and transit countries that he has certified as fully cooperative with the United States in controlling drugs. If the President fails to certify that a country is cooperative, then that country is "decertified" and it becomes ineligible for U.S. foreign aid and other economic and trade benefits. It also tends to paint the "decertified country" as something of a pariah state, hopefully, embarrassing the government into being more cooperative with the United States. If any member of Congress disagrees with the President's certification of a particular country, a resolution of disapproval can be introduced to overturn the President's decision. This triggers a painful and often ugly debate in Congress which rubs salt into an already raw relationship.

The whole purpose of this statute is to encourage countries to cooperate with the United States in stopping narcotics trafficking. Does it work? No! Not even close. Countries subject to review resent the judgmental, unilateral nature of our certification process. Rather than increasing cooperation, it creates a political backlash against the United States, a backlash which often hampers the prospects for progress.

The process is also highly sensitive to the prevailing political winds. A few years ago, largely because of the arrest of Gutierrez Rebollo just days before the President was required to make his decision, there was enormous political pressure on Clinton to decertify Mexico. Only with a tremendous effort were we able to turn the tide.

But let's stop and think for a minute what decertification of Mexico would mean. Yes, drugs are a serious problem in our society. Yes, the majority of narcotics flowing into the United States come from Mexico. And yes, Mexico does have some deep-rooted problems with corruption. But is the answer to decertify the country and make them ineligible for assistance in their, and our, struggle against drugs?

When we threaten to impose unilateral sanctions on friendly countries such as Mexico, we are jeopardizing cooperation on a large number of issues. The United States needs Mexican cooperation on a number of issues, from illegal immigration to cross-border pollution. Decertification of Mexico is not likely to help solve the drug problem. But one thing is certain: it would definitely poison our bilateral relations and hamper cooperation on a number of important bilateral issues.

A Suggested Solution

The problem of unilateral sanctions is real; they are becoming an increasingly popular tool of foreign policy despite their limited utility. It's time we in Congress reexamined our use of this tool. That is why I am proud to be a co-sponsor of

H.R. 1244, the Enhancement of Trade, Security, and Human Rights through Sanctions Reform Act.

Now there is some criticism aimed at this legislation and the sanctions reform movement, most notably in two recent articles, one by Senator Jesse Helms and the other by Elliot Abrams. Both authors question whether the proliferation of legislation has actually resulted in any increase in the use of sanctions. They also assert that depriving the United States of the ability to utilize sanctions will ultimately lead to more draconian responses to foreign policy problems, including war. Although I respect the opinions of both authors, I believe their conclusions are wrong on both fronts.

First, of the 115 unilateral sanctions since World War I, 60 have been imposed in the last five years. Second, it is worth noting that this rise in the use of unilateral sanctions comes during the same five years that U.S. military forces have been engaged more often and in more places than the previous 40 years combined.

I think both Senator Helms and Mr. Abrams miss the fundamental point of the sanctions reform bill. The legislation being considered does not deprive either the administration or the executive branch of the ability to impose unilateral sanctions. It only requires that a deliberative, methodical process be rigorously applied before they are imposed. If, after undertaking this process, either the administration or Congress feels that unilateral sanctions are the most appropriate method of achieving our foreign policy goals, they can still be applied.

Conclusion

By now, it should be clear that my position is very clear! The United States cannot retreat from the world stage or the world economy. Nor can we shrink from the leadership role which is thrust upon us. But it is equally obvious that unilateral sanctions are a poor tool of foreign policy. If there is any lesson I would want you to take from these remarks today, it is this: acting alone, the United States can neither cope with all the challenges presented by today's international environment nor can it take advantage of all of the opportunities it presents. There needs to be recognition of the limits of unilateralism and greater deference given to multilateral approaches.

In the end, world engagement and multilateralism do not reduce America's influence, but extend it. They do not reduce respect for America's power. They enhance it.

Thank you.

III. Defending Human Rights

Fulfilling the Promise of America[1]

Goliath J. Davis III

Chief of Police, St. Petersburg, FL, 1997– , and Adjunct Professor of Criminology, University of South Florida, St. Petersburg; born St. Petersburg, FL, 1951; B.A., Rollins College, 1973; M.S., University of South Florida, 1977; Ph.D., Florida State University, 1984; graduate of Harvard University's John F. Kennedy School of Government, 1993; Certified Police Officer/Fire Fighter, St. Petersburg, FL, beginning 1973; assigned to that department's Field Training and Evaluation Program, 1979; served department in Patrol, Training, Vice and Narcotics, and Research and Development; Division Chief assigned to Training and Research Division, 1980; Deputy Chief, 1984; Deputy Chief of Patrol Division, 1989; Assistant Chief of Administrative Services Bureau, 1990; Fifth Annual Tampa Bay Ethics Award from University of Tampa, Center for Ethics, 1999; Brownlow Award for best article in Public Administration Review, 1998.

Editors' introduction: Dr. Goliath J. Davis III addressed some 775 students, parents, faculty, union members, employees, and politicians at the University of South Florida commencement convocation in Mahaffey Theater. Concerned that "America's promise may be in jeopardy," Chief of Police Davis advised that, "while law enforcement has its place, the law enforcement community too often is forced to respond in a punitive or coercive way when other institutions of social control fail . . . ." This speech was printed in the *St. Petersburg Times*, May 6, 1998. Responses to the speech were "positive" and "powerful."

Goliath J. Davis III's speech: President Castor, Dean Heller, members of the faculty and staff, the graduating class, award recipients and honorees, dignitaries, family members and friends, it is an honor to stand before you today to deliver the commencement address. I have chosen to speak to you briefly on the subject "Fulfilling the promise of America."

No one doubts that America is a great nation. Economically, militarily and intellectually, America has consis-

---

1. Delivered in St. Petersburg, Florida, on May 3, 1998, at 2:00 p.m. Reprinted with permission of Goliath J. Davis III.

tently demonstrated its capacity to compete and succeed. Yet, by other indices, America's promise may be in jeopardy. As we enter into the new millennium, we must question whether or not we have lost sight of the fundamental principles which are the very foundation of our commitment to be "one nation . . . . indivisible, with liberty and justice for all."

On July 4, 1776, the Founding Fathers introduced a document which proclaimed, "We hold these truths to be self-evident, that all men are created equal, that they are endowed by their creator with certain inalienable rights, that among these are life, liberty, and the pursuit of happiness."

America's courage rests with the fact that, since the signing of the Declaration of Independence, the American people have struggled and toiled to realize the intent of this great proclamation. This struggle has manifested itself in the form of civil war and civil unrest at home, and world war abroad. The significance of the Declaration of Independence is so pervasive that while standing on one of the great battlefields of the Civil War, President Abe Lincoln in his Gettysburg Address reminded those present and all of mankind to follow the promise of America. He reflected on the Declaration of Independence stating, "Four score and seven years ago, our fathers brought forth on this continent a new nation, conceived in liberty and dedicated to the proposition that all men are created equal."

Like others engaged in the struggle for freedom and equality, Lincoln knew that neither comes without costs, and the struggle itself may jeopardize the existence and future of those who collectively form this democracy we call the United States of America. For he further stated in his address, "Now we are engaged in a great civil war, testing whether that nation or any nation so conceived and so dedicated can long endure . . . ."

Lincoln's great address was delivered on November 19, 1863, approximately one hundred thirty-five years ago, and while the nation survived the Civil War, it still seeks to fulfill the promise of America. If America is to continue to be a nation of hope, a nation of vision, and a nation of prosperity, if it is to continue to be that nation so conceived, and so dedicated to the founding principles of equality, liberty, and justice for all, then we the people must wake up and realize that, while we have made considerable progress, the journey is not yet complete.

Lincoln's crisis of the 1860s was civil war. As the journey continued, the crisis of the 1960s was civil rights, civil unrest, riots, and, once again, considerable debate regarding the inconsistencies between the promise of America and the realities of the American experience for those denied opportunities to participate fully in all that America offers. Like Lincoln, Americans devoted to securing the promise of

America for all of its people were assassinated—John [F.] Kennedy, Martin [Luther] King, and Robert [F.] Kennedy. Additionally, blacks and whites alike lost their lives in pursuit of America's promise.

The 1968 Kerner Commission report found that our nation was moving toward two separate societies: one white and one black. Recently, the Millennium Breach report revealed that we have reached two societies in America, separate and unequal—the rich are getting richer and the poor are getting poorer.

Ironically, as we observe the 30th anniversary of the assassination of Dr. Martin Luther King Jr., and the garbage strike here in St. Petersburg, the push to declare victory and roll back the accomplishments and enabling legislation from the civil rights era has intensified. Proposition 209 in California and other comparable initiatives designed to dismantle affirmative action are being implemented and applauded.

Confused by the relative success of social integration, many fail to realize that economic integration is far from being a reality, and as we move towards a society marked by haves and have-nots, African Americans and others who have been locked out economically are as a group adversely impacted.

Locally, we have experienced civil unrest and continue to seek solutions. Some among us believe that the only solution is more prisons, the only solution is intensified law enforcement, the only solution is more laws. As police chief and one with a doctorate in criminology, I continually strive to communicate that, while law enforcement has its place, the law enforcement community too often is forced to respond in a punitive or coercive way when other institutions of social control fail to effectively accomplish their objectives.

Recently, Florida lawmakers proposed modifying the criteria for the Bright Futures Scholarship, an initiative which makes awards to Florida students utilizing monies from the Florida lottery. The proposal, if approved, would raise the current SAT score needed from 970 to 1100 by the year 2001. If the revised SAT score had been in place during the first year the scholarships were awarded, over eleven thousand students would not have been able to obtain scholarships, disproportionately impacting minority and low-income families. Sadly, the reason for modifying the criteria has nothing to do with the probability of success, but rather with the fact that legislators feel the current program is too expensive. Yet, few question the expense of incarceration when clearly it is cheaper to educate our children.

Schools sit idle, in this and other communities, after the official closing times while children fail because they do not have access to libraries, computers, and other resources. We must rethink how we deliver our services if we are to realize the promise of America. For every time schools, churches,

We must rethink how we deliver our services if we are to realize the promise of America.

and families fail the probability of a police or criminal justice system success is heightened. We must change this dynamic. We must educate more and incarcerate less. We must prepare our children to compete in this and the global society and ensure everyone an opportunity at the table of economic prosperity.

Regrettably, as we have moved towards a society of haves and have-nots, selfish interests have heightened; and race, ethnicity, and gender issues have become more pronounced. Have we lost our collective will to be our brother and sister's keepers? And are we more and more, either explicitly or implicitly, endorsing measures and initiatives which neglect the plight of those who are less fortunate?

Regrettably, as we have moved towards a society of haves and have-nots, selfish interests have heightened; and race, ethnicity, and gender issues have become more pronounced.

Some argue against what is perceived as unfair preferential treatment as it relates to affirmative action, while ignoring the issue of privilege in our society. The question has never been whether or not African Americans, Latinos, and others can compete if afforded the opportunity; but rather would they be allowed to compete or forced to comply with standards and rules that are not true predictors of one's capacity or probability of success. The truth of the matter is that, even with the institution of affirmative action and civil rights, we have yet to realize the moment when self-interest will allow African Americans and others equal access without legal intervention and oversight. Thus, the question of affirmative action is a moral one.

Recent experiences at Denny's and Texaco clearly illustrate the extent to which, although much has been accomplished, there is still much to do. African American secret servicemen entrusted with the responsibility of protecting the most prominent leader of the free world were denied opportunities to be served at a Denny's restaurant in Maryland. Further investigation found discriminatory practices widespread in the Denny' s organization.

Texaco oil company executives characterized fully capable, competent African American employees as black jelly beans, stuck in the bottom of the jar; and actively denied them opportunities for advancement, based not on character, not on competence, but on ethnicity.

So, while the signs of discrimination, segregation, Jim Crow, and preference have changed and are more difficult to read than before, they are nonetheless still present. Some are now in the form of Proposition 209, charter schools, unitary status, reverse discrimination, and other initiatives which reflect our frustration with our inability to create a perfect society since the civil rights movement, more than thirty years ago.

In the face of a recent development in the sports world, one must ask, "Are we the people truly opposed to quotas and preferences as a means of righting prior wrongs?" American race officials demoralized by Kenya's dominance in distance track and field events changed the rules and established quotas restricting to three the number of Kenyan and foreign runners. The number of American competitors is unrestricted.

In 1903, poet Emma Lazarus penned the sonnet "The New Colossus." It is testimony to her faith in America as a haven for the oppressed, and is inscribed on the base of the main entrance to the pedestal of the Statue of Liberty. All of us are familiar with the words:

"Give me your tired, your poor, your huddled masses yearning to breathe free, the wretched refuse of your teeming shore. Send these, the homeless, tempest-tossed to me, I lift my lamp beside the golden door."

The sincerity of this invitation is being questioned today as we close our borders in Texas and California to Mexicans desiring to enter our country because they believe in the promise of America.

Competition for goods and commodities seem to be draining us of our will to fulfill the requirements of America's promise. I am reminded of Adam's fall from grace in the Garden of Eden, and the report that he hid himself from God. As I stand before you today, I can imagine God calling out to America as he called out to Adam saying, "America, oh, America, where art thou? Where art thou on the issue of human rights? Where art thou on the issue of liberty? Where art thou on the issue of justice and equality?" And unlike Adam, I do not believe we are going to hide. I believe America is going to wake up and fulfill its moral imperative.

As I stand before you today, I am concerned but I am not without hope. I am worried but I am not without faith. For I believe America will answer the call and fulfill its promise. For the promise of America does not rest solely with words scribbled on historical documents or at the base of statues and monuments; but rather the promise of America lies in the hearts and souls of all who profess to be American.

Dion, the songwriter asked, "Has anybody here seen my old friends Abraham, Martin, John, and Bobby? Can you tell me where they have gone? They freed a lot of people but it seems the good, they all die young, I just looked around and they were gone."

And I, a man of hope and idealism, ask, Have we lost all of the dreamers? Have we lost all of the warriors for peace, justice, equality, and harmony? I believe the answer is a resounding no. I believe the class of 1998, at this university and others across this land, represent the dreams of America. Sitting among you are the future doctors who will conquer AIDS, the economists who will provide the guidance and leadership needed to ensure economic prosperity, the social scientists who will craft a new society, the philosophers and religion majors who will assist with the moral dilemmas we face, the educators who will revolutionize the manner in which we deliver educational services, and the criminologists who will assist citizens and policy makers in understanding the nexus between crime, education, economics, and power.

I will never give up on America. Therefore, I will endeavor for all the days of my life to continue the process which has made America a great nation. That process is one of self-criticism. And I encourage you, as I always encourage my students, to do the same. Let us never fail to hold this country up to the mirror and evaluate its progress in light of the intent of that great document, the Declaration of Independence.

The new civil rights frontier as we enter into the year 2000 is economic empowerment for all Americans; and our challenge will be constructing the bridge to economic parity.

As I close, I leave you with the words of Dr. King and ask that you, the class of 1998, and all others within the sound of my voice adopt them as I have, as a guiding vision. Dr. King stated, "I have the audacity to believe that people everywhere can have three meals a day for their bodies, education and culture for their minds, and dignity, equality and justice for their spirits. I believe that what self-centered men have torn down, other-centered men can build up."

My challenge to the class of 1998 is that you move forward, rekindle the flame of hope, justice, and equality, and continue the struggle to realize the fulfillment of the promise of America.

Thank you!

Hate Crimes: A Model Response[2]

Eric H. Holder Jr.

U.S. Deputy Attorney General, 1997– ; born January 21, 1951, New York City; B.A., Columbia College, 1973; J.D., Columbia Law School, 1976; Department of Justice, 1976–1988; Associate Judge, Superior Court, District of Columbia, 1988–1993. U.S. attorney, Department of Justice, District of Columbia, 1993–1997. As a law student, clerked for the NAACP Legal Defense Fund and Department of Justice Criminal Division.

Editors' Introduction: Speaking before a summit on hate crimes, Deputy Attorney General Eric H. Holder Jr. pointed up the need to recognize that "hatred starts oftentimes in an individual who feels alone, confused and unsupported. Hatred starts with someone who believes he has no control over his life and who illogically lashes out at others." He urged his audience to "craft effective ways to redirect the anger that fuels hate."

Eric Holder Jr.'s speech: Thank you for such a warm welcome. I am delighted to be a part of this extraordinary summit on hate crimes sponsored by the United States Attorney's office for the Southern District of Ohio and its Hate Crimes Working Group. I thank my friend United States Attorney Sharon Zealey for extending me an invitation. To everyone who worked so hard to make this day a reality, I offer you my sincerest congratulations on a job well done. I know that we will all come away inspired and enriched. And to those who have been involved in the effort to combat hate crimes in this area I offer my thanks. Only when more people like yourselves become involved in similar efforts in other parts of our great nation will the problem of hate crime be ended.

Eliminating hate crimes and eliminating bigotry and bitterness are among this country's most important, and enduring, challenges. There is never an excuse for violence against innocent persons. And we must all understand that these kinds of attacks—committed because the victims look different, practice a different faith, or have a different sexual orientation—threaten America's most cherished ideals. They represent an attack not just on the individual victim but also on the victim's community—and they diminish us all. And their impact is broader because they send a message of hate. They are intended to create fear.

Tragically, bias-related crimes and the hatred that fuels them remain a fundamental problem in our society. My expe-

We must all understand that these kinds of attacks—committed because the victims look different, practice a different faith, or have a different sexual orientation—threaten America's most cherished ideals.

---

2. Delivered at the Sharonville Convention Center Sharonville, Ohio, June 21, 1999. Reprinted with permission.

rience has been that the virus of hatred has spread far beyond its historical roots of racism. As a former United States Attorney for the District of Columbia, I found that Asian merchants were often targeted for robberies and assaults not only because they were shopkeepers, but also because they were Korean or Chinese or Vietnamese. The brutality of some of these attacks seemed at least partly motivated by misplaced resentment against their success, and rank prejudice against their nationalities.

My office also witnessed an alarming number of violent incidents against individuals based on their sexual orientation. In one case, a man approached two individuals sitting on a park bench and repeatedly asked them in a loud voice, "Are you homosexual?" He then picked up a stick and broken bottles and started beating one of them. The defendant proudly testified at trial that "When homosexuals die, they will burn in hell."

These incidents and other hate crimes like them are not just a law enforcement problem. They are a problem for the entire community: for our schools, for our religious institutions, for our civic organizations, and for each one of us as individuals. And when we come together to respond to these crimes, as you have done over the months and as we do today, we help build communities that are safer, stronger, and more tolerant.

These incidents and other hate crimes like them are not just a law enforcement problem. They are a problem for the entire community: for our schools, for our religious institutions, for our civic organizations, and for each one of us as individuals.

Our first step is to gain a better understanding of the problem. The truth is the data we have now is inadequate. As a result of the Hate Crimes Statistics Act, enacted in 1990, the FBI began collecting information from law enforcement agencies around the country. In 1991, the first year that the FBI reported its findings, 2,700 law enforcement agencies reported 4,560 hate crimes. In 1997, the last year for which we have statistics, 11,211 law enforcement agencies participated in the data collection program and reported 8,049 hate crime incidents.

These numbers alone are a significant concern. Eight thousand forty-nine hate crime incidents represent almost one hate crime incident per hour. One incident per hour. But we know that even this disturbing number significantly underestimates the true level of hate crimes. Many victims do not report hate crimes. Many police departments do not collect any hate crime data. And about 80 percent of those that do, even some in large metropolitan areas, report few or no hate crimes in their jurisdictions, even when most observers conclude a larger problem exists.

There are many ways to improve our data collection. First and foremost, increased hate crime training for law enforcement officials is essential. Police officers must know how to identify the signs of a hate crime. What might appear to some as a crime like so many others, upon investigation can turn out to be one that is motivated by bias.

As many of you know, about a year and a half ago the Department of Justice launched a multi-faceted Hate Crimes Initiative. Improving data collection and enhancing law enforcement training are key components of the initiative. To meet these goals, we recently commissioned a study by Northeastern University to survey some 2,500 law enforcement agencies in order to better understand and improve upon police reporting practices, and we brought together state police academies, police chiefs, state attorneys general, and others around the country to develop uniform curricula for hate crime training.

As a result of these efforts, the Department now has available three law enforcement training curricula on hate crimes—for all levels of investigators. I am very proud of these curricula. They offer each level of officer an "A to Z" handbook for approaching hate crimes as well as a general overview of the topic. Moreover, we have held three regional "train-the-trainer" sessions to instruct qualified trainers on the ins and outs of these new curricula. In each state, there is at least one team of three trainers available to teach these curricula.

But increased opportunities for law enforcement training are only one piece of the reporting puzzle. We must encourage victims to report incidents of hate crime. The reasons for underreporting of hate crime by victims are varied. In some immigrant communities, there is a fear that reporting crimes may lead to reprisals. Language and cultural barriers may also impede reporting. Many gay and lesbian crime victims do not report incidents to the police because they fear mistreatment or disclosure of their sexual orientation.

Generally it can be said that too often the victim is the forgotten person in our criminal justice system. This is especially true where the victim has suffered through a hate crime. Throughout the system, we have to make the process understandable for all, so that all victims are encouraged to report the crime. Our local working groups, which I will turn to in a few moments, can help in this endeavor.

Identification and reporting are, of course, not a complete answer. We must also ensure that potential hate crimes are investigated thoroughly, prosecuted swiftly, and punished appropriately. We must give lie to the notion that there is no difference between an assault and an assault that is motivated by bias. The differences are very, very real.

One thing we know for certain is that we are most effective when we work together. Just as hate crimes are a community problem, they require community solutions. The centerpiece of the Department's Hate Crime Initiative is the formation of local working groups in each of the United States Attorney districts. Here in the Southern District of Ohio and throughout the country, these task forces are hard at work bringing together the FBI, the U.S. Attorney's office, local law enforcement, community leaders and educators to coordinate our response to hate crimes. These working groups recognize that while local law enforcement has the primary role in responding to and pursuing these crimes, federal law enforcement can provide additional resources and can assist with training.

By convening this summit, your working group is a shining example to others. In bringing together local, state, and federal law enforcement as well as community leaders for education and training, you are modeling the coordinated community effort so essential to an effective hate crimes response.

As Southern Ohio has learned firsthand, by involving community organizations in our local working groups, we are enhancing our ability to prosecute these crimes. Quite simply we are more effective when we enjoy the trust and support of the community. Community support makes it easier to uncover information, to enlist witnesses to testify, and to solve cases. But involving the community is not just about effective enforcement, it's about better prevention efforts as well. As a United States Attorney—I learned that prosecutors feel better about themselves and their jobs if they get involved at the front end of these crimes—before they occur—rather than waiting on the sidelines to become involved only afterwards. This feeling is one that I also found shared by others in law enforcement as well.

As many of you are aware, there is federal jurisdiction for prosecuting hate crimes, and we have made these cases a top priority. While most hate crimes are investigated and prosecuted at the state level, we want to make sure that federal jurisdiction to prosecute hate crimes covers everything that it should. Over the past few years, we have taken a comprehensive look at one of our principal federal hate crime laws and decided that it needs to be strengthened. To this end, we proposed to Congress last year, and reintroduced again this year, a bill that would expand our ability to prosecute.

Current law prohibits certain hate crimes committed on the basis of race, color, religion, or national origin. Under the proposed Hate Crimes Prevention Act, federal law would be expanded to cover acts committed on the basis of gender, sexual orientation, or disability. The Act will also remedy a second deficiency in current law. Right now, we must prove not only that a defendant committed an offense because of the victim's race, color, religion, or national origin, but also because of the victim's participation in one of six narrowly defined "federally protected activities." This extra intent requirement, which was written into the law some 30 years ago, is neither appropriate nor necessary in our modern society. And it can lead to truly bizarre results.

For example, federal jurisdiction will probably be upheld if a racially-motivated assault occurs on a public sidewalk. But we may not be able to bring a federal charge if the same attack occurs in a private parking lot across the street. And if a crime takes place in a convenience store, our jurisdiction over places of entertainment may not be triggered unless there is a video game inside the store. Federal jurisdiction should not hinge upon such unnecessary and illogical distinctions.

This new bill is a good fix. Last April, in a Roosevelt Room ceremony, President Clinton joined with a bipartisan group of legislators to urge its swift passage. Testifying before the United States Senate Judiciary Committee last month, I was pleased to join my voice with his to offer my strong support of this bill.

But the battle must be fought not just for changes in our laws but for changes in our hearts as well.

We must look at, we must come to understand the root causes of hate crime. Intolerance often begins not with a violent act, but with a small indignity or bigoted remark. To move forward as one community, we must work against the stereotypes and prejudices that spawn these actions. We must foster understanding and respect in our homes and our neighborhoods, in our schools and on our college campuses. We must not lose sight of the fact that integration—integration by race, ethnicity, sexual orientation—integration is a very good thing. We seemed to know this thirty-five years ago—we fought for it. And now at the close of this century we must battle for it again because social interaction does not allow the virus of stereotyping to grow.

Hate is learned. Hate can be unlearned. We must engage our schools in the crucial task of combating hate by teaching our children moral values and social responsibility. Educators can play a vital role in preventing the development of the prejudice and the stereotyping that leads to hate crime. I am pleased that the Department will be assisting a new partnership announced recently by the president in its efforts to develop a program for middle-school students on tolerance and diversity.

Americans must simply learn to communicate with each other. Not in advertisement cliches and 30-second TV sound bites, but in honest words of thought and feeling. This interaction will not always be pleasant at first but if we are to truly talk to one another we must be prepared to hear things we may not understand or agree with. This is the first step in talking to one another and not at one another and is the initial step in combating stereotypes and fighting hate. We must learn to solve problems together. We must start early in our schools teaching our children how to resolve conflicts and disagreements without knives, guns, and fists.

But we must also understand that this kind of education is an ongoing process and must be continued outside the classroom and throughout the course of our lives.

We must look at, we must come to understand the root causes of hate crime. Intolerance often begins not with a violent act, but with a small indignity or bigoted remark.

Where does hatred start? Hatred starts oftentimes in an individual who feels alone, confused, and unsupported. Hatred starts with someone who believes he has no control over his life and who illogically lashes out at others. I look at a young hate crime perpetrator and I know that, at many points along the way, we could have intervened and helped him take a different path. We must recognize those points and craft effective ways to redirect the anger that fuels hate. We have to invest in our children. We have to help them grow in strength, to acquire positive values, and to have respect for others. These are the things that are the true basis of a good education.

As you leave this summit, pledge to go back to your communities and continue this effort. Hate, though learned, is one of man's most enduring traits. You must persevere in your struggle against it and must be steadfast in your determination to see the battle through. The problem will not be solved in weeks or months or even over a few years. But it can be solved, for this is a man-made problem susceptible to man-made remedies. Your courage, your commitment to this cause will be needed in the years ahead, for in your works, and in your hearts, lie the ultimate solutions.

Thank you.

150th Anniversary of the First Women's Rights Convention[3]

Hillary Rodham Clinton

First Lady of the United States, 1992– ; born Chicago, IL, 1947; B.A., Wellesley College, 1969; J.D., Yale University, 1973; attorney, Children's Defense Fund, 1973–74; assistant professor of law, University of Arkansas, 1974–77; partner, Rose Law Firm, 1977– ; lecturer, University of Arkansas Law School, 1979–80; leader, Rural Health Advisory Committee, 1979-80; author, It Takes a Village: And Other Lessons Children Teach Us, *1996.*

Editors' introduction: At the first Women's Rights Convention at Wesleyan Chapel, in Seneca Falls, New York, on July 19 and 20, 1848, delegates resolved that, "All men and women are created equal" and "endowed by their Creator with certain inalienable rights." In her address to some 16,000 in the heat of a high-school football field, on the 150th anniversary of that convention, Ms. Clinton insisted that, "If we are to finish the work begun here— then no American should ever again face discrimination on the basis of gender, race, or sexual orientation anywhere in this country."

Hillary Rodham Clinton's speech: Thank you for gathering here in such numbers for this important celebration. I want to thank Governor Pataki and Congresswoman Slaughter and all the elected officials who are here with us today. I want to thank Mary Anne and her committee for helping to organize such a great celebration. I want to thank Bob Stanton and the entire Park Service staff for doing such an excellent job with the historic site. I want to thank our choirs . . . I want to thank our singers whom we've already heard from and will hear from because this is a celebration and we need to think about it in such terms.

But for a moment, I would like you to take your minds back a hundred and fifty years. Imagine if you will that you are Charlotte Woodward, a nineteen-year-old glove maker working and living in Waterloo. Every day you sit for hours sewing gloves together, working for small wages you cannot even keep, with no hope of going on in school or owning property, knowing that if you marry, your children and even the clothes on your body will belong to your husband.

But then one day in July, 1848, you hear about a women's rights convention to be held in nearby Seneca Falls. It's a convention to discuss the social, civil, and religious condi-

---

3. Delivered in Seneca Falls, New York, July 16, 1998.

tions and rights of women. You run from house to house and you find other women who have heard the same news. Some are excited, others are amused or even shocked, and a few agree to come with you, for at least the first day.

When that day comes, July 19, 1848, you leave early in the morning in your horse-drawn wagon. You fear that no one else will come; and at first the road is empty, except for you and your neighbors. But suddenly, as you reach a crossroad, you see a few more wagons and carriages, then more and more, all going towards Wesleyan Chapel. Eventually you join the others to form one long procession on the road to equality.

Who were the others traveling that road to equality, traveling to that convention? Frederick Douglass, the former slave and great abolitionist, was on his way there and he described the participants as "few in numbers, moderate in resources, and very little known in the world. The most we had to connect us was a firm commitment that we were in the right and a firm faith that the right must ultimately prevail." In the wagons and carriages, on foot or horseback, were women like Rhoda Palmer. Seventy years later in 1918, at the age of one hundred and two, she would cast her first ballot in a New York State election.

Also traveling down that road to equality was Susan Quinn, who at fifteen will become the youngest signer of the Declaration of Sentiments. Catharine F. Stebbins, a veteran of activism starting when she was only twelve going door to door collecting anti-slavery petitions. She also, by the way, kept an anti-tobacco pledge on the parlor table and asked all her young male friends to sign up. She was a woman truly ahead of her time, as all the participants were.

I often wonder, when reflecting back on the Seneca Falls Convention, who of us—men and women—would have left our homes, our families, our work to make that journey one hundred and fifty years ago.

I often wonder, when reflecting back on the Seneca Falls Convention, who of us—men and women—would have left our homes, our families, our work to make that journey one hundred and fifty years ago. Think about the incredible courage it must have taken to join that procession. Ordinary men and women, mothers and fathers, sisters and brothers, husbands and wives, friends and neighbors. And just like those who have embarked on other journeys throughout American history, seeking freedom or escaping religious or political persecution, speaking out against slavery, working for labor rights. These men and women were motivated by dreams of better lives and more just societies.

At the end of the two-day convention, one hundred people, sixty-eight women and thirty-two men, signed the Declaration of Sentiments that you can now read on the wall at Wesleyan Chapel. Among the signers were some of the names we remember today: Elizabeth Cady Stanton and Lucretia Mott, Martha Wright and Frederick Douglass, and young Charlotte Woodward. The "Seneca Falls 100," as I like to call them, shared the radical idea that America fell far short of her ideals stated in our founding documents, denying citizenship to women and slaves.

Elizabeth Cady Stanton, who is frequently credited with originating the idea for the Convention, knew that women were not only denied legal citizenship, but that society's cultural values and social structures conspired to assign women only one occupation and role, that of wife and mother. Of course, the reality was always far different. Women have always worked, and worked both in the home and outside the home for as long as history can record. And even though Stanton herself had a comfortable life and valued deeply her husband and seven children, she knew that she and all other women were not truly free if they could not keep wages they earned, divorce an abusive husband, own property, or vote for the political leaders who governed them. Stanton was inspired, along with the others who met, to rewrite our Declaration of Independence, and they boldly asserted, "We hold these truths to be self-evident, that all men and women are created equal."

"All men and all women." It was the shout heard around the world, and if we listen, we can still hear its echoes today. We can hear it in the voices of women demanding their full civil and political rights anywhere in the world. I've heard such voices and their echoes from women, around the world, from Belfast to Bosnia to Beijing, as they work to change the conditions for women and girls and improve their lives and the lives of their families. We can even hear those echoes today in Seneca Falls. We come together this time not by carriage, but by car or plane, by train or foot, and yes, in my case, by bus. We come together not to hold a convention, but to celebrate those who met here one hundred and fifty years ago, to commemorate how far we have traveled since then, and to challenge ourselves to persevere on the journey that was begun all those many years ago.

We are, as one can see looking around this great crowd, men and women, old and young, different races, different backgrounds. We come to honor the past and imagine the future. That is the theme the President and I have chosen for the White House Millennium Council's efforts to remind and inspire Americans as we approach the year 2000. This is my last stop on the Millennium Council's Tour to Save America's Treasures—those buildings, monuments, papers and sites—that define who we are as a nation. They include not only famous symbols like the Star Spangled Banner and not only great political leaders like George Washington's revolutionary headquarters, or creative inventors like Thomas Edison's invention factory, but they include also the women of America who wrote our nation's past and must write its future.

Women like the ones we honor here—and, in fact, at the end of my tour yesterday, I learned that I was following literally in the footsteps of one of them, Lucretia Mott, who, on her way to Seneca Falls, stopped in Auburn to visit former slaves and went on to the Seneca Nations to meet with clan mothers, as I did.

Last evening, I visited the home of Mary Ann and Thomas McClintock in Waterloo, where the Declaration of Sentiments was drafted, and which the Park Service is planning to restore for visitors if the money needed can be raised. I certainly hope I can return here sometime in the next few years to visit that restoration.

Because we must tell and retell, learn and relearn these women's stories, and we must make it our personal mission, in our everyday lives, to pass these stories on to our daughters and sons. Because we cannot—we must not—ever forget that the rights and opportunities that we enjoy as women today were not just bestowed upon us by some benevolent ruler. They were fought for, agonized over, marched for, jailed for and even died for by brave and persistent women and men who came before us.

We must tell and retell, learn and relearn these women's stories, and we must make it our personal mission, in our everyday lives, to pass these stories on to our daughters and sons.

Every time we buy or sell or inherit property in our own name—let us thank the pioneers who agitated to change the laws that made that possible.

Every time, every time we vote, let us thank the women and men of Seneca Falls, Susan B. Anthony and all the others, who tirelessly crossed our nation and withstood ridicule and the rest to bring about the 19th Amendment to the Constitution.

Every time we enter an occupation—a profession of our own choosing—and receive a paycheck that reflects earnings equal to a male colleague, let us thank the signers and women like Kate Mullaney, whose house I visited yesterday, in Troy, New York.

Every time we elect a woman to office—let us thank groundbreaking leaders like Jeannette Rankin and Margaret Chase Smith, Hattie Caraway, Louise Slaughter, Bella Abzug, Shirley Chisholm—all of whom proved that a woman's place is truly in the House, and in the Senate, and one day, in the White House, as well.

And every time we take another step forward for justice in this nation—let us thank extraordinary women like Harriet Tubman, whose home in Auburn I visited yesterday, and who escaped herself from slavery, and then risked her life, time and again, to bring at least two hundred other slaves to freedom as well.

Harriet Tubman's rule for all of her underground railroad missions was to keep going. Once you started—no matter how scared you got, how dangerous it became—you were not allowed to turn back. That's a pretty good rule for life. It not only describes the women who gathered in Wesleyan Chapel in 1848, but it could serve as our own motto for today. We, too, cannot turn back. We, too, must keep going in our commitment to the dignity of every individual—to women's rights as human rights. We are on that road of the pioneers to Seneca Falls; they started down it 150 years ago. But now, we too, must keep going.

We may not face the criticism and derision they did. They understood that the Declaration of Sentiments would create no small amount of misconception, or misrepresentation and ridicule; they were called mannish women, old maids, fanatics, attacked personally by those who disagreed with them. One paper said, "These rights for women would bring a monstrous injury to all mankind." If it sounds familiar, it's the same thing that's always said when women keep going for true equality and justice.

Those who came here also understood that the Convention and the Declaration were only first steps down that road. What matters most is what happens when everyone packs up and goes back to their families and communities. What matters is whether sentiment and resolutions, once made, are fulfilled or forgotten. The Seneca Falls one hundred pledged themselves to petition, and lit the pulpit and used every instrumentality within their power to affect their subjects. And they did. But they also knew they were not acting primarily for themselves. They knew they probably would not even see the changes they advocated in their own lifetime. In fact, only Charlotte Woodward lived long enough to see American women finally win the right to vote.

Those who signed that Declaration were doing it for the girls and women—for us—those of us in the twentieth century.

Elizabeth Cady Stanton wrote a letter to her daughters later in life enclosing a special gift and explaining why. "Dear Maggie and Hattie, this is my first speech," she wrote; "it contains all I knew at that time; I give this manuscript to my precious daughters in the hopes that they will finish the work that I have begun." And they have. Her daughter, Harriot Blatch, was the chief strategist of the suffrage movement in New York. Harriot's daughter, Nora Barney, was one of the first women to be a civil engineer. Nora's daughter, Rhoda Jenkins, became an architect. Rhoda's daughter, Colleen Jenkins-Sahlin, is an elected official in Greenwich, Connecticut. And her daughter, Elizabeth, is a thirteen-year-old who wrote about the six generations of Stantons in a book called *33 Things Every Girl Should Know.*

So, far into the twentieth century, the work is still being done; the journey goes on. Now, some might say that the only purpose of this celebration is to honor the past, that the work begun here is finished in America, that young women no longer face legal obstacles to whatever education or employment choices they choose to pursue. And I certainly believe and hope all of you agree that we should, every day, count our blessings as American women.

I know how much change I have seen in my own life. When I was growing up back in the fifties and sixties, there were still barriers that Mrs. Stanton would have recognized—scholarships I couldn't apply for, schools I couldn't go to, jobs I couldn't have—just because of my sex. Thanks to federal laws like the Civil Rights Act of 1964 and Title IX, and the Equal Pay Act, legal barriers to equality have fallen.

But if all we do is honor the past, then I believe we will miss the central point of the Declaration of Sentiments, which was, above all, a document about the future. The drafters of the Declaration imagined a different future for women and men, in a society based on equality and mutual respect. It falls to every generation to imagine the future, and it is our task to do so now.

If all we do is honor the past, then I believe we will miss the central point of the Declaration of Sentiments, which was, above all, a document about the future.

We know, just as the women 150 years ago knew, that what we imagine will be principally for our daughters and sons in the 21st century. Because the work of the Seneca Falls Convention is just like the work of the nation itself—it's never finished, so long as there remain gaps between our ideals and reality. That is one of the great joys and beauties of the American experiment. We are always striving to build and move toward a more perfect union, that we on every occasion keep faith with our founding ideals, and translate them into reality. So what kind of future can we imagine together?

If we are to finish the work begun here—then no American should ever again face discrimination on the basis of gender, race, or sexual orientation anywhere in our country.

If we are to finish the work begun here—then $0.76 in a woman's paycheck for every dollar in a man's is still not enough. Equal pay for equal work can once and for all be achieved.

If we are to finish the work begun here—then families need more help to balance their responsibilities at work and at home. In a letter to Susan B. Anthony, Elizabeth Cady Stanton writes, "Come here and I will do what I can to help you with your address, if you will hold the baby and make the pudding." Even then, women knew we had to have help with child care. All families should have access to safe, affordable, quality child care.

If we are to finish the work begun here—then women and children must be protected against what the Declaration called the "chastisement of women," namely domestic abuse and violence. We must take all steps necessary to end the scourge of violence against women and punish the perpetrator. And our country must join the rest of the world, as so eloquently Secretary Albright called for on Saturday night here in Seneca Falls, "Join the rest of the world and ratify the Convention on the Elimination of Discrimination Against Women."

If we are to finish the work begun here—we must do more than talk about family values; we must adopt policies that truly value families—policies like a universal system of health care insurance that guarantees every American's access to affordable, quality health care. Policies like taking all steps necessary to keep guns out of the hands of children and criminals. Policies like doing all that is necessary at all levels of our society to ensure high quality public education for every boy or girl no matter where that child lives.

If we are to finish the work begun here—we must ensure that women and men who work full-time earn a wage that lifts them out of poverty and all workers who retire have financial security in their later years through guaranteed Social Security and pensions.

If we are to finish the work begun here—we must be vigilant against the messages of a media-driven consumer culture that convinces our sons and daughters that what brand of sneakers they wear or cosmetics they use is more important than what they think, feel, know, or do.

And if we are to finish the work begun here—we must, above all else, take seriously the power of the vote and use it to make our voices heard. What the champions of suffrage understood was that the vote is not just a symbol of our equality, but that it can be, if used, a guarantee of results. It is the way we express our political views. It is the way we hold our leaders and governments accountable. It is the way we bridge the gap between what we want our nation to be and what it is.

Can you imagine what any of the Declaration signers would say if they learned how many women fail to vote in elections?

But when will the majority of women voters of our country exercise their most fundamental political right? Can you imagine what any of the Declaration signers would say if they learned how many women fail to vote in elections? They would be amazed and outraged. They would agree with a poster I saw in 1996. On it, there is a picture of a woman with a piece of tape covering her mouth and under it, it says, "Most politicians think women should be seen and not heard. In the last election, 54 million women agreed with them."

One hundred and fifty years ago, the women at Seneca Falls were silenced by someone else. Today, women, we silence ourselves. We have a choice. We have a voice. And if we are going to finish the work begun here we must exercise our right to vote in every election we are eligible to vote in.

Much of who women are and what women do today can be traced to the courage, vision, and dedication of the pioneers who came together at Seneca Falls. Now it is our responsibility to finish the work they began. Let's ask ourselves, at the 200th anniversary of Seneca Falls, will they say that today's gathering also was a catalyst for action? Will they say that businesses, labor, religious organizations, the media, foundations, educators, every citizen in our society came to see the unfinished struggle of today as their struggle?

Will they say that we joined across lines of race and class, that we raised up those too often pushed down, and ultimately found strength in each other's differences and are resolved in our common cause? Will we, like the champions at Seneca Falls, recognize that men must play a central role in this fight? How can we ever forget the impassioned plea of Frederick Douglass, issued in our defense of the right to vote?

How can we ever forget that young legislator from Tennessee by the name of Harry Burns, who was the deciding vote in ratifying the 19th Amendment. He was planning on voting "no," but then he got a letter from his mother with a simple message. The letter said, "Be a good boy Harry and do the right thing." And he did! Tennessee became the last state to ratify, proving that you can never, ever overestimate the power of one person to alter the course of history, or the power of a little motherly advice.

Will we look back and see that we have finally joined the rest of the advanced economies by creating systems of education, employment, child care, and health care that support and strengthen families and give all women real choices in their lives?

At the 200th anniversary celebration, will they say that women today supported each other in the choices we make? Will we admit once and for all there is no single cookie-cutter model for being a successful and fulfilled woman today, that we have so many choices? We can choose full-time motherhood or no family at all or, like most of us, seek to strike a balance between our family and our work, always trying to do what is right in our lives. Will we leave our children a world where it is self-evident that all men and women, boys and girls are created equal? These are some of the questions we can ask ourselves.

Help us imagine a future that keeps faith with the sentiments expressed here in 1848. The future, like the past and the present, will not and cannot be perfect. Our daughters and granddaughters will face new challenges which we today cannot even imagine. But each of us can help prepare for that future by doing what we can to speak out for justice and equality, for women's rights and human rights, to be on the right side of history, no matter the risk or cost, knowing that eventually the sentiments we express and the causes we advocate will succeed because they are rooted in the conviction that all people are entitled by their creator and by the promise of America to the freedom, rights, responsibilities, and opportunity of full citizenship. That is what I imagine for the future. I invite you to imagine with me and then to work together to make that future a reality.

Thank you all very much.

Protect Me and Respect Me[4]

Charles E. Schumer

United States Senator, 1998– ; born 1951; attended public schools, Brooklyn, NY; graduate of Harvard College and Harvard Law School; elected to New York State Assembly at 23, and to the U.S. Congress at 29, where he represented the Ninth Congressional District in Brooklyn and Queens for nine terms; U.S. Senate Committees on Banking and Financial Services, the Judiciary, and Rules.

Editors' introduction: In United States Congress, Congressman Charles E. Schumer sponsored and helped pass the Omnibus Crime Bill of 1994, and authored and passed the Violence Against Women Act. Schumer sponsored the Hate Crimes Statistics Act, which organized data on crimes of bigotry, and the Hate Crimes Prevention Act, which would allow federal authorities to prosecute these insidious offenses. In his maiden speech on the floor of the United States Senate, printed below, Schumer addressed "the rift between minorities and the police."

Charles Schumer's speech: Mr. President, like many New Yorkers, I have spent a great deal of time in the aftermath of the Amadou Diallo killing reflecting about our city, our police, our country, and our people.

During my career, I think I have been considered a friend of both law enforcement and the minority community. But I have always been troubled by the rift between minorities and the police. And I have always felt that this rift has caused pain and harm to both communities.

There are men, women and children, black and white, alive today because of the work of the New York City Police Department—their fine work. New Yorkers are proud of that fact. Most cops are decent, honorable, and hardworking—and it is wrong to judge all cops by the actions of the bad few.

But what we all must realize is that the momentous drop in crime and the model behavior of many officers does not undo the plain truth that black men and women in New York City who have never broken the law and who should have absolutely no reason to fear law enforcement are all too often hassled and made to feel like lawbreakers, and that it is different for minorities than for the average white person in the city.

Many whites seem to feel that widespread frisking and patting down is a small price to pay for a steep reduction in

---

4. Delivered in Washington, D.C., on March 25, 1999, at 11:00 a.m.
Reprinted with permission of Charles E. Schumer.

crime. But most white people have never been frisked and have no conception of how pervasive the practice is.

But if you talk to black stockbrokers on Wall Street and black lawyers downtown—people who wear a suit and a tie every day—to a person they have a story of being stopped, frisked, and harassed by a police officer.

If you talk to minority co-workers or attend services at African American churches and ask the men and women from the congregation about their interaction with the police—they talk about how they or their law-abiding children were stopped, questioned, and searched by the police.

And they will tell you, as they have said to me, that they know this doesn't happen as often to white people. They know that white people are treated differently.

All people, black and white, want very much for their neighborhoods to be safe and to feel confident that when they send their children or grandchildren to the corner store for a carton of milk they will come home safely. But in addition to these feelings, minorities are humiliated and angered by the indignity of being treated all too often as presumptive criminals.

And if you take the time to listen, the views of minorities about the relationship they want to have with the police can be summed up in five words: "Protect me, *and* respect me."

This poem was left on the shallow doorway where Amadou Diallo was killed:

When you look at me what do you see;
Am I innocent until proven guilty;
Am I your enemy;
Or were you sent here to protect me.
Protect me *and* respect me.

Whatever facts emerge from the killing of Amadou Diallo, or, for that matter, the killing of a Syracuse man, Johnny Gammage, by the Pittsburgh police—whether it is guilty, not guilty, suspension, or removal—our society must deal with the underlying problem of race and law enforcement.

There has been a great deal of rhetoric and anger in the aftermath of the Diallo shooting. I can understand why. But I wish to take a different approach.

I offer today what I believe are constructive solutions that transcend any one set of circumstances and will allow both the "protect me *and* respect me" parts of the equation to coexist and even flourish.

First, for the sake of the city and for the sake of the police force, the NYPD must immediately put in place a system that more quickly gets bad cops off the street.

It was well-known among police, for example, that Justin Volpe, one of the cops who tortured Abner Louima, was a bad, bad seed with multiple complaints against him. It was well-known that Officer Francis Livoti was a ticking time bomb for years before he strangled Anthony Baez in 1994.

The force knew it and did nothing about it. That attitude of silence, protecting your own, sweeping problems under the rug has got to end, not only for the sake of future victims, but for the police department itself.

The tens of thousands of good, honest, hardworking officers pay a price when the Volpes are not removed. For that reason, it is in their interest to end any policy of silence.

The mayor, the police chief, police union leaders, community leaders, and church leaders should all urge police officers to come forward when there is a bad element on the force. It should be an honorable action, not a shameful action, to come forward.

Second, minority recruitment at the NYPD must improve. The force is more than two-thirds white; the city is nearly three-fifths minority.

When mostly white cops patrol high-density, minority neighborhoods resentment is bound to follow.

The city should at last fully fund the Cadet Corps to recruit qualified, college-educated minority applicants through the City University. The program is on the books, but until this crisis was basically ignored.

Also, the city should take advantage of a program created last year by Reverend Johnny Ray Youngblood and me to recruit and train young minority applicants through the churches and to help them become police officers who will patrol the neighborhood from where they came.

Next, beyond minority recruitment, New York City should look to what works in other places.

Two efforts stand out: Boston's Ten-Point Coalition and the military's Defense Equal Opportunity Management Institute.

Boston had the same problems as New York: a rift between police and the African-American community, several high-profile incidents of abuse by certain officers, and clergy that took on the role of police critics.

Their hatred exploded into the open with the stabbing death of Carol Stuart, a pregnant white woman. The husband, Charles Stuart, told police that a black man committed the crime.

The Boston Police hit the streets in full force. They stopped and searched every black male that fit the general description. The neighborhood residents complained about the tactics, but the crime was so horrible no one listened.

They arrested William Bennett, a black man. Carol Stuart's husband, it was learned months later, was the killer. Bennett was innocent.

And Boston was on the verge of a meltdown.

With no place else to go, the police and the clergy agreed to stop fighting and to sit down to develop a plan to stop crime on the one hand, and preserve dignity on the other.

They initiated a five-point contract.

That attitude of silence, protecting your own, sweeping problems under the rug has got to end, not only for the sake of future victims, but for the police department itself.

The heart of it was this: the ministers and respected community leaders agreed to help identify those in the neighborhood who were the real troublemakers. They took the responsibility of telling the police who was dealing drugs and committing violent crime.

The flip side is that when ministers and community leaders took responsibility and identified the troublemakers, others were left alone. And because most crime in each neighborhood is caused by just a few people, the use of the standard stop-and-frisk procedure that the community found so oppressive greatly diminished.

If an officer is abusive or disrespectful, ministers and community leaders have an open line to the police. If the police did not act, or if they refused to address the problem, the ministers and community leaders were free to go to the media.

The plan worked. The crime rate in Boston has dropped even faster than in New York. Serious youth crime is almost non-existent. And the important but difficult relationship between police and the minority community is vastly improved.

Last month in the Bronx, 100 members of the clergy met in the office of the Bronx Borough President and said they have always wanted to work with the police. They said, "We could be a resource. But they're not using us. The police don't even know us. They don't come and talk to us."

The Boston model will work in New York and we should move quickly to implement it here.

The military—and our prayers are with the American soldiers fighting over Kosovo—has also found a way to confront bigotry while increasing effectiveness. The Defense Equal Opportunity Management Institute, developed in the early 1970s to confront segregation and racial hostility among soldiers in Vietnam, is one of the reasons that the armed forces is the most integrated institution in America.

The military learned that, unless bigotry was ended in the armed forces, America could not have an effective military. So by necessity they developed a program that lasts to this day.

Officers and supervisors take a course to confront their own stereotypes and to identify problems within their unit. They have a simple goal: change people's behavior. The rule is that if you've got a problem with race, it better not show up in your words or actions.

The thrust of the program is this: DEOMI, as it is called, continuously surveys enlisted soldiers and officers about race relations on their base. The results are made known only to the commanding officer and to people at DEOMI. When there is a problem on a base, a mobile team of trainers moves in to solve it.

The model has been so successful that DEOMI has signed contracts to work with police organizations. New York City should sign a contract as soon as possible.

In conclusion, this has been one of the most trying and emotional times in New York in years. We are a city, right now, divided. No good has ever come from divisiveness. No job was ever created. No street made safer. No school made better by pulling ourselves apart.

I worry about two things:

First is that division in ours, the most diverse city on earth, has the potential to pull us down.

Second, failure to deal with this problem will ultimately weaken our efforts to fight crime and, perhaps, forfeit the gains we made in crime reduction. That is unacceptable and unnecessary given that options abound if we choose them.

New York City is undoubtedly a safer place in every neighborhood from the far end of the Bronx to the tip of the Rockaways. But it is not necessarily a better place for every neighborhood.

Dr. Martin Luther King taught us that "We are tied together in the single garment of destiny, caught in an inescapable network of mutuality. And whatever affects one directly affects all directly."

The killing of Amadou Diallo, the killing of Johnny Gammage affects us all directly.

We all love our city. Let's each side—as hard as it is to do—put aside our frustration and distrust so we can move past confrontation and collaborate constructively on solutions that protect *and* respect.

No good has ever come from divisiveness. No job was ever created. No street made safer. No school made better by pulling ourselves apart.

Race Relations in America[5]

Bill Bradley

U.S. Senator from New Jersey, 1978–1996; born July 28, 1943, in Crystal City, Missouri; Bachelor's degree, Princeton University; Master's degree, Oxford University (Rhodes Scholar); Air Force Reserves (first lieutenant), 1967–1971; player for the New York Knicks, 1967–1977; author, Life on the Run, 1976; Time Present, Time Past, 1996; Values of the Game, 1998.

Editors' introduction: As he made his way along the campaign trail in 1999 during his bid for the Democratic party nomination, former senator Bill Bradley spoke at length on numerous social issues plaguing America at the end of the century. In this speech, Bill Bradley addressed the subject of racial harmony and emphasized that the true mission of race relations "is to vanquish racial discord from our hearts and spirit."

Bill Bradley's speech: Today I want to talk about race in America, and I'm going to start at home, by talking about race and my own family.

Let me tell you a story about my uncle Cecil and aunt Bub. My uncle Cecil worked in a lead factory for 40 years. He worked next to African Americans, made the same wage, took the same risks, but when my beloved aunt Bub spoke, she didn't talk about African Americans with respect. She'd say, "I just come from another time, I guess but . . ." and then she'd go off on some tirade that would appall me. She didn't hate, but her language was abusive. I often wondered how I could love someone who was so flagrantly wrong on the fundamental moral issue our nation confronted. I'd get angry with her. I'd argue with her. She'd be reduced to tears. Then she'd say to me, "But you're still my baby, aren't you?" Then, I'd leave the room or I'd plead with her that whatever she did, don't hurt me, don't use the language, change.

After I left the hometown I grew up in for college, I began to see her less and less. I'd talk with her on the phone occasionally. "Don't forget, you're still my baby," she'd say, "no matter how big you get." Or she'd pop in at some New York Knick game somewhere on the road in America often ready with a post-game comment about my black teammates that would distress me anew. Yet, I knew I couldn't forget that she'd been my second mother while I was growing up. I wouldn't have dreamed of withholding my love. The conflict was never resolved.

---

5. Delivered on April 20, 1999. Reprinted from http://www.billbradley.com.

One of the last times I saw aunt Bub was in 1988. She weighed about 100 pounds. We sat in the living room of her two-room apartment in a small town in Missouri and she told me about the chemotherapy and the doctors and how Medicare paid her bills and how she was able to live on Social Security. She showed me a picture of her newborn grandson, recalled the good old days, and commented how life was actually pretty good. "Remember," she said, "whatever happens, you're still my baby."

Then right out of the blue, Aunt Bub said, "I'm sure glad you didn't run for President."

"Why?" I asked.

"Because you would have probably chosen Jesse Jackson as your Vice President and then the blacks"—she used another word—"would have killed you."

Then my aunt's funeral took place, and a surprising thing occurred. The most moving tribute at the funeral was a song sung by a black friend of hers—the wife of a local doctor whom my aunt had obviously loved and who, it was also obvious, had loved my aunt.

It was a friendship I never knew about.

After I told the story about Aunt Bub for the first time in a public audience, my press secretary, who was African American, came up to me and said, "You know something, Bill?" I said, "What?" He said, "I've got an Aunt Bub, too."

Race relations in America are never simple. When confronted with the legacy of fear surrounding the issue of race, what can we do beyond deploring violence, enforcing anti-discrimination laws, toughening hate crime laws? How can we peel back the layers of denial and defense that all races bring to the table of multiracial dialogue? How can we overcome our divisions to get to a time when, in Toni Morrison's words, "race exists, but it doesn't matter"?

For starters, we can look deeper into the soul of America.

If we did, we might see four young African American girls in white dresses talking prior to Sunday services in the ladies lounge of the 16th Street Baptist Church in Birmingham, Alabama. The year, 1963. Suddenly, the church is ripped apart by a bomb, killing the young girls instantly. There had been other bombings in Birmingham aimed at halting blacks' progress toward racial equality, but they had not penetrated the national consciousness. But, after that Sunday's explosion, people of all races and all political persuasions throughout the country were sickened in spirit.

Coming 18 days—just 18 days—after Dr. Martin Luther King Jr. had shared his dream for America from the steps of the Lincoln Memorial, the bombing was a stark reminder of how violently some Americans resisted racial healing. Yet the sense of multiracial outrage and solidarity that came out of this tragedy, combined with the seminal leadership of President Lyndon Johnson, led to the Civil Rights Act of 1964 and

When confronted with the legacy of fear surrounding the issue of race, what can we do beyond deploring violence, enforcing anti-discrimination laws, toughening hate crime laws?

to the hope that the search for racial equality would lead to the emergence of a spiritually transformed America.

In the summer of 1994, 30 years later, I was reminded again that slavery was our original sin and race remains our unresolved dilemma and that the bombers were back. From an urban church in Knoxville, Tennessee, to countless rural church burnings in South Carolina, Virginia, Georgia, Tennessee, Texas, North Carolina, and Alabama, the flames and the hatreds of racism burned again. Just as they did in 1982, when Vincent Chin, a 27-year-old Chinese American, was bludgeoned to death in Detroit by two unemployed auto workers who blamed their layoffs on Japan and could not see beyond eye shape to recognize Vincent Chin as an American. Just as they did in 1987, when Navrose Mody, an Asian Indian American, was killed by a hate group called Dot-Busters, which refers to a red dot that many Hindus wear on their foreheads. Just as they did in 1989, when another Chinese American named Minghi Jin Lu was beaten to death in Raleigh, North Carolina, by a number of white men who blamed him for the Vietnam War. Just as they did last summer in Jasper, Texas, when an African American named James Byrd was "chained to a pick-up truck and dragged along a country road until his body literally was torn apart." Just as they did last year in Buffalo, New York, when a group of black teenagers attacked a white man who was gay and stomped him to death. Violence is often just below the surface of race relations in America and fear follows as sure as the night follows the day.

The need for racial healing should be a common-sense impulse. If you believe you are your brother's keeper, if that's your morality, you've got to walk your talk. But, if morality doesn't convince you, how about self-interest?

America is increasingly a mixture of races, languages, and religions. Four to five million Latinos and over five million Pacific Asians have arrived in America since 1980.

- In my home state of New Jersey, schoolchildren come from families that speak 120 different languages.
- Detroit has absorbed over 200,000 people of Islamic Middle Eastern descent in the last decade.
- In San Jose, California, when you look in the phone book for the Vietnamese surname Nguyen, it outnumbers the Joneses.

In Houston, one Korean immigrant restaurant owner oversees Hispanic immigrant employees who prepare Chinese-style food for a predominantly black clientele.

By the year 2010 in America less than 60 percent of the people entering the workforce are going to be native-born white Americans. That means that the economic future of the children of white Americans will depend increasingly on the talents of non-white Americans. That's not ideology; that's demographics.

Even though our American future so evidently depends upon finding common ground, people of different races often do not listen to each other on the subject of race. For example, too often black Americans ask of Asian Americans, What's the problem? You're doing great economically. Many black Americans believe that Latinos don't properly appreciate the historic civil rights struggle. And some Latino Americans question whether the civil rights model of blacks and whites is the best path to progress. Meanwhile, many white Americans continue to harbor absurd stereotypes about all people of color. And many black Americans take white criticism of individual acts as an attempt to stigmatize all black Americans. In other words, we seem to be more interested in defending our racial territory than in recognizing it could be enriched by another person's racial perspective.

Yet the desire to be a part of one national community—even a noble community—persists. Last year, I was in Santa Cruz, California, meeting with the leaders of an extraordinary organization called Barrios Unidos, which aims to avoid violence among local Latinos, to generate jobs, and to bring people together. After touring the area I sat and talked with seven young women from the neighborhood. Most came from families that had worked from dawn to dusk in the lettuce fields of California's Central Valley. After a while I asked them what they hoped for. One, a junior in the local college and president of her class, said, "What I hope for"—she began to choke up as tears rushed to her eyes—"is that someday I can be treated like everyone else in America." Unfortunately, we have constructed a society in which the deadwood of superstition, fear and fantasy continues to stave off racial understanding. For many Americans race means difference. It means we see humanity divided into kinds—white, black, yellow, brown, red. Worse, race means we see these kinds as absolutely, eternally, essentially different, and worst of all, we're infected by the idea that God or the devil or nature created these kinds of human beings and intended some kinds to be better than others. Too many of us believe that each kind is stuck with its particular characteristics and that if you mix the different kinds you usually get the worst of both. It is this mind-set—this lens of perception—that we must overcome.

Over the last 35 years there has been much progress on race relations in America. The walls of legal segregation have been dismantled. I sometimes imagine what Dr. Martin Luther King Jr. would observe if he were to return today. He had always predicted that if America removed the shackles of overt discrimination, African Americans would ascend to

Even though our American future so evidently depends upon finding common ground, people of different races often do not listen to each other on the subject of race.

positions of excellence in practically every field of endeavor in America. That has come to pass.

The task, for those of us who want better racial understanding today, is not the same task as those who led the great civil rights revolution of the 1960s. It is not the same task as those of us who fought the affirmative action battles of the 1980s. It is not the same task of those of us who tried to push up the glass ceilings in the 1990s. Our task is more difficult and more subtle and—if we're successful—more long-lasting. It is to vanquish racial discord from our hearts and spirit.

While legal barriers are down, divisions still remain, but they are divisions of the heart more than of the law. The law is only a framework. It cannot control the most important things in life. It can't improve and enrich all the ways that we relate to human beings of a different race: the spirit with which we interact with them, the love we can muster for them simply because they are human beings, the openness we have to them including the acceptance of good and evil, strengths and weaknesses in the same person. The law can tell people what's right for them and then force them to do it, but it can't change the way they feel. It can't generate forgiveness or lessen hatred. It can't bury the old stereotypes and prevent new ones from taking root. It can't force people to see beyond the material events of a day to the deeper meaning of spiritual renewal through brotherhood.

I care about vanquishing racial discord from our hearts and spirit. I care about getting beyond the stupidity of racial division to a time when we can accept each other for who we are. Whenever I speak to a classroom of multiracial faces, whenever I watch a naturalization ceremony that includes new citizens from all the continents of the world, whenever I sit in a black church and feel the power of shared sorrow and shared enthusiasm, whenever I sense the optimism of young Latino political organizers or see the pain on the faces of Asian Americans stigmatized by false suspicions in the 1996 presidential fundraising scandals—when I experience all these things I'm reminded by how much I care. For something so palpably right to be so demonstrably hard to accomplish only strengthens my determination. In running for President, I'm betting that far more than a majority of people in America want to achieve a deeper racial unity. I'm betting that the goodness that's in each of us can win out over our more base impulses and that together we can unleash our national potential and live the promise of our Declaration that "all men are created equal."

It is with all of these thoughts in my mind that I reflect on the crisis that engulfed black and white relations in New York recently and what this reveals about some truths and some needs in our life.

> *The task, for those of us who want better racial understanding today, is not the same task as those who led the great civil rights revolution of the 1960s.*

Amadou Diallo, a 22-year-old immigrant from Guinea, was shot on the night of February 4, 1999. Four police officers fired 41 bullets, 19 hitting him. He lay dead in the entryway of his apartment building. He was unarmed. Protests and marches ensued. Approximately seven and a half weeks later four police officers were indicted for second-degree murder. The trial will dominate the news media in New York during the coming months.

This tragic event was in most ways different from the church burnings of 1994 or the James Byrd murder of last summer. It was not an act of senseless hatred. It cannot be dismissed as an act of aberrant individuals. Rather, it was a grievous error by those charged with protecting the very person they shot and in that sense it tells a story about all of us.

Issues about race in the criminal justice system are among the hardest of all to resolve. Communities need the police to protect them from crime and give them a feeling of security in their neighborhoods. There are thousands of excellent police officers of all races who serve their communities with sensitivity and effectiveness. Many have built up strong ties to community institutions, and even more exercise great restraint in performing their difficult duties to pursue those who break the law.

All neighborhoods have the same desire for a life without fear of violence and violation. All neighborhoods benefit when the police and the community join together to reduce crime. The question is, how do we get equal security for all communities? How can we make sure that the pursuit of criminals who terrorize citizens in one neighborhood doesn't lead to wholesale violations of citizens' rights in another neighborhood?

The reason the Diallo event ignited immediate outrage in the black community is that it was only an extreme example of the targeting that most African Americans have experienced with the police at some time in their lives. Even Mayor Giuliani's highest appointed African American recalled a time when his car was stopped and he was given a rough time by the police in Queens simply because he was black. Or, as Harvard Law Professor Charles Ogletree has said, "If I'm dressed in a knit cap and a hooded jacket, I'm a probable cause."

If you're black, you know that being within the radar of white fear and suspicion can be dangerous. You also know that getting outside that radar is a relentless task because you have to keep doing it every day. A noted African American male once told me that whenever he got into an elevator with a white woman he would whistle Beethoven's Fifth so that she could be sure that he was no threat. Ask any middle-class black family about the talk they have with their children before they loan them the family car. The conversation is called DWB—Driving While Black. The chance is great that at some time a young African American who is driving a car will be stopped by the police, usually on the road at night. Mothers want to make sure that their children know how to act—don't be too nervous or too calm, say yes sir, offer no complaint, indulge in no talk-backs; if asked to get out for a body search cooperate fully and don't make any quick movements; if the police want to look in the trunk forget the Constitution, and don't protest, just open it. That way the police will hopefully see your innocence and let you go unscathed both in body and record. Every black mother dreads the call from the police department in the middle of the night.

Is a Diallo-like event a potential catalyst, not just toward police reform, but toward deeper understanding? If you're the mother of a white 22-year-old, imagine your son unarmed and riddled with bullets. Why can't this stark tragedy come across in a compelling-enough way to open the eyes of all of us today—just like the church explosion in Birmingham did 36 years ago? The answer lies in white indifference and black suspicion. Our perceptions of what's possible have been shaped by years of life experience in a tough world full of stereotypes, shocking behavior, and more than a few people of both races with an inability to forgive. This predicament makes it hard for whites to talk calmly about the fear of young black men and equally hard for blacks to grant any validity to the white concerns.

White indifferences comes in many forms. It can be indifference to the suffering of others or what Martin Luther King Jr. called "the silence of good people." It can be indifference to the need for racial healing. It can be the inability to see that most black parents are just like most white parents—struggling against circumstances that would test the very best of us to provide their children with a good home, an education, health-care, and the chance to avoid the traps of teenage pregnancy and drug abuse. It can also be found in the inability of whites to understand what they possess for no reason other than the color of their skin.

White skin privilege is the flip side of discrimination. While discrimination is negative and overt, white skin privilege is negative but passive. It's a great blind spot more than a painful boil, but in a subtle way the result is often similar. Most whites are unaware of it. What I call privilege seems normal to them. It seems normal because it is not seen in contrast with the experience of someone who doesn't possess it.

For example, a few years ago ABC's Diane Sawyer devoted a segment on the program *Prime Time Live* to the experience of a white couple and a black couple who were looking for apartments in St. Louis. Each couple was dressed the same, had the same type of job and income, and maintained relatively the same demeanor through all of the apartment visits.

The black couple was turned down at virtually every stop. The white couple was accepted at nearly all the stops. When a white goes to look for an apartment, it doesn't occur to him/her that it will be lost because of race. That's white skin privilege.

Another example: when I was a rookie in the NBA, I got a lot of offers to do advertisements, even though I wasn't the best player on the team. My black teammates, some of whom were better, got none. I felt the offers were coming to me not only because of my biography, but because I was white. Thus, white skin privilege.

Finally, white skin privilege means that if your kids are stopped by police at night you don't fear they will be mistreated by the police because of the color of their skin. There is no need for classes in DWW—Driving While White.

Black suspicion comes from multiple sources. Many African Americans are frustrated with years of having to answer for the violent actions of a few African Americans while white Americans never have to answer for the violent actions of a few whites. African Americans seem to think, "When can we ever be accepted for who we are individually?" Sharing the agony of violence committed by their own brothers and sisters in their own neighborhoods, they yearn for police action that stabilizes but doesn't stigmatize. Other African Americans try to engage in racial education conversations only to find whites basically uninterested. The fatigue from these attempts and these experiences has often led to a reduced effort to get whites to understand, even an anger toward whites for not understanding, and finally a resentment for having to be the party who shoulders the bulk of the effort. The result is sometimes an unwillingness on the part of African Americans to give white Americans the benefit of the doubt. And white Americans know it. Sometimes these feelings produce a bitterness that hardens as if it were cement, making candid talk about race with whites impossible. When black suspicions are so high, a Diallo event can never bring us all together.

The media conveyed the Diallo tragedy as an Al Sharpton–Rudy Giuliani problem—another episode in the long-standing conflict between two bitter political foes. But why, when such horrific acts take place, do not all of us spontaneously and instinctively rise up together regardless of race and express our sadness, our sympathy, and our determination that it won't happen again? Why do we not take what is hidden from view—the underlying tension, fear, and anger—and bring them into the sunlight where the wounds can heal? Why in the aftermath of such a shooting does not someone of stature focus on the pain and not on the politics? Why doesn't some public official ask our schoolchildren to observe the tragedy with a moment of silence in memory of another life lost to senseless violence and tell all of us that, if we want to, we can change our lives, our relationships, and our communities for the better? Why can't we see that by framing it as just a conflict between two interest groups, the police and the blacks, we diminish our chances for healing and in so doing are losing the idealistic part of ourselves that is most genuine, most soulful, and most hopeful?

The best way to get beyond the divisions and tensions is to unite for a deeply felt common goal. Police accountability, yes—but I'm thinking of something larger. One in five children in America live in poverty. Among black children 40% are destitute. There is no reason why a multiracial coalition cannot be built to lift up our poorest children—to make sure they have a healthy start, a nurturing childhood, and a chance for a good education. If that became our shared purpose, millions of Americans from all races could join the effort. Working side by side—as we did in fighting for civil rights in the 1960s and rebuilding burned-out black churches in the 1990s—we could reaffirm our common humanity. It would necessarily involve the parents of the children. They offer the leverage for whatever the rest of us will do. The coalition effort would challenge the national government to do more, utilize the rich, untapped human resources of the community, mobilize the money of those moved to give, and attract the goodwill of the nation.

Improving the life chances of children who are poor can become the North Star of our society—a reference point by which we measure our actions, our progress, and our self-respect.

To say that such an objective is right or left misses the point. Ideas about how to save children can come from both sides of the political spectrum and all should be invited to participate. Improving the life chances of children who are poor can become the North Star of our society—a reference point by which we measure our actions, our progress, and our self-respect.

And now I'd like to address the next generation—those in the hall today and those across the country who are working and attending school—for it is your generation that can harvest the fruits of our rich diversity.

The poet Vachel Lindsey once wrote, "The tragedy is not death. The tragedy is to die with commitments undefined, with convictions undeclared, and with service unfulfilled."

There is no issue in which commitment, conviction, and service is as desperately needed as race in America. Today I've described how it has divided us in stupid and often lethal ways since the beginning of our country. Skin color, eye shape, and even ethnic origin have too often in American history resulted in humiliation, and even sometimes death, for the ones that looked different. We have to accept those painful chapters about who we are as a people, just as we have to accept some painful facts about who each of us is as an individual. But then we must move on and build a better world. The question is, how can the people with the best intentions from all races find a way to move forward together?

For me the quest for racial unity remains the defining
moral issue of our time. It's the reason I first ran for the public office. I can still remember sitting in the Senate galley as a
college intern one hot June night in 1964 and watching the
Civil Rights Act pass—the one that desegregated public
accommodations—and thinking something happened here
that made America a better place tonight for all Americans
and maybe someday I can be here to help make America a
better place. This "commitment" and this "conviction" filled
my Senate years with purpose. I can still remember walking
into the Senate chamber the day of the Rodney King verdict
and in a silent chamber taking pencils and hitting my lectern
56 times in two minutes to symbolize the blows King
received at the hands of the Los Angeles Police Department.
Afterwards the hate mail flowed but so did a letter that lifted
my spirit from a man in Philadelphia who in honor of my
speech wrote a symphony called "56 Blows."

That's my story. What's yours?

Do you care about race? If you do, then do something
about it.

Don't just listen to the old folks who tell you about the
glory of the civil rights movement—even though it was glorious. Don't conceive of race as just affirmative action—even
though narrow-minded politicians and ambitious journalists
will seek to reduce it to that. Don't tolerate business people
who claim they can't find minorities of talent—even though
they make little attempt to try. Don't coddle excuse makers
of any race—even though there are plenty reasons to grab an
excuse. Don't believe that making money is a sufficient con-
tribution to solving our national problems—even though
money with an open heart can make great progress and
launch a thousand ships of hope.

I say to you who are young, take this issue and find a way
of making it yours—of blowing away the acrid odor of racism
as well as the stultifying pessimism that nothing will change.
We are on the eve of the 21st century. Let us affirm that
when we get to its third decade the racial divisions of America will be mended. Pledge that it will be your generation
that will put these stupid attitudes behind us. Then, it won't
matter whether the doctor is black, white, yellow, or brown
but only whether he's a good doctor. Then, it won't matter
whether you are black, white, yellow, or brown the taxicab
will stop for you in the dead of night. Then, it won't matter
whether two people are black, white, yellow, or brown, love
will conquer all. Start with your life and the life of a friend.
Go from there to your parents, your dorm, your club, your
team, and more friends. Make racial unity a part of your
being. See that difference which enriches is good, but difference that divides becomes self-defeating. If you believe that
you are your brother's keeper—that's your morality—then
walk your talk. If you like the idea of America leading the

world by the power of our example as a multiracial society that works—then help bring it about. If you want a bright economic future for your children—then remember that it will increasingly be dependent on non-white Americans. We are truly at a time when we will all advance together or each will be diminished.

I believe that integration and racial unity are central to our American future. They are not merely programmatic issues. They are not political trends. They are more than identity conundrums. They are fundamental questions of attitude and action, questions of individual moral courage and the moral leadership of our nation.

James Baldwin, counseling his nephew in a letter not to be afraid during the civil rights demonstrations of the early 1960s, concludes with this:

The question is, can we see ourselves and the promise of our future clearly enough so that we can see how good it could be and then want to move ahead?

> I said that it was intended that you should perish in the ghetto, perish by never being allowed to go behind the white man's definitions, by never being allowed to spell your proper name. You have, and many of us have, defeated this intention; and, by a terrible law, a terrible paradox, those innocents who believed that your imprisonment made them safe are losing their grasp of reality. But these men are your brothers—your lost, younger brothers. And if the word integration means anything, this is what it means: that we, with love, shall force our brothers to see themselves as they are, to cease fleeing from reality and begin to change it. For this is your home, my friend, do not be driven from it; great men have done great things here, and will again, and we can make America what America must become.

Our path ahead cannot be clear if we believe the journey has been completed. Denial of the distance we must travel will never allow us to vanquish racial discord from our hearts. The question is, can we see ourselves and the promise of our future clearly enough so that we can see how good it could be and then want to move ahead? By honestly accepting one another, we can get to a new place where fear and hostility give way to the acceptance of goodness in each of us no matter what race.

Only leadership will get us there—from the President, and from hundreds of thousands of leaders across the country who are waiting for the call. They are the Americans who even now lead racial unity forums. They are the ones who take a moment to look beyond people's skin color, eye shape, or ethnicity, to get to know them as human beings. From the President, it starts with making sure that everyone knows just how important this issue is to him, and how fundamental it is to our nation's future.

When Ronald Reagan was President, everyone knew that if you wanted to please the boss, you cut taxes, increased military spending, and fought communism. If I'm President, I want one thing to be known: if you want to please the boss, one of the things you'd better show is how in your department or agency you've furthered tolerance and racial understanding.

When I was in Iowa earlier this year, I spoke at a diversity forum at the University of Iowa—mostly white students. Later that evening, in the home of two professors, a woman asked me, "Why are you speaking about the need for racial progress to a group of white Iowans?" And I answered, "Why not to you? I talk about it everywhere I go."

I will continue to talk through this campaign about the importance of deciding whether we will be a collection of 265 million individuals, or 265 million individuals living together as one nation. One nation—not immigrants and natives, not women and men, not heterosexual and homosexual, not urban and suburban and rural. One nation. Indivisible—not pitted group against group, English-speaking versus Spanish-speaking, black versus white, but indivisible. One nation—where all men—and all women—are created equal, and where each advances and prospers, not because of what they are, but because of who they are, as individuals and as part of that one nation.

IV. Concern for Civil Morals and Ethics

Loss of Sense of Self[1]

Anthony J. Brankin

Pastor of Saint Thomas More Parish, Chicago, IL; born Chicago, IL, 1949; Pontifical Licentiate of Sacred Theology, St. Mary of the Lake University, 1975; Accademia di Belle Arti, University of St. Thomas Aquinas, Rome, 1981–83; Vice President, Catholic Church Extension Society, 1984–86; pastor since 1989.

Editors' introduction: The Reverend Anthony J. Brankin spoke at an annual evening of spiritual renewal to 250 Catholic parishioners of Saint Thomas More Parish, on the southwest side of Chicago, mostly the women of the Tabernacle Society of Our Lady of Charity Parish, as well as a number of men. Brankin concluded that, "If 60–70% of Americans don't really care how their President conducts his private life, it is obvious that his impiety . . . is only a reflection of . . . our prideful unwillingness to order our lives under God." Brankin received a number of requests for reprints of the speech.

Anthony J. Brankin's speech: May I first of all express my thanks to the women of the Tabernacle Society for inviting me to this evening of recollection. I remember a long time ago, there was a particular part in the ceremony for the installation of the officers when the president of the society was told in no uncertain terms that all successes belonged to the society members, and all failures belonged to her. Well, I am here tonight to accept all the blame if this talk fails. Don't blame Sheila. Don't blame Elaine. Just blame me.

You know, of the thousand and one things a priest might do during the course of a day or week or year, he ought to do nothing unconsciously. He ought to watch, think, analyze, and theorize about everything he experiences, that he might gain just a hint of understanding about the world in which he finds himself. Of course, no one is really absolved from the responsibility of being as aware as possible of the events and people that fashion our lives.

Maybe, therefore, you have been watching, too. Maybe you have been picking up on changes that have been taking place. Maybe you have been discerning that somehow, in

---

1. Delivered in Cicero, Illinois, on March 31, 1998, at 7:00 p.m.
Reprinted with permission of Anthony J. Brankin.

some way, things are different—more different today than they were even ten years ago and certainly more different than they were thirty years ago.

Now, I certainly do not mean superficial changes—new kinds of cars, clothing styles, neighborhood changes, though these can always signify some deeper kind of change. What I mean is the sense that we ourselves are not the same people that we were years ago. There has taken place an evolution or a mutation of which we are aware only when we step back and look at ourselves from afar.

This mutation perhaps involves our sensitivities, our morals, our beliefs, certainly; but, most importantly, it denotes a change in that which we consider important and vital to our lives. Indeed the change in ourselves is discovered when we realize that even though we may adhere to a certain body of beliefs, the violation of those beliefs by ourselves or others is so far down on our list of things which bother us that we might as well not even bother to believe.

There has taken place an evolution or a mutation of which we are aware only when we step back and look at ourselves from afar.

The item that causes this meditation in my fevered brain is the last two months of "President Clinton news." Now, mark me well, I do not gloat in any man's sin. I feel bad for him as well as for his family. It is only a typical modern perversion to receive satisfaction from another's personal degradation— "delectatio morosa" elevated to the status of a virtue.

The question which begs to be asked—and it is not even about President Clinton—but rather about us: how is it possible that, according to the polls, the President's approval rating continues to hover around sixty to seventy percent? How is it possible that, citizen after citizen interviewed on the radio, television, or in the newspaper declares that they simply do not care what the president might do in his private life; that his personal morality has nothing to do with any success he might have as president or with the way in which he is running the country?

Well, aside from the fact that it is doubtful that he is actually running the country—I know many mothers and fathers who barely have a fraction of the time he has and they are only running a household. Those things which ought to stop us cold are not the accusations, are not the alleged immorality, but the polls and talk shows that indicate that Americans do not care if the charges are true or not. We simply do not care. And that is stunning. That is saddening.

Years ago, as a boy, I remember the disgust with which one particular Hollywood matinee idol was regarded—at least by some adults— when it became known that some woman in his life had posed naked. His status as hero immediately plummeted to where he was now considered just another Hollywood pervert. In fact, another star from that era was jailed for smoking marijuana; and I remember, as a boy, listening to the adults refer to him as nothing more than a dope fiend.

In the 30s, 40s, and 50s, these kinds of things were cause for outrage and no small amount of embarrassment and shame. No one would ever say that sins were not committed in those earlier days; but those who committed such transgressions were embarrassed. And those who heard about them were shamed. Hence the outrage! Something innocent, the soul, the fabric of our country was being dirtied, and it would not be endured by the public. But there is no longer any outrage! Everything is fine. No one can do anything that bothers us anymore—at least for more than 2 or 3 days.

So my analysis is this: some of us are no longer outraged at the shameful behavior of our public figures, because we no longer have a sense of shame. And we no longer have a sense of shame, for we no longer care about God; and no longer caring about God, we lose our sense of self as something that is precious and beautiful—something to be treasured and protected. Ugly behavior, therefore, whether it comes from our President or sports or entertainment celebrities—or even from our children or grandchildren—is simply accepted, shrugged off, or ignored.

Let us look first at "shame" and its relationship to modesty and then to both shame and modesty's dependence upon piety. It may very well be true that the only animal capable of blushing is the human being—you know the feeling where the blood rushes to your face, and you feel warm, and you wish you were somewhere or someone else. I would suspect that the reason no other species can blush is that no other species can feel shame—neither embarrassment nor guilt. Oh! Sometimes birds or dogs if they lose their feathers or their coat will shrink away. But that is more from a sense they do not look right—certainly not from a sense of modesty, shame, or embarrassment.

When humans blush, it is because they feel shamed; but shame is possible only where there is a sense of modesty. We could define modesty as that virtue by which we try to maintain on the outside the dignity that is within. For example: by our dress, our demeanor, our language and comportment, we try to convey the beauty and dignity of the person within—the beauty and dignity of the soul! We always say modesty is attractive and "becoming." And it truly is, because it is a mirror of that beauty and innocence, originally created by God, which we try to preserve. It is a visual manifestation of that which should be going on inside the soul.

Immodesty, however, is the visual or behavioral display for all the world to see, that for this person or in this situation there is nothing to conceal. It's all, embarrassingly enough, on the surface; for there is nothing beautiful or good within to protect or treasure or hide.

Shame, therefore, is that faculty in the soul whereby we know, sense, or feel that modesty has been or is in danger of

My analysis is this: some of us are no longer outraged at the shameful behavior of our public figures, because we no longer have a sense of shame.

being violated in us or in others; and we fear that violation. Now, shame is necessary for us. It is akin to the ability to feel pain. If our nerves did not convey the message of pain to our brains, we'd never pull our hands back from the fire until it was too late. We'd never let go of an electrical wire until it were impossible to do. Pain is the news flash to the mind that one's life is in danger.

By the same token, shame is the message to the soul that the soul's innocence, modesty, and beauty is in danger of being compromised, sullied, or dirtied—or that the soul has already been so violated by sin that it has betrayed its natural beauty and dignity. We feel embarrassed that something that should have been treasured and protected for being so beautiful is now beheld as cheap and ugly. We are shamed.

But thank God for shame, for the ability or capacity to be shamed convinces us instinctively that something is wrong. Yet the only place that shame can exist is in a soul where the comparison between sin and goodness, light and darkness can still be discerned.

Do you remember when Christ calmed the waves and the storm and St. Peter fell to his knees? He wouldn't even look up at Jesus, crying out, "Depart from me, Lord, for I am a sinful man." Peter recognized two things: the utter beauty and goodness and innocence of Christ, and his own sinfulness, highlighted by the presence of Christ. Peter could not have recognized his own corruption. He could not have been shamed if first he hadn't recognized Christ and His beauty. Because Peter still had a sense of shame, he could recognize that his soul should have been more beautiful than it was.

And so, while we never wish to be shamed, we should be grateful that we can be shamed for that will drive us to confession, urge us to contrition, help us maintain our refound innocence, and help keep the beauty that is within beautiful.

Essayists, in many modern journals, often ask the question, "Have we lost our sense of shame?" In view of all the awful things that continue to happen in modern public life —from President Clinton's escapades to 11-year-olds machine gunning their classmates; from basketball players who dress like girls to 35 million abortions in 25 years — it is obvious that we have lost our sense of shame.

The next question, however, is how is it that we have lost this shy sense? And with it our dignity and nobility? How have we gotten to this point where modesty no longer even exists? How is it that no one is even embarrassed to hear what goes on in the Oval Office or to see what is broadcast to us every day on television and radio? If we learn how we've lost our capacity for shame, we can learn how to regain it.

We perhaps have lost our capacity for shame because we have lost our sense of piety. By piety I do not mean what we usually mean by "piety," i.e., someone who prays just a little more outwardly than the rest. What we mean by piety is the old ancient Roman understanding of the word by which emperors and popes, kings and heroes were named Pius. Piety, originally, meant the capacity within to hear a warning voice that we must think as mortals—that it is not for us either to know all or control all. It did not mean "holy" or ostentatious in holiness. When for example it was used of popes and emperors, it meant that, in spite of the great strength of their heroic character, despite the incredible power and authority of their office, they had to recognize that they were mere mortals—that there was a supernatural order above them—a God to whom they must offer sacrifice and a universal law under which they must place themselves or face the most disastrous of consequences.

It was considered imperative that everyone in public or private life recognize that they are not all-knowing, not all powerful, but mortal; and they must constantly refer their policies, their life, their position to a God who is all-knowing, all powerful, and immortal. That's how our fathers and mothers were pious. They knew always there was a God and it was to Him they would have to answer. They may not have gone to church every day of the week, or may not have spent every waking hour on their knees; but they were pious for they understood their relationship to God and to the world.

How unlike our society and culture where we see ourselves as immortal and our science as all-powerful—our knowledge as all-seeing, our future totally of our own making—and we can do whatever we want to whomever we want for there really is no higher power than we ourselves.

Sharpen your sense of modesty and capacity to be shamed, for that will enable you to discern right from wrong, good from bad, ugly from the beautiful.

Do you, therefore, see how totally lacking in modesty that is? How immodest is our society? There is no hidden beauty within—nothing to treasure or protect because we do not reflect God. We are like gods—everything on the outside displayed for all the universe to see—our sins, our failings, our perversions. We think those are our virtues and that they should be displayed. But they are actually our vices and they are shaming us before God and before each other, revealing how empty we are within. If 60–70% of Americans don't really care how their President conducts his private life, it is obvious that his impiety—his prideful unwillingness to admit a God higher than he—is only a reflection of our own impiety, our prideful unwillingness to order our lives under God. What irony that the pagan Romans were more pious in their own way and perhaps even closer to God than we who profess to be Christians. Yes, there has been a change. We are in for some rough times. Therefore, maintain your piety and your prayer life; for that will maintain your position with God. It will also enhance the beauty of your soul.

Sharpen your sense of modesty and capacity to be shamed for that will enable you to discern right from wrong, good from bad, ugly from the beautiful. And it is only that ability that might save our nation!

America at a Moral Crossroads[2]

Jesse Helms

United States Senator, 1973– ; born Monroe, NC, 1921; attended Wingate (NC) Junior College, and Wake Forest College; honorary degrees from Bob Jones University, Grove City College, Campbell University, and Wingate University; U.S. Navy, World War II, 1942–45; city editor, Raleigh Times; Executive Director, North Carolina Bankers Association, 1953–60; Raleigh City Council, 1957–61; CEO of Capitol Broadcasting Co., Raleigh, NC, 1960–72; Chairman, Committee on Foreign Relations; member of Committee on Agriculture, Nutrition, and Forestry; member of Rules Committee; Freedoms Foundation Award, 1962 and 1973; Grand Lodge of Masons of NC; Masons Grand Orator, 1965, 1982, and 1991; Gold Medal of Merit from Veterans of Foreign Wars; North Carolina American Legionnaire Award; Most Admired Conservative in Congress, 1980, 1981, and 1983.

Editors' introduction: Concerned with the "moral and spiritual crisis" in the United States, in this speech Senator Jesse Helms, Dean of the United States Senate, reminded colleagues in that body of the "connection between the business we do in Congress and the state of public morality in our society." Believing that elected officials should be the "caretakers of our own culture," Helms introduced legislation he argued would "promote what is right and prevent what is wrong in our society."

Jesse Helms' speech: Mr. President, I have sent to the desk a slate of legislation that addresses a number of our nation's most pressing social problems. I have introduced a great many of these bills in prior congressional sessions and senators who have been around for a while will find these proposals familiar.

Nonetheless, I shall devote a few minutes to explain the importance of these bills and why it is so crucial to address permissive social policies that are creating a moral and spiritual crisis in our country.

I am delighted, Mr. President, that our nation's economy has grown and prospered for the last two years—helped along, not incidentally, by the responsible fiscal policies insisted upon by the Republican Congress. But the good news on the financial pages is too often overshadowed by utterly horrifying stories elsewhere, stories which detail a moral sickness at the heart of our culture, stories which chronicle the devaluation of human life in our society, sym-

---

2.   Delivered in the United States Senate, Washington, D.C., on January 19, 1999. Reprinted with permission of Jesse Helms.

bolized by the tragic 1973 Supreme Court decision, *Roe v. Wade.*

The most notorious of these appalling stories was the episode involving a young New Jersey woman who in May of 1997 gave birth to an infant in a public bathroom stall during her senior prom. She then strangled her newborn baby boy, placed the body in a trash can, adjusted her makeup, and returned to the dance floor.

Mr. President, this chilling tale cries out that something is badly wrong in the culture that produced it. The American people were justifiably stunned by the furor surrounding this crime—and they are surely even more shocked to learn that this is not an isolated incident.

Consider this: in November of 1997, in Tucson, Arizona, a 15-year-old boy found a newborn in a 3-pound coffee can. After an investigation, police arrested the boy's sister, then 19 years of age. She had given birth to the baby and promptly drowned it in the toilet, covered its little head with a plastic ice cream wrapper, wrapped the body in a flannel shirt, and hidden it. She said she had intended to bury it later.

Despite these largely uncontested facts, an Arizona jury—browbeaten into submission by a defense team suggesting that its client was in fact the victim of a strict Catholic upbringing—returned a guilty verdict only on a charge of negligent homicide, the least severe conviction applicable. This woman, who had murdered her own baby, received a sentence of one year, and during her prison term she will be released during daytime hours on a work furlough program.

This is the tip of the iceberg, Mr. President. National Public Radio recently reported that the bodies of about 250 newborns are callously discarded each year. In some of these cases the babies were stillborn, but in others the newborns were murdered.

Lest anyone think I am exaggerating, pick up almost any newspaper in America, and a distressing story is likely to be found. For example:

- The *Pittsburgh Post-Gazette*, August 12, 1997: Teenage Mother Admits Slaying: Newborn was Found Dead in Gym Bag in Garage of Home
- The *Record*, Northern New Jersey, December 24, 1997: 12 Years for Mom Who Killed Baby: Newborn Tossed From Window
- Associated Press, Atlantic City, New Jersey, July 14, 1997: Baby Born in Toilet Stall, Left in Atlantic City Bus Terminal
- *St. Petersburg Times*, December 20, 1997: Girl Charged who Left Baby in Trash
- *Dallas Morning News*, October 29, 1997: Teen Jailed in Baby's Death Hid Pregnancy, Parents say Newborn Boy

Was Found Suffocated in Garbage Bag

Should we really be surprised, Mr. President, that a nation that not only tolerates, but actively defends the practice of partial birth abortion would produce these gruesome headlines? And the extraordinary level of disrespect for human life to which America has fallen isn't limited to the horrible practice of neonaticide on the part of young mothers. It pervades every part of our society.

In Pennsylvania, two teenagers were stabbed during a showing of a so-called "horror movie" that itself featured two characters being brutally stabbed to death watching a horror film. In Oregon, much of the nation watched in disbelief as news reports described the case of a young man who, after killing his parents, walked into a crowded school cafeteria and opened fire on his fellow students.

Can it be denied that the decline in moral values in American culture helped set the stage for these notorious crimes?

No one act of Congress or court decision is solely responsible for these tragedies, of course. But can it be denied that the decline in moral values in American culture helped set the stage for these notorious crimes? The American people believe this is true. Last year, CBS and CNN/Time both conducted polls indicating more Americans believe that a lack of moral values was the most important problem facing the United States—more important than crime, more important than taxes, more important than health care, more important than education.

Too often, however, the mainstream media doesn't seek to remedy our decaying culture; they actively celebrate it. Just last fall, the supposedly responsible news magazine *60 Minutes* elected to show the videotaped death of a man via Dr. Jack Kevorkian's so-called "suicide machine." In voice-over, Kevorkian was allowed to comment on the procedure—no, strike that, the murder—that the viewer was watching. All the while he defended his abhorrent belief in assisted suicide. And instead of responding with outrage, a portion of the American public rewarded the program with its highest ratings of the year.

Has America become so hard-hearted and callous, Mr. President? Or is it just responding to so-called cultural elitists who celebrate abortion, euthanasia, and promiscuity, while with unrestrained zeal endeavor to destroy all traces of religion in American public life.

Too many politicians blithely suggest that government and morality are not and should not be related; too many producers in Hollywood claim that the filth that passes for entertainment does not corrupt our culture; and too many educators claim the academy does not have a place in addressing the difference between right and wrong.

Mr. President, *they* are the ones who are wrong. We fool ourselves and we fool the public if we suggest that there is no connection between the business we do in Congress and the state of public morality in our society. We are the caretakers of our own culture. And we must not shrink from the responsibility of passing laws that promote what is right and prevent what is wrong in our society.

We make judgments between right and wrong every day, Mr. President, in every vote we cast and every action we take. And when we judge correctly, the positive results can be wonderfully encouraging. Consider this: on August 1, 1996, the Senate passed the Personal Responsibility and Work Opportunity Reconciliation Act. It was subsequently enacted into law. This landmark legislation, commonly referred to as "welfare reform," injected the time-honored values of hard work and personal responsibility into our social welfare system.

Welfare reform has been successful beyond even its supporters' wildest expectations—and, in my view, has tangible indirect benefits as well.

The numbers are stunning: according to the Department of Health and Human Services, the percentage of Americans receiving welfare benefits has plunged from 5.5% in 1995 to 3.3% in 1998. In three short years—and aided by the polices of a number of creative, innovative governors and state leaders—welfare reform almost halved the welfare rolls.

The success of welfare reform is not limited to the dramatic decline of the welfare recipients, though the numbers are impressive indeed. Putting people back to work has started to mend other social problems. The January/February 1999 edition of *The American Enterprise* reports the following good news:

- The number of homicides has dropped from 11 Americans per 100,000 in 1990 to only 7 in 1998, with a noticeably steep decline in the curve since 1995.
- Poverty among black Americans has declined sharply, to a 30-year low of 27%. (U.S. Bureau of the Census)
- Divorce rates in the last three years are dropping, while marriage rates over the same time period are inching upward. (U.S. National Center for Health Statistics)

I for one do not doubt that welfare reform is partially responsible for these encouraging statistics.

In short, Mr. President, good laws help make good societies. And that is the reason I continue to introduce bills in each and every Congress that limit the modern tragedy of abortion and its insidious effects; that allow for prayer in schools while taking steps to ease the scourge of drug use among our children; that protect the rights of federal employees to speak their minds about moral issues; and that make sure our civil rights laws treat Americans as individuals rather than faceless members of racial groups, religious groups, or of a certain gender.

Mr. President, I send seven bills to the desk and ask unanimous consent that the text of each bill be printed in the Record at the conclusion of my explanation of it.

Unborn Children's Civil Rights Act

Mr. President, the Unborn Children's Civil Rights Act has several goals. First, it puts the Senate on record as declaring that, one, every abortion destroys deliberately the life of an unborn child; two, that the U.S. Constitution sanctions no right to abortion; and three, that *Roe v. Wade* was incorrectly decided.

Second, this legislation will prohibit federal funding to pay for, or promote, abortion. Further, this legislation proposes to de-fund abortion permanently, thereby relieving Congress of annual legislative battles about abortion restrictions in appropriation bills.

Third, the Unborn Children's Civil Rights Act proposes to end indirect federal funding for abortions by, one, prohibiting discrimination, at all federally funded institutions, against citizens who as a matter of conscience object to abortion, and, two, curtailing attorney fees in abortion-related cases.

Fourth, this bill proposes that appeals to the Supreme Court be provided as a right if and when any lower federal court declares restrictions on abortion unconstitutional, thus effectively assuring Supreme Court reconsideration of the abortion issue.

Mr. President, I believe this bill begins to remedy some of the damage done to America by the Supreme Court's decision in *Roe v. Wade.* I continue to believe that a majority of my colleagues will one day agree, and I will never give up doing everything in my power to protect the most vulnerable Americans of all: the unborn.

Civil Rights of Infants Act

In 1989, our distinguished colleague from New Hampshire, Senator Gordon Humphrey, first called attention to the incredibly brutal practice of abortions performed solely because prospective parents prefer a child of a gender different from that of the baby in the mother's womb.

The Civil Rights of Infants Act makes sure nobody could ever act upon this unthinkable decision by specifically amending Title 42 of the United States Code governing civil rights. Anyone who administers an abortion for the purpose of choosing the gender of the infant will be subject to the same laws which protects any other citizen who is a victim of discrimination.

Nobody—even the most radical feminists—can ignore the absurdity of denying a child the right to life simply because the parents happened to prefer a child of the opposite gender. I hope the 106th Congress will swiftly act to fulfill the desires of the American people, who rightfully believe it is immoral to destroy unborn babies simply because the parents demand a child of a different gender.

Federal Adoption Services Act of 1999

I am also pleased to introduce the Federal Adoption Services Act of 1999. This bill proposes to amend Title X of the Public Health Service Act to permit federally funded planning services to provide adoption services based on two factors: (1) the needs of the community in which the clinic is located, and (2) the ability of an individual clinic to provide such services.

Under this legislation, no woman will be threatened or cajoled into giving up her child for adoption. Family planning clinics will not be required to provide adoption services. Rather, this legislation will make it clear that federal policy will allow or even encourage adoption as a means of family planning. Women who use Title X services will be in a better position to make informed, compassionate judgments about the unborn children they are carrying.

With so many loving, caring parents available to care for unwanted children, the federal government should do everything it properly can to make sure that adoption is an alternative for expectant mothers. I hope my colleagues will join me in supporting this reasonable proposal.

Voluntary School Prayer Protection Act

Mr. President, the Voluntary School Prayer Protection Act will make sure that student-initiated prayer is treated the same as all other student-initiated free speech—which the U.S. Supreme Court has upheld as constitutionally protected so long as it is done in an appropriate time, place, and manner such that it "does not materially disrupt the school day." [*Tinker v. Des Moines School District*, 393 U.S. 503]

Under this bill, school districts could not continue—in constitutional ignorance—enforcing blanket denials of students' rights to voluntary prayer and religious activity in the schools. For the first time, schools would be faced with real consequences for making uninformed and unconstitutional decisions prohibiting all voluntary prayer. The bill creates a complete system of checks and balances to make sure that school districts do not shortchange their students one way or the other.

This proposal, Mr. President, prevents public schools from prohibiting constitutionally protected, voluntary, student-initiated prayer. It does not mandate school prayer and suggestions to the contrary are simply in error. Nor does it require schools to write any particular prayer, or compel any student to participate in prayer. It does not prevent school districts from establishing appropriate time, place, and manner restrictions on voluntary prayer—the same kind of restrictions that are placed on other forms of speech in the schools.

With so many loving, caring parents available to care for unwanted children, the federal government should do everything it properly can to make sure that adoption is an alternative for expectant mothers.

What this proposal will do is prevent school districts from establishing official policies or procedures with the intent of prohibiting students from exercising their constitutionally protected right to lead, or participate in, voluntary prayer in school.

Safe Schools Act of 1999

Mr. President, government has no higher obligation than the protection of the most vulnerable among us—our children. Outside of their own home, there is no place that a child should feel more secure and protected than while at school.

That is why I joined with several other senators last Congress in introducing the Safe Schools Act. This legislation directly confronts the issue of illegal drug use and juvenile violence by requiring schools that accept federal education funds to adopt a "zero tolerance" policy when a student is found in possession of illegal drugs at school.

The Safe Schools Act provides a logical and commonsense extension of 1994's Gun-Free Schools Act by conditioning receipt of federal education dollars on state adoption of a policy requiring the expulsion for not less than one year of any student who brings illegal drugs to school.

Anyone who questions the link between school violence and drugs should merely turn their attention to the results of a recent National Parents' Resource Institute for Drug Education survey, or PRIDE survey as it is called, which found that:

- Gun-toting students were *twenty times* more likely to use cocaine than those who didn't bring a gun to school;
- Gang members were *twelve times* more likely to use cocaine than non-gang members;
- And students who threatened others were *six times* more likely to be cocaine users than others.

These frightening statistics combined with students' own reports that drugs are the number one problem they face and that illegal drugs are readily available to students of all ages illustrate the need for immediate action. The Center on Addiction and Substance Abuse (CASA) at Columbia University has documented that two thirds (66%) of students report that they go to schools where students keep, use, and sell drugs and that over half (51%) of high-school students believe the drug problem is getting worse. In contrast, CASA has found that most principals see drugs "virtually nowhere."

Mr. President, the Center for the Prevention of School Violence in North Carolina tracks the incidence of criminal acts on school property. For the last four years, "possession of a controlled substance" has been either the first or second most reported category of incident. It is past time that we restore an environment that is secure and conducive to the education of the vast majority of students who are eager to learn. Our students and teachers deserve nothing less.

Freedom of Speech Act

Mr. President, I am also pleased to introduce the Freedom of Speech Act, which makes sure that federal employees are not forced to check their moral beliefs at the door when they arrive at the federal workplace.

This bill attempts to make sure that President Clinton is not allowed to do by Executive Order what Congress has declined to enact in the past two congressional sessions— namely, to treat homosexuals as a special class protected under various titles of the Civil Rights Act of 1964. Last year, President Clinton signed such an Executive Order, and in so doing infringed upon the constitutional rights of federal employees who wish to express their moral and spiritual objections to the homosexual lifestyle.

President Clinton has instructed federal agencies and departments to implement a policy that treats homosexuals as a special class protected under various titles of the Civil Rights Act of 1964. This necessarily prevents federal employees who have strong religious or moral objections to homosexuality from expressing those beliefs without running afoul of what amounts to a workplace speech code. Apparently, when the President's desire to write his belief system into federal workplace regulations conflicted with the First Amendment right to free speech, the Constitution lost.

Congress should jealously protect its constitutional prerogative to make laws, and prevent the executive branch from creating special protections for homosexuals, particularly in a way that doesn't take into account the constitutional right of freedom of speech enjoyed by all federal employees. That is the purpose of the legislation I offer today.

Under this bill, no federal funds could be used to enforce President Clinton's Executive Order #13807. Further, no federal department or agency would be able to implement or enforce any policy creating a special class of individuals in federal employment discrimination law. This bill will also prevent the federal government from trampling the First Amendment rights of federal employees to express their moral and spiritual values in the workplace.

Mr. President, for many years the homosexual community has engaged in a well-organized, concerted campaign to force Americans to accept, and even legitimize, an immoral lifestyle. This bill is designed to prevent President Clinton from advancing the homosexual agenda at the expense of both the proper legislative role and the free speech rights of federal workers.

Mr. President, the last of these bills is entitled the Civil Rights Restoration Act of 1999. Specifically, this legislation prevents federal agencies and the federal courts from interpreting Title VII of the Civil Rights Act of 1964 to allow an employer to grant preferential treatment in employment to any group or individual on account of race.

This proposal prohibits the use of racial quotas once and for all. During the past several years, almost every member of the Senate—and the President of the United States—have proclaimed that they are opposed to quotas. This bill will give senators an opportunity to reinforce their statements by voting in a roll call vote against quotas.

Mr. President, this legislation emphasizes that from here on out employers must hire on a race-neutral basis. They can reach out into the community to the disadvantaged and they can even have businesses with 80 percent or 90 percent minority workforces as long as the motivating factor in employment is not race.

This bill clarifies section 703(j) of Title VII of the Civil Rights Act of 1964 to make it consistent with the intent of its authors, Hubert Humphrey and Everett Dirksen. Let me state it for the Record:

> It shall be an unlawful employment practice for any entity that is an employer, employment agency, labor organization, joint labor–management committee subject to this title to grant preferential treatment to any individual or group with respect to selection for, discharge from, compensation for, or the terms, conditions, or privileges of, employment or union membership, on the basis of the race, color, religion, sex, or national origin of such individual or group, for any person, except as provided in subsection (e) or paragraph (2). It shall not be an unlawful employment practice for an entity described in paragraph (1) to recruit individuals of an underrepresented race, color, religion, sex, or national origin, to expand the applicant pool of the individuals seeking employment or union membership with the entity.

Specifically, this bill proposes to make part (j) of Section 703 of the 1964 Civil Rights Act consistent with subsections (a) and (d) of that section. It contains the identical language used in those sections to make preferential treatment on the basis of race (that is, quotas) an unlawful employment practice.

Mr. President, I want to be clear that this legislation does not make outreach programs an unlawful employment practice. Under language suggested years ago by the distinguished senator from Kansas, Bob Dole, a company can recruit and hire in the inner city, prefer people who are disadvantaged, create literacy programs, recruit in the schools, establish day care programs, and expand its labor pool in the poorest sections of the community. In other words, expansion of the employee pool is specifically provided for under this act.

Mr. President, this legislation is necessary because in the 33 years since the passage of the Civil Rights Act, the federal government and the courts have combined to corrupt the spirit of the Act as enumerated by both Hubert Humphrey and Everett Dirksen, who made clear that they were unalterably opposed to racial quotas. Yet in spite of the clear intent of Congress, businesses large and small must adhere to hiring quotas in order to keep the all-powerful federal government off their backs. This bill puts an end to that sort of nonsense once and for all.

Mr. President, I do not pretend that enaction of this legislation will solve all of the pathologies of modern society. But, taken as a whole, they seek to turn the tide of the increasing apathy—and, in some cases, outright hostility—toward moral and spiritual principles that have marked late-twentieth century social policy.

The Founding Fathers knew what would become of a society that ignores traditional morality. I have often quoted the parting words of advice our first President, George Washington, left his beloved new nation. He reminded his fellow citizens:

> Of all the dispensations and habits which lead to political prosperity, religion and morality are indispensable supports. In vain would that man claim the tribute to patriotism who should labor to subvert these great pillars of human happiness.

Mr. President, that distinguished world leader, Margaret Thatcher, highlighted for us the words of Washington's successor, John Adams, who said, "Our Constitution was designed only for a moral and religious people. It is wholly inadequate for the government of any other."

Our Founding Fathers understood well the intricate relationship between freedom and responsibility. They knew that the blessings of liberty engendered certain obligations on the part of a free people—namely, that citizens conduct their actions in such a way that society can remain cohesive without excessive government intrusion. The American experiment would never have succeeded without the traditional moral and spiritual values of the American people—values that allow people to govern themselves, rather than be governed.

Moral Values[3]

Lee H. Hamilton

U.S. Representative from Indiana, 1965–1999; born April 20, 1931, in Florida; Bachelor's degree, DePauw University, 1952; studied at the Goethe University, Frankfurt; Indiana University School of Law, 1953–1956; as a congressman, Hamilton chaired the Committee on Foreign Affairs, the Joint Committee on the Organization of Congress, the October Surprise Task Force, the Select Committee to Investigate Covert Arms Transfers with Iran, the Permanent Select Committee on Intelligence, and the Joint Economic Committee.

Editors' introduction: In this speech, former U.S. Representative Lee H. Hamilton addressed the issue of moral values in America. Hamilton asserts that the government's role in improving moral culture and fostering "attitudes like civility and respect" is limited. Instead, he urged citizens to look toward activities such as civic and artistic involvement to "strengthen our society and build character."

Lee H. Hamilton's speech: Mr. Speaker, I would like to insert my Washington Report for Wednesday, July 29, 1998, into the Congressional Record.

I've often been impressed in talking with Hoosiers about the concern that many of them have that the state of moral values in the country is weak. With all of the tough issues of the day, like the problems of campaign finance or how to maintain solid economic growth in the economy, the moral concern of Hoosiers comes through repeatedly. They worry about moral decline and about the character and values exhibited by Americans today.

More generally, the polls show that by substantial majorities the public believes that the United States is in a long-term moral decline. They see behavior that weakens family life, widespread disrespect for authority, an inclination towards self-indulgence, and a lessening of personal responsibility. They see a lot of behavior around them they do not approve of: a professional athlete spits on an umpire or abuses women, a movie star says she wants a baby but not a husband, and a politician makes a lot of money on a book deal from a personal scandal. They do not like to see children being mistreated or ignored, marriages disintegrating, high levels of violence and drug use, deteriorating educational systems, less emphasis on responsibility and accountability, increasing coarseness and incivility in popu-

---

3. Delivered in Washington, D.C., at the House of Representatives, on July 29, 1998

lar culture and politics, too much emphasis on making money, not enough concern about the distinction between right and wrong, less concern with the truth.

I think most Hoosiers understand too that there is only so much government can do to improve the moral culture of the country. Certainly government actions can make it either harder or easier for families to prosper, or for children to get a good education, for example. Government can punish actions which threaten the social order. It can fund programs to fight drugs and crime, pass laws against discrimination and pornography, and hold congressional hearings to spotlight moral issues. Public officials can be positive or negative role models. But government's power to foster attitudes like civility and respect is limited.

Fortunately there are many institutions which strengthen our society and build character and citizenship. It is not surprising then that the country is becoming more concerned about civil society—that is, the relationships and institutions that are not controlled by the government but are essential, like families, neighborhoods, and the web of religious, economic, educational, and civic associations that foster character in individuals and help children become good people and good citizens.

By all odds, the most important is the family, where children first learn or fail to learn the simple virtues: honesty, trust, loyalty, cooperation, self-restraint, civility, compassion, personal responsibility, and respect for others.

Religion is very important in the lives of most Americans, and our churches foster the values that are essential to good quality of life in America. They emphasize personal responsibility, respect for moral law, and concern for others. They remind us of the timeless and transcendent virtues toward which we all must strive.

A large number of voluntary civic organizations help define our country and help us achieve social goals. All of us know the importance that civic organizations like Little League, the Chamber of Commerce, service clubs, the Future Farmers of America, Boy and Girl Scouts, and hundreds of others play in improving our lives. People want to be able to play in the parks, go to the library, learn from and help each other, and participate in all sorts of activities and relationships that make life meaningful.

In every community there are people who push for greater exposure to music, poetry, literature, and the other arts. The arts strengthen our communities by affirming important, core values: creativity, sensitivity, integrity of expression, craftsmanship.

Schools, of course, are crucial. They shape the lives of students and at their best require basic standards of good conduct: responsibility, respect for teachers' authority, respect for other students. They pass on the culture of the country

Public officials can be positive or negative role models. But government's power to foster attitudes like civility and respect is limited.

and the responsibilities of citizenship, thereby sustaining our democratic values.

Business enterprises of all kinds and descriptions are increasingly playing a prominent role in our civil society, quite apart from their critical economic role. Labor and management both have a role to play in ensuring honest value in return for fair reward, in promoting ethical business practices and in enforcing standards of conduct in the workplace. Businesses also can provide vital support for all sorts of community efforts.

One institution demands special mention because of its size and influence, but also because it is widely criticized as undermining civic life, and that is the media. Often I hear that the media—including movies, video games, Internet sites, and television—are hostile to the values that parents want for their children.

These and other institutions are in no small measure responsible for the country's success. The concern is that many of them are eroding.

I frequently ask Hoosier audiences what the United States is all about. One theme that comes through is that this is a country that should permit every person the opportunity to become the best they can become. Civil society helps advance that goal. The purpose of government and the other institutions of our society is to help foster the conditions to permit individuals to achieve their highest potential, to flourish and to prosper, and live positive and constructive lives.

So a primary challenge in the country today is neither governmental nor economic, but moral. It is to strengthen our families, improve our communities, permit our religious institutions to flourish, encourage voluntary civic organizations, support the arts, and place great emphasis on education, including character education programs. We must ensure that business, labor, and other community leaders understand their role in providing for the overall health of society, and encourage the media to be mindful of the effects of inappropriate violent and sexual content on young people.

The Founding Fathers were not afraid to speak of virtue and the role that individuals must play for a democratic society to flourish. The essential product in the foundation of a democratic nation is good and responsible people.

V. Religious Faith and Freedom

Keeping the Faith: Religion, Freedom, and International Affairs[1]
Paul Marshall

Senior Fellow, Freedom House's Center for Religious Freedom, Washington, D.C.; born Liverpool, UK; permanent resident of U.S.A.; B.S, University of Manchester, 1969; M.S., University of Western Ontario; M. Phil., Institute for Christian Studies, Toronto, 1980; M.A. and Ph.D., York University, Toronto; instructor in geology, University of Western Ontario, London, Ontario, 1969–71; Lecturer in political philosophy, York University, Toronto, 1977–81, 1983; Academic Vice President, Institute for Christian Studies, Toronto, 1985–87; adjunct faculty, Ontario Theological Seminary, 1987–95; Emma Kaufmann Award, 1989; Visiting Professor, Catholic University, Washington, D.C.; Visiting Fellow, Claremont Institute, California, 1996–97; presently adjunct professor at Free University of Amsterdam, Claremont Institute, California, and Fuller Theological Seminary, Pasadena; columnist for News Network International, Christian Week, *and* Christian Courier; *author,* Just Politics; *Heaven is Not My Home; Stained Glass: World Views and Social Science; Their Blood Cries Out; Thine is the Kingdom; Labor of Love: Essays on Work; and* A Kind of Life Imposed on Man: Vocation and Social Order from Tyndale to Locke; *Gold Medallion Award, 1997.*

Editors' introduction: Dr. Paul Marshall addressed a seminar on "Faith and Freedom Around the World," sponsored by Hillsdale College's Center for Constructive Alternatives and the Sage Foundation. Marshall spoke to some 300 students, faculty, and members of the community in the college auditorium. Questions and discussion followed the address for twenty-four hours after the speech. Marshall contends that "it is absurd to examine any political order *without* attending to the role of religion."

Paul Marshall's speech: At the end of 1997, former *New York Times* executive editor A. M. Rosenthal confessed, "I realized that in decades of reporting, writing, or assigning stories on human rights, I rarely touched on one of the most important. Political human rights, legal, civil, and press rights, emphatically often; but the right to worship

---

1. Delivered at Hillsdale College, Hillsdale, Michigan, fall 1998.

where and how God or conscience leads, almost never."

The habit of ignoring religious persecution is all too common in the West. On August 22, 1998, for example, seven leaders of underground churches in China released an unprecedented joint statement calling for dialogue with the communist government. The U.S. media virtually ignored the statement, despite the fact that these leaders represent the *only* nationwide group in China not under government control. Their membership of 15 million is several times larger than the population of Tibet and hundreds of times larger than the number of China's democracy and human rights activists. But the press just isn't interested.

Nor is it interested in religious persecution in Sudan, the largest country in Africa, which still practices crucifixion. After enduring more than forty years of civil war, the predominantly Christian population in southern Sudan is subject to torture, rape, and starvation for its refusal to convert to Islam. Christian children are routinely sold into slavery. Muslims who dare to convert to Christianity are faced with the death penalty.

In the last 15 years, Sudan's death toll of more than 1.9 million is far greater than Rwanda's (800,000), Bosnia's (300,000), and Kosovo's (1,000) *combined.* The United Nations' special rapporteur on Sudan, Gaspar Biro, produced five official reports documenting the carnage, declaring "abuses are past proving . . . these are the facts." He resigned when his reports were consistently ignored.

Not a week goes by that Freedom House's Center for Religious Freedom does not learn of major stories of religious persecution abroad. Christians are usually the victims, but so are many others, such as Buddhists in Vietnam, Baha'i's in Iran, and Shiite Muslims in Afghanistan. These stories rarely make headlines or penetrate the consciousness of journalists and foreign policy professionals.

Secular Myopia

One main cause for this ignorance is what I call "secular myopia," that is, "an introverted, parochial inability even to see, much less understand, the role of religion in human life." It is a condition that mainly afflicts the "chattering classes," which include diplomats, journalists, political commentators, and policy analysts. As strategic theorist Edward Luttwak has observed, the chattering classes are eager to examine economic causes, social differentiations, and political affiliations, but they generally disregard the impact of faith upon the lives of individuals and the lives of nations.

Secular myopia can have painful consequences. Remember how little the U.S. knew about the Ayatollah Khomeini and his followers in Iran during the late 1970s? Luttwak notes that there was only one proposal for the CIA to examine "the

Secular myopia can have painful consequences. Remember how little the U.S. knew about the Ayatollah Khomeini and his followers in Iran during the late 1970s?

attitudes and activities of the more prominent religious leaders" and that this proposal was vetoed as an irrelevant exercise in sociology.

As the Shah's regime was collapsing, U.S. political analysts kept insisting that everything was fine. True to their training, they focused on economic variables, class structure, and the military, and they concluded that, since businessmen, the upper classes, and the military supported the Shah, he was safe. There were, of course, many *mullahs* (religious teachers and leaders) arousing Islamic sentiment, but the analysts believed that religious movements drew only on folk memories, were destined to disappear with "modernization," and were irrelevant to the real forces and institutions of political power.

Consequently, the U.S. did not clear its embassy of important documents or staff. When Khomeini seized power, his followers captured both. They used the former to attack American personnel throughout the Middle East and the latter to precipitate a hostage crisis that paralyzed our nation for two years.

According to Luttwak, during the Vietnam War, "Every demographic, economic, ethnic, social, and, of course, military aspect of the conflict was subject to detailed scrutiny but the deep religious cleavages that afflicted South Vietnam were hardly noticed." He added that the "tensions between the dominant Catholic minority [and] a resentful Buddhist majority . . . were largely ignored until Buddhist monks finally had to resort to flaming self-immolations in public squares, precisely to attract the attention of Americans so greatly attentive to everything else in Vietnam that was impeccably secular."

Similar tales can be told of our myopic view of conflicts in Bosnia, Nicaragua, Israel, Lebanon, India, the Philippines, and Indonesia.

Misunderstanding Religion

Religion as Ethnicity

In 1997, when Malaysian Prime Minister Mahathir Mohamed railed against speculators with the outrageous claim, "We are Muslims, and the Jews are not happy to see the Muslims progress," the *Los Angeles Times* described him as "race-obsessed." Perhaps the *Times* took its cue from media descriptions of former Yugoslavia. In this tortured land, the war raging between the Orthodox, Catholics, and Muslims is always referred to as "ethnic," and attacks on Bosnian Muslims are always referred to as "ethnic cleansing."

There are many such examples of media misunderstanding. The *Economist* headlined a 1997 story about attacks on 25 churches and a temple in eastern Java that were prompted by a Muslim heresy trial as "Race Riots." A 1998

New York Times editorial on rampant violence in Indonesia cited "tensions between Indonesia's Muslim majority and Chinese minority" as if there were no Chinese Muslims and no non-Muslims except for the Chinese.

Religion as Irrationality

Western opinion makers and policymakers consider themselves the heirs of the "Enlightenment," an 18th-century intellectual movement that stressed rationalism and science over faith and other forms of "superstition." To them, all contemporary peoples, events, and issues fall into Enlightenment categories, which are most often political or ideological.

Muslims are identified as "right-wing," even when they advocate leftist economic controls. Hindus who propose to build a temple on the site of the Babri mosque in India and Jews who propose to build a Third Temple on the site of the Dome of the Rock in Jerusalem are also labeled "left-wing" or "right-wing" without any regard to religious context.

> *When ethnicity and psychology fail to subsume religion, the alternative is to treat it, in quasi-Marxist fashion, as the sublimation of drives that supposedly can be explained by poverty, economic changes, or the stresses of modernity.*

When the vocabulary of "left" and "right" has run its tired course, we are left with that old standby, "fundamentalist"— a word dredged up from the American past, despite dubious provenance. What "fundamentalist" means when applied to Christians, Buddhists, Hindus, or Muslims is hard to understand. Using the term is a sign of intellectual laziness. If what believers believe does not easily fall into an Enlightenment category, then it is assumed that they must be "irrational." Thus, "fundamentalist" is now merely shorthand for "religious fanatic"—for someone who is to be categorized rather than heard, observed rather than comprehended, dismissed rather than respected.

Religion as Sublimated Anxiety

When ethnicity and psychology fail to subsume religion, the alternative is to treat it, in quasi-Marxist fashion, as the sublimation of drives that supposedly can be explained by poverty, economic changes, or the stresses of modernity. Of course, these factors do play a role, but, all too often, what we encounter is an a priori methodological commitment to treating religion as secondary—as a mildly interesting phenomenon that can be explained, but that is never an explanation in and of itself.

So great is this bias that when the *Journal of International Affairs* devoted its 1996 edition to studies of religious influences, it apologized in part for even mentioning faith with the admission, "Religion may seem an unusual topic for an international affairs journal." The editors added that "it is hardly surprising that scholars . . . have, for the most part, ignored [religion]."

Taking Religion Seriously

Religion and War

If we *do* start to take religion seriously in international affairs, then we will learn a great deal about war, about democracy, and about freedom of all kinds.

It was pointed out by religion scholars long before political scientist Samuel Huntington's recent book, *The Clash of Civilizations and the Remaking of World Order*, that chronic armed conflict is concentrated on the margins of the traditional religions, especially along the boundaries of the Islamic world. The Middle East, the southern Sahara, the Balkans, the Caucasus, Central Asia, and Southern Asia are where Islam, Christianity, Judaism, Buddhism, and Hinduism intersect. It is also where most wars have broken out in the last 50 years.

These are not explicitly religious wars. But since religion shapes cultures, people in these regions have different histories and different views of human life. Regardless of the triggers for conflict, they are living in unstable areas where conflict is likely to occur—in religious fault zones that are also prone to political earthquakes.

Religion and Democracy

Religion also shapes governments. In Eastern Europe, authoritarian governments are finding it easier to hold on in areas where the Orthodox church, with its long history of association with the state, has had special influence. The new boundaries of Eastern and Western Europe are tending to fall along the old divide between Orthodox and Catholic/Protestant.

Huntington makes a strong case that, in the 1970s–80s, a "third wave of democracy" swept over Portugal, Spain, Eastern Europe, Latin America, and the Philippines, in part because of important changes in the dominant nongovernment institution—the Catholic Church. (He concludes that changes made after the Second Vatican Council inspired a major movement toward democracy and human rights.)

The role of the Church in the fall of communism may not be clear to Western observers afflicted with secular myopia, but it is all too clear to Chinese government officials. As brutal practitioners of Communism, they are perversely aware of the power of human spirituality, and so they regard religion with deadly seriousness. In 1992, the Chinese press noted that "the Church played an important role in the change" in Eastern Europe and the former Soviet Union and warned, "If China does not want such a scene to be repeated in its land, it must strangle the baby while it is still in the manger."

Underground Church or "house church" leaders consistently report that the current government crackdown is due to fears prompted by religious events in the former Soviet bloc. Even Chinese government documents actually implementing the crackdown state that one of their purposes is to prevent "the changes that occurred in the former Soviet Union and Eastern Europe."

Each year, Freedom House conducts a comparative survey of political rights and civil liberties around the world. The 1998–99 survey finds that, of the 88 countries rated as "free," 79 "are majority Christian by tradition or belief." Clearly, correlations are not causalities, so this does not imply any direct link between Christianity and democracy (the survey also finds a connection between Hinduism and democracy). However, the existence of such a relationship is significant, not least because it is far greater than material factors such as economic growth, on which theorists and analysts lavish attention.

Politics and the Nature of the Church

One reason for the modern correlation between Christianity and political freedom lies in the nature of the Church. From the beginning Christians, while usually loyal citizens, necessarily have an attachment to "another king" and a loyalty to a divine order that is apart from and beyond the political order.

In the Latin churches of the West, the two realms of *sacerdotium* (church) and *regnum* (state) emerged. Henceforth, there were two centers of authority in society. As political philosopher George Sabine reminds us, the Christian Church became a distinct institution, independent of the state, entitled to shape the spiritual concerns of mankind. This, he adds, "may not unreasonably be described as the most revolutionary event in the history of Western Europe, in respect both to politics and to political thought."

It is not that the church or the state directly advocated religious freedom or any other freedom—they did not, and often inquisitions were defended. But people in both realms always believed that there *should be* boundaries, and they struggled over centuries to define them. This meant that the church, whatever its lust for civil control, had always to acknowledge that there were forms of political power which it could and should not exercise. And the state, whatever its drive to dominate, had to acknowledge that there were areas of human life that were beyond its reach.

The very existence of the modern church denies that the state is the all-encompassing or ultimate arbiter of human life. Regardless of how the relationship between God and Caesar has been confused, it now at least means that, contra the Romans and modern totalitarians, *Caesar is not God.* This confession, however mute, sticks in the craw of every authoritarian regime and draws an angry and bloody response.

Faith and Freedom

This confession also suggests that people interested in democracy should heed religion. For example, attention to China's courageous pro-democracy activists is certainly deserved, but it must be remembered that their following is quite small.

Therefore, more attention should be paid to China's dissident churches, which, at a conservative estimate, number some 25 million members (apart from 15 million members in official churches) and which are growing at a rate of 10–15 percent a year.

In a 1997 cover story, "God Is Back," the *Far East Economic Review* quoted the words of one Beijing official: "If God had the face of a 70-year-old man, we wouldn't care if he was back. But he has the face of millions of 20-year-olds, so we are worried."

Clearly, the rapid growth of the only nationwide movement in China not under government control merits *political* attention.

Religion and International Relations

Apart from some of the horrific situations already described in Sudan, the Balkans, and elsewhere, the following religious trends also merit political reflection:

- The rise of large, militant religious parties, such as the Welfare Party in Turkey and the Bharatiya Janata Party (BJP) in India, and the growth of radical Islam all over the world.

- The rapid growth of charismatic Protestantism and Catholicism in Latin America. As Cambridge sociologist David Martin has shown, these indigenous developments represent one of the largest religious changes of the century. They also produce personal reform and provide a major impetus toward entrepreneurial activity.

- The pattern of violence and warfare along the sub-Saharan boundary from Nigeria to Ethiopia. This constitutes a huge Christian/Muslim breach that must be addressed before peace is possible.

- Massive rates of Christian conversions in Korea (now 25 percent of the population), China (a minimum of 40 million, up from one million in 1980), Taiwan, and Indonesia.

- Increasing religious tensions in trouble spots such as Nigeria and Indonesia. There is widespread religious violence in the northern and central regions of Nigeria, with thousands dead in recent years. There could be all-out religious war. In Indonesia, escalating religious strife precedes and has some separate dynamics from recent anti-Chinese violence: 200 churches were destroyed in Java alone in a recent 15-month period, and most of them were not attended by ethnic Chinese. Such incidents threaten to undermine what has been one of the world's best examples of interreligious toleration and cooperation.

- In both of these regions, there is the possibility that

instability and violence will spread far beyond the religious communities themselves.

- The exodus of Christians from the Middle East—some two million in the last five years. Currently some 3 percent of Palestinians are Christians, compared to an estimated 25 percent 50 years ago. Similar mass flight from Egypt, Syria, Lebanon, Turkey, and Iraq has occurred.
- The emergence of the Orthodox Church as a unifying symbol in Russia, the Balkans, and other parts of the former Soviet Union.
- The increasing prominence of religion in the conflicts between India and Pakistan, which now possess nuclear weapons.

I am not making the absurd suggestion that religion—apart from other cultural, ethnic, economic, political, or strategic elements—is the only or the key factor in international affairs. Societies are complex. But I am saying that it is absurd to examine any political order *without* attending to the role of religion. We consistently need to deal with religion as an important independent factor. Analyses that ignore religion should be inherently suspect.

The Centrality of Religious Freedom

In the West, there are now hopeful signs of a new awareness of the importance of religion and religious freedom. On October 9, 1998, the U. S. Senate passed the landmark International Religious Freedom Act. The following day, the House did the same. On October 27, President Clinton—a strong opponent—cut his losses and signed the act, which establishes a commission appointed by Congress and the White House to monitor global religious persecution and recommend responses. This is a small step, but it *is* a step, and in a vital area where few have trod. It is vital that *we* take similar steps—as concerned citizens.

We must support policies, programs, and organizations that promote and defend religious freedom.

We must support people such as Pope John Paul II, a man with no military or economic resources who is nonetheless daily aware of the spiritual dynamics of the world and who, for this reason, is perhaps its most important statesman.

We must make religious freedom a core element of "human rights." This is not a parochial matter. Historically, it is the first freedom in the growth of human rights, and it is the first freedom in the First Amendment to the U. S. Constitution.

While all human rights pressures make "geopolitical realists" nervous, religion carries the additional burdens of touching on deeply felt commitments, of facing confused domestic claims about "separation of church and state," and of feeding fears that the U.S. is an imperial Christian power. But this is no reason to hesitate. Religious rights must be at the forefront of any sound human rights policy. And unless

we understand this, our ability to fight for any freedom at all
is compromised.

Freedom of Thought, Conscience, Religion, or Belief [2]

Laila Al-Marayati

Member, U.S. Commission on International Religious Freedom, 1999– ; Member, U.S. State Department Advisory Committee on Religious Freedom Abroad 1996– ; Clinical Assistant Professor, University of Southern California School of Medicine, Department of Obstetrics and Gynecology, 1992– ; born May 12, 1962 in Los Angeles, California; B.S., University of California, Los Angeles, 1984; Doctor of Medicine, University of California, Irvine, California College of Medicine, 1988; Resident, Los Angeles County University of Southern California Medical Center, Women's Hospital, 1988–1992; President, Muslim Women's League 1995–1998;

Editors' introduction: In October 1998 Doctor Laila Al-Marayati joined the U.S. delegation to the Conference on Human Dimension Issues of the Organization for Security and Co-operation in Europe, which was held in Warsaw, Poland. She spoke at length on the topics which the delegation felt were most critical to international respect of human rights and religion, focusing on laws and governmental actions that restrict religious freedom.

Laila Al-Marayati's Speech: At previous OSCE meetings, the U.S. Delegation has applauded the expansion of religious liberty in this historic decade. At the same time, we want to address concerns we have regarding the increasing intolerance toward religious and belief groups in many OSCE participating states. The U.S. Delegation has three areas of concern:

Laws That Hinder Religious Practice and Discriminate Among Religious Groups

Recently, several participating states have enacted legislation disproportionately and adversely affecting minority religious communities. The enactment of these laws, the progression toward more state control of religious institutions, and the similarity of these legal provisions in restricting religious communities considered less desirable reflects disturbing intolerance of minority faiths.

Since our last meeting, two new laws have been enacted that restrict religious liberty in Uzbekistan. On May 1, 1998, the parliament of Uzbekistan passed amendments to the 1991 law on religious organizations and the Criminal Code,

2. Statement of Dr. Laila Al-Marayati, U.S. Delegation to the OSCE Implementation Meeting on Human Dimension Issues on October 27, 1998.

which blatantly violate virtually every Helsinki commitment on religious liberty. Among other restrictions, the amendments now require 100 Uzbek citizens to sign a religious community's application for registration, criminalize any unregistered religious activity, and penalize free speech based on its religious content. The new amendments particularly affect both non-Russian Orthodox Christian minorities and Muslim communities who want to practice their faith outside Uzbekistan's religious establishment.

Observers note that these amendments to the law merely legalize what has been the practice of the government of Uzbekistan toward religious groups over the last few years. In December 1997, the government engaged in a series of crackdowns in the Farghona Valley, in gross violation of human rights and Helsinki principles. Muslims were arbitrarily arrested, detained, tortured, and confessions were forced while in police custody. A number of well-documented cases exist of Muslim leaders who have simply disappeared, under extremely suspicious circumstances. The U.S. Delegation calls on the government of Uzbekistan to repeal the new law and insure that governmental practices comply with international law and Helsinki principles.

In August 1997, the Parliament of Macedonia passed a religion law that prohibits religious work and rituals from being performed by unregistered communities or groups and requires the signature of 50 citizens for registration. One of the more disturbing sections of the law prohibits the existence of two "religious communities" with the same creed, which in effect establishes the government as the arbiter between religious factions. Some harassment of non-Orthodox religious groups has been reported and Protestant groups complain of being unable to register their churches and obtain regular employment status for their employees in violation of Macedonia's commitment in Paragraph 16.3 of the Vienna Concluding Document to "grant upon their request to communities of believers, practicing or prepared to practice their faith within the constitutional framework of their states, recognition of the status provided for them in the respective countries."

On September 26, 1997, President Boris Yeltsin signed a law containing discriminatory provisions against "new" religious faiths, onerous registration requirements, and vague criteria for "liquidating" religious organizations. Although this law has not led to widespread repression of religious believers and sections of the law are being challenged in the Constitutional Court, it is clear that Russian citizens now have less religious freedom than in 1991. Furthermore, it is clear that certain local officials in Russia are using this law arbitrarily to discriminate against religious organizations whose presence or practices are not to their taste. The Lutheran Church in Tuim, Khakassia, is experiencing a series of harassing lawsuits under the rubric of violation of this law, and was recently ordered closed by local officials. Even in Moscow city officials have commenced a civil court case to ban a local Jehovah's Witness organization under Article 14 of the law presumably because the Jehovah's Witnesses believe they should not accept blood transfusions. The U.S. Delegation acknowledges that there are instances when a government may contravene a fundamental right in the interest of health and safety of society. However, as agreed in the Copenhagen Concluding Document Paragraph 24, any restriction on a fundamental freedom is an exception [that] must be limited and narrowly tailored to the problem. Banning a religious group based on an aspect of their belief violates this OSCE principle of proportionality.

While no new laws have been passed in Greece and in Turkey, it should be noted that these countries have had constitutional provisions, laws and government policies for many years that violate OSCE commitments on religious liberty. With respect to Greek law, especially onerous are the anti-proselytism provisions, including Article 13 of the Constitution and the Metaxas-era Laws of Necessity 1363/1938 and 1672/1939, which have been used almost exclusively against religious minorities. These statutes have an adverse impact on religious liberty in the Hellenic Republic and are inconsistent with numerous OSCE commitments, including Paragraph 16 of the Vienna Document and Paragraph 9 of the 1990 Copenhagen Document. We urge repeal of these laws in order to help ensure the freedom of all individuals in Greece to profess and practice their religion or belief.

We are well aware of the controversy surrounding the selection of individuals to serve as Mufti in the Hellenic Republic and understand that relevant Muslim practices vary from country to country. In this regard, we stress the importance of respecting the right of members of the Muslim community to organize themselves according to their own hierarchical and institutional structure, including in the selection, appointment, and replacement of their personnel in a manner consistent with relevant OSCE commitments. We are particularly disturbed over the lengthy prison sentences—a total of 49 months—handed down against Mehmet Emin Aga for "usurping the title of Mufti."

We are also concerned by the burdensome Greek requirements imposed on minority religious communities to obtain special permits issued by "competent ecclesiastical authorities" and the Ministry of National Education and Religious Affairs for the establishment or operation of churches, including places of worship. Reportedly, permission for the construction or repair of places of worship is often difficult or impossible to obtain despite the commitment of OSCE participating states to respect the right of religious communities

While no new laws have been passed in Greece and in Turkey, it should be noted that these countries have had constitutional provisions, laws and government policies for many years that violate OSCE commitments on religious liberty.

to establish and maintain freely accessible places of worship or assembly.

Historically non-Orthodox churches have encountered difficulties in securing so-called "House of Prayer" permits, although it appears the record for approval of permits is improving. Members of the Muslim community have similarly reported difficulty in securing permission for the repair of mosques, including the Suleymaniye Mosque on Rhodes. The rights of individuals belonging to minority religions or beliefs must be fully respected without discrimination or subordination. In this regard, we are aware of the pending request submitted by a community of the Macedonian Orthodox Church seeking to open a church building to conduct worship services in the Florina area.

The United States remains concerned over the inclusion of religious affiliation on Greek national identity cards. The inclusion of such information on this widely used document could lead to discrimination against individuals from minority religions or beliefs. Accordingly, we urge the repeal of the 1993 identity law. In addition, we urge further action to implement the recommendations of the advisory committee on anti-Semitic references in public school textbooks.

In a positive development, we note the Greek law on conscientious objection that came into force earlier this year and understand that the authorities are instituting arrangements whereby those objectors imprisoned under the old law will be given the option of engaging in alternative civilian social service.

The situation in Turkey remains largely unchanged. Minority religious communities face significant challenges and are occasionally targeted for acts of violence and vandalism. Members of the majority Muslim community may even face restrictions on some religious practices or customs in certain settings. Minority religions not recognized under the 1923 Lausanne Treaty, for example, generally may not acquire additional property for worship services. Even some recognized communities are prevented from fully utilizing existing facilities, such as the Ecumenical Patriarchate's Halki Seminary and the Armenian Apostolic Orthodox Church's Holy Cross Seminary, both closed to theological studies since 1971. In other cases, property of religious communities has been confiscated by the state without compensation. Securing the necessary permission to build new houses of worship or the renovation of existing churches is often difficult, if not impossible, to secure.

While proselytism is not outlawed per se, activist Muslims and evangelical Christians have been jailed in Turkey on the pretext of disturbing the peace for sharing their faith in public. Eight Americans were arrested briefly in March for handing out New Testaments on the streets of Eskisehir.

> *While prose-lytism is not outlawed per se, activist Muslims and evangelical Christians have been jailed in Turkey on the pretext of disturbing the peace for sharing their faith in public.*

The United States also takes note that, even among states with a long-standing tradition of support for human rights and fundamental freedoms, there have been unfortunate developments legalizing discrimination among religious groups. For example, in December 1997, the Austrian Parliament passed legislation on the "Legal Status of Religious Belief Communities" that established a two-tier system for receiving state funds and other privileges. In the first tier are 12 legally recognized communities, only a few of which could satisfy the prerequisites to gain such recognition under the new law. For instance, the religious community must have existed for at least twenty years and have a minimum number of members, equal to 0.02% of the population or about 16,000 members.

Organizations that place themselves under government observation for a period of time with the hope of becoming legally recognized comprise the second tier. During the observation period, legal status is denied and the religious organization is liquidated if the government ascertains that the beliefs of the group violate, among other criteria, democratic interests, public security, public order, health and morals, or the protection of the rights and liberties of others. The groups in this tier cannot sponsor foreign religionists for visas and do not have other privileges that the 12 legally recognized communities enjoy. The requirement that the statutes of a religious body must include a description of religious doctrine which is different from the doctrines of existing religious belief communities or churches is of concern to the U.S. Delegation because this establishes the government as the arbiter in theological disputes.

Some religious groups, including a number of independent Protestant churches, are granted the status of "association" and have rudimentary juridical personality to open bank accounts and own property. However, they do not have visiting rights in prisons or hospitals, cannot sponsor foreign co-religionists for visas, and do not have other privileges that the 12 legally recognized communities enjoy. A few groups have been denied "association" status, including the Unification Church, which is barred from countering potentially libelous reports in the press because they do not have legal status under Austrian law. The inherent inequality of this legal structure is of concern to the U.S. Delegation, especially in light of Austria's own authorship of the language in Paragraph 16 of the 1989 Vienna Concluding Document, which calls on the participating states to "foster a climate of mutual tolerance and respect" for all religious groups.

Governmental Actions that Perpetuate Discrimination Against Minority Religious Groups

Several Western European parliaments, most notably France, Belgium and Germany, have investigated and reported on the beliefs and activities of minority religious groups in the last few years. These parliamentary investigations have had a detrimental effect on religious liberty, as many groups being investigated or labeled "dangerous" have experienced a public backlash. The French Parliament's 1996 report contained a list of "dangerous" groups in order to warn the public against them. The Belgian Parliament's 1997 report had a widely circulated, informal appendix that listed 189 groups and included various allegations against many Protestant and Catholic groups, Quakers, Hasidic Jews, Buddhists, and the YWCA (Young Women's Christian Association).

In Belgium, some public officials have relied upon the unofficial appendix to justify denial of access to publicly rented buildings for Jehovah's Witnesses and Bahai'is merely because they were identified in this appendix. A German Bundestag "Enquete Kommission" on June 18, 1998, issued a report on its two-year investigation into "so-called sects" and "psycho-groups." While concluding that such groups pose no danger to German society, the report did recommend continued investigation and surveillance of Scientology. A number of religious and belief groups, such as the Jehovah's Witnesses, the Church of Scientology, and independent Pentecostal Protestant churches, have complained about harassment, discrimination, and biased media reports in Germany in connection with this commission and its work.

Also of concern is the establishment of government information centers to alert the public about groups deemed by the government to be "dangerous." The Austrian and French governments have set up hotlines for the public and, through government-sponsored and funded advisory centers, distribute information on groups. The German Enquete Kommission recommended that such a center be created there as well. The Belgian information is scheduled to open in early 1999. We note that the government of France, only this month, created a new, Interministerial Mission to Battle Against Sects" ("Mission interministérielle de lutte contre les sectes"). The very name of this mission suggests confrontation with religious minorities rather than tolerance.

The U.S. Delegation notes that characterizations of religious beliefs by government-operated centers, particularly the publication of unproved or potentially libelous materials, create a climate of intolerance towards members of groups. Government dissemination of information that may be construed as propaganda through these centers calls into questions the commitments that Austria, France, Belgium, and Germany have made to "foster a climate of mutual tolerance and respect." Furthermore, these activities excessively entangle the government in the public discussion on religious beliefs that foists the government into the role of religious arbitrator.

Religious Liberty of Muslims and Other Minorities in the OSCE Participating States

The status of both immigrant and indigenous Muslim minorities and majorities in the OSCE participating states is often precarious. Many countries, such as Spain, Austria, and Belgium, are adopting a variety of measures to accommodate and integrate their Muslim populations. Elsewhere, religious persecution and intolerance of Muslims in the OSCE region is closely linked to racial and ethnic hatred, xenophobia, social malaise, and international political conflicts. Fear of potential violence or terrorism spawned by "Islamic" fundamentalism or extremism is often used as a pretext to justify gross violations of the human rights of Muslims who are practicing their faith. Mindful of the broad spectrum of religious and ethnic oppression of Muslims in several participating states, the U.S. Delegation calls on those countries to reexamine their policies in light of existing OSCE commitments. We are not seeking special rights for Muslims or any other group for that matter. We seek to uphold the human rights and fundamental freedoms of all of our citizens without distinction of any kind.

> *The status of both immigrant and indigenous Muslim minorities and majorities in the OSCE participating states is often precarious.*

A combination of ethnicity and religion underlie human rights violations against Muslim populations in Europe. The most extreme form of anti-Muslim sentiment manifested in Europe was the brutal assault against Bosnian Muslims, today increasingly referred to as Bosniaks, by Serbian forces of the former Yugoslavia. Recently, the inhabitants of Kosovo, the vast majority of whom are ethnic Albanians and Muslims, have suffered mass killings, arbitrary detention, rape, destruction of property, and forced migration at the hands of the Belgrade regime. These atrocities yet again test the will of the international community to take a strong stand against such assault.

Muslims who are members of an ethnic minority, such as North Africans in France, and Turks in Germany, are subjected to violent crimes often perpetrated by racists and sometimes by police. Indo-Pakistanis have occasionally been the subject of racist attacks in the United Kingdom. Inadequate efforts to convict the perpetrators of these violent acts contribute to a climate of impunity for such crimes.

Religious education is often abridged or denied to Muslims in the OSCE region in direct violation of OSCE commitments expressed in Paragraph 16 of the 1989 Vienna Concluding Document. In Turkey, the Parliament enacted measures designed to eliminate the system of state-funded Islamic education by extending compulsory primary secular education. In Uzbekistan, religious teachers Obidkhon Nazarov, Rahim Otagulov, Olinjon Glofurov have been harassed, evicted, and arrested by government authorities repeatedly over the past 2 years. In addition, unofficial Islamic teaching institutions have been closed.

Economic and political discrimination against Muslims is common in the OSCE region. In Greece, particularly in Thrace, Muslims experience discrimination through loss of promotion opportunities, confinement to low-paying jobs, inadequate political representation, and prevention from advancement in the military. Similarly, in the Bulgarian military, Muslims are consistently assigned only to construction units. The Muslim minority in Russia, which represents 10% of the population, also faces societal discrimination in the workplace and in housing. Some Muslim minorities, like other minorities, have difficulty obtaining citizenship in countries such as Germany, Croatia, Serbia, and Greece. There are numerous reports that Muslims in Serbia, particularly in the Sandzak region and in Montenegro, are arbitrarily fired from their jobs and often driven from their homes.

In Turkey, some Muslims are labeled by the military and the government as "extremist" and thereafter experience widespread discrimination. Political participation is significantly denied, most notably by the banning of the Welfare (Refah) Party earlier this year and the recent conviction and banning of Istanbul Mayor Erdogan. Observant Muslims are excluded from certain jobs, demoted or expelled from the military, and marginalized politically.

Throughout much of the OSCE area, wearing the hijab in a particular way is interpreted as a sign of extremism, although the wearing of the hijab normally represents to the woman modest dress and an expression of faith. In Uzbekistan, Muslim women in hijab have been expelled from universities. In France, the Ministry of Education issued a decree stating that a headscarf is an "ostentatious display of a religious symbol" that should be strongly discouraged in public schools. There has been a controversy in Baden-Württemberg regarding a proposal to ban headscarves worn by teachers, reflecting societal trends of intolerance against Muslims. In Turkey, women who wear headscarves may become targets of discrimination and be banned from public-sector jobs, such as nursing, teaching, and judicial posts, and are prohibited from registering at public universities.

Efforts to respond to global threats of terrorism may lead to further restrictions and continued marginalization of Muslim populations in the OSCE region. The U.S. Delegation notes the disturbing tendency of some OSCE participating states to assume arbitrarily that Muslims are responsible for violence and threats to national security. In the United States, Muslims are too often victims of negative stereotypes in the media, as seen in the recent movies *GI Jane* or *True Lies*, which contributes to societal assumptions equating violence and terrorism with Islam. Arbitrary detention of over 100 North African Muslims in France at the opening of the World Cup similarly reflects a disregard of rights in the name of security. The United States supports freedom of religion, not criminal behavior. The blanket condemnation of Muslims, or any other marginalized group, is not only a violation of Helsinki principles, but is counterproductive and dangerous policy. Such policies could contribute to desperation in some quarters and lead to radicalization that might not have occurred otherwise. If this growing problem is to be addressed, OSCE participating states must comply fully with their OSCE obligations, the core of which is that the government cannot and should not control all aspects of society and certainly not matters of faith and must accept religious groups as a positive, integral part of society.

Conclusion

The U.S. Delegation calls on the governments of Uzbekistan, Russia, and Macedonia to repeal or amend significantly their laws on religious associations to comply with OSCE commitments; calls on the governments of Turkey and Greece to ensure that their laws and practices conform with OSCE principles of freedom of belief, association, and expression; calls on the government of Austria to recognize the potential that its law has for encouraging other states to enact prejudicial legislation and urges the government to amend its current law; calls on the governments of Austria, Belgium, France, and Germany to foster a climate of tolerance and respect toward minority religion or belief groups and insure through law and governmental practice that religious freedoms for minorities are protected; calls on all OSCE participating states to reexamine their laws, governmental practices, and societal trends that discriminate against Muslims and other religious minorities.

We Are Many, We Are One[3]

Elizabeth C. LaRocca-Pitts

United Methodist Minister, 1983 , and Assistant Professor of Old Testament Studies, Duke Divinity School, 1996–; born Athens, GA, 1959; B.A., Duke University, 1980; M.Div., Garrett-Evangelical Theological Seminary, 1984; Ph.D., Harvard University, 1994; pastor of Bishop, Farmington, High Shoals, and Salem United Methodist Churches, Oconee County, GA, 1984–87; adjunct professor of Old Testament Studies, Andover Newton Theological School, 1990–92; associate pastor, First United Methodist Church, Athens, GA, 1993–96; adjunct professor of Old Testament Studies, Candler School of Theology, 1994, and the University of Georgia, 1995.

Editors' introduction: Professor Elizabeth C. LaRocca-Pitts spoke at a Communion Service opening the 1998 session of the North Georgia Annual Conference of the United Methodist Church. She addressed some 2,200 clergy, lay persons, spouses, children, youth delegates, and visitors from local churches in the Augusta-Richmond County Civic Center. The conference is both religious and political, as delegates convene for Bible study, worship services, and to make Church policy, review reports from affiliated agencies, plan and approve new programs, and compose new legislation for ratification nationally at the next general conference. Confronted with divisive issues challenging Methodist and other denominations, this sermon contributed to a more harmonious consideration of them. LaRocca-Pitts counseled, "Once each voice has been heard and weighed, we must allow the hand of Jesus to touch us, heal our hurts, and give us one voice . . . ."

Elizabeth C. LaRocca-Pitts' speech:

They came to the other side of the sea, to the country of the Gerasenes. And when he had stepped out of the boat, immediately a man out of the tombs with an unclean spirit met him. He lived among the tombs; and no one could restrain him any more, even with a chain; for he had often been restrained with shackles and chains, but the chains he wrenched apart, and the shackles he broke in pieces; and no one had the strength to subdue him. Night and day among the tombs and on the mountains he was always howling and bruising himself with stones.

---

3. Delivered in Augusta, Georgia, on June 16, 1998, at 2 p.m. Reprinted with permission of Elizabeth C. LaRocca-Pitts.

When he saw Jesus from a distance, he ran and bowed down before him; and he shouted at the top of his voice, "What have you to do with me, Jesus, Son of the Most High God? I adjure you by God, do not torment me." For he had said to him, "Come out of the man, you unclean spirit!" Then Jesus asked him, "What is your name?" He replied, "My name is Legion; for we are many." They begged him earnestly not to send them out of the country. Now there on the hillside a great herd of swine was feeding; and the unclean spirits begged him, "Send us into the swine; let us enter them." So he gave them permission. And the unclean spirits came out and entered the swine and the herd, numbering about two thousand, rushed down the steep bank into the sea; and were drowned in the sea.

The swineherds ran off and told it in the city and in the country. Then people came to see what it was that had happened. They came to Jesus and saw the demoniac sitting there, clothed and in his right mind. The very man who had had the legion; and they were afraid. Those who had seen what had happened to the demoniac and to the swine reported it. Then they began to beg Jesus to leave their neighborhood. As he was getting into the boat, the man who had been possessed by demons begged him that he might be with him. But Jesus refused and said to him, "Go home to your friends, and tell them how much the Lord has done for you and what mercy has been shown you." And he went away and began to proclaim in the Decapolis how much Jesus had done for him and everyone was amazed. (Mark 5: 1-20, *New Revised Standard Version*)

If we have heard these words, so that they take root in our hearts, and change the way we live our lives, then they will become for us, and for all who know us, truly the words of the living God.

Praised be our Lord and Savior Jesus Christ and blessings upon this His Annual Conference! On behalf of my brothers and sisters in ministry at Duke Divinity School, and on behalf of all of us serving in extension ministries around our country and our world, I bring you greetings and say, it's good to be home.

In a way, I had a visit from all of you last fall when our Bishop came to Duke for the installation of our new Dean. It was on this visit, after taking the four of us North Georgia-related Dukies out for a barbecue, that he did me the great honor of inviting me to break the bread of life for you, here, this afternoon. You know, most people when given almost a year to prepare such a sermon would have prayed and reflected on this day and allowed the Holy Spirit to lead them to the passage in scripture that best seemed to reflect what God was communicating to them concerning this specific occasion. I, however, am a hopeless radical about certain things—a genuine true believer. You know people like me. I won't name names, but we are sitting all around you. We are single-minded, uncompromising, bullheaded, set in our ways, and intractable. We're . . . We're . . . lectionary preachers.

Yes, that's right! We are those people who, regardless of the occasion, regardless of the lead time provided, will mechanistically, even slavishly, follow the weekly scripture menu provided by the lectionary. In this case, the gospel reading we have heard today is the one for this coming Sunday. But let me reassure you, good friends, that it really isn't true that lectionary preachers simply refuse to be guided by the Holy Spirit. Rather, we believe deeply that it was none other than the Holy Spirit who chose this passage for us today. I know I didn't choose it. It reminds me too much of the time, in my first appointment, when I used the world's most inappropriate pulpit joke in a sermon on this very passage, and no, I'm not going to tell it again today! Even though it was one of Med Roach's jokes, and very funny when he told it to me in the lobby of Annual Conference one year. Maybe it was my delivery?

But seriously. I might have been tempted never to risk reliving that embarrassing moment by preaching on this passage again. But today, the Holy Spirit set this miracle story out for us—selected it specifically for this day, ages and ages ago, before the daily paper arrived. Before the evening news was broadcast. Although it was prepared for us long ago, now it is become the lens through which God wishes us to see ourselves and our world, as we are today. It is now our daily share of the bread of life which has been broken for us. Will you pray with me before we partake of it together?

Prayer for illumination: May the words of my mouth and the meditations of our hearts be acceptable in your sight, oh Lord our Rock, and our Redeemer. Amen.

You know, if you had seen the other lectionary passages for Sunday, you would know that I am in danger of losing my Old Testament Professor's union card because I'm not preaching on 1 Kings Chapter 19, which is one of the most important passages in all of Hebrew scripture. It is the story of Elijah in the cave, waiting to hear a word from God. It affirms Israel's faith in the God who is beyond natural phenomena, the God who is greater than the storm, God of Canaan, the God who speaks not in fire, or wind, or earthquake, but in the still voice whispered directly into the prophet's ear. It is a miracle, this passage! It is beauty! It is power! But there is a greater word waiting for us. An even greater word.

I'm also in danger of losing my "left-of-center, golly-darned feminist, bleeding-heart liberal" union card as well this afternoon because I'm not preaching on Galatians 3:23-29. How could a person like me not preach on these words of St. Paul: "In Christ there is no longer Jew nor Greek, Slave nor Free, Male nor Female but you are all one in Christ Jesus!" Oh, what could make a person with my politics turn their eyes from this wonder, this blessing, this great gift of God? (Not to mention the fact that it goes perfectly with my sermon title!?) But believe it or not, beloved, there is an even greater word awaiting us, and it is beauty and power, blessing and healing, healing for us, yes, even us.

You see, Our Lord once arrived by boat across the Galilee, to a town on a cliff above the eastern shore. As soon as he stepped out of the boat, a tortured soul ran up to greet him. A man with demons, so many demons that he called himself Legion, as if he were possessed by an army of voices. So marred was this man, so filled with confusion, that he was burdened with the anger and infuriated power of two thousand captured souls. Their number did not give him greater wisdom, or greater insight, or greater faith, but only torment and destruction as they railed against the frame that was too small to contain them. No chain was strong enough. No shackle sound enough, to immobilize the terrible chaos that seethed within him. Barely a human being, he was exiled to the graveyard, to the place where only silence and the dead reside.

So striking was the story of the Lord's encounter with this wretched man that both Matthew and Luke tell the story as well as Mark, but perhaps because of the unusual nature of this man's affliction, St. Matthew remembers the story with not one demoniac, but two! How many people was he? How many voices came from him? He was many, so very many, that he seemed a monster who could not be understood or cared for by normal people. But the miracle in our story today comes, as it always does, in the person of Jesus. Christ saw this man as we do, bruised and tattered and twisted. Christ heard the voices of the legion, but Christ also saw something else. When Christ gazed upon him, he saw what no one else could see. He saw the one blessed child of God whom this poor man once had been.

As those of you who know me know, one of the great miracles of my life has been my relationship with my eldest sister. She it was who taught me what it meant to pray. What it meant to love asking nothing in return. What it meant to be beloved of God, and, as many of you know, my sister Mary Blair is mentally retarded. In fact, she lives nearby here. She has lived at Gracewood now nearly 40 years. Over and over God has taught me great lessons of compassion, great les-

sons of mercy because of her. One of the greatest happened
some twelve years ago, when doctors told us she had cancer.
Strange, but I had never imagined she could get cancer, on
top of all her other illnesses, but they told us she had cancer,
and that she would die of it. They were wrong, thank the
Lord, she is well even today. But twelve years ago we
thought she was dying, so we all began to prepare.

My brother Carl, who had not seen her in over 20 years,
decided that he would overcome his distaste for hospitals
and travel down to Gracewood to see her one more time.
Even though they were only about two years apart in age,
they had not lived together since she was 11 and he was 13
and now they were both in their late 30s. I should tell you
that Mary Blair does not have language, her mind is frozen at
about the age of 18 months. Her life consists of enjoying
music, and food, and sunlight on a swing set. So Carl had no
idea whether Mary Blair would even recognize him when he
came to see her. When they were there in the hospital unit,
Mom and Dad and Carl sat around the room and talked
together while Mary Blair, as always, watched and rocked
and listened from the bed. But all the time she was staring at
Carl, at that 40-something-looking man, with greying hair, a
widening midsection, and a beard on his face. She stared at
him a long time.

Then she suddenly did something extraordinary. She got
out of her bed and went over to him. She grabbed him by the
wrist and started dragging him toward the door and down
the hall. She can be very persuasive when she wants something, so he went with her, and Mom and Dad followed, as
she dragged him into the patient lounge near the nurses station, which was really little more than a glass booth with a
television set and a long vinyl sofa. Once in the room, Mary
Blair sat on the sofa in front of the TV, and pulled Carl down
next to her so they were sitting side by side.

In that one action she had said everything she needed to
say. She had made it clear to all of them that she had recognized Carl and she knew who he really was. He wasn't just
some 40-something-year-old man, some strange grey-haired
person. She had seen past the weight of the years, she had
seen past what time had done. Under the changes of two and
a half decades and the tracks of life upon his face, she saw
the boy she had once sat next to on the sofa back at home.
Here was the boy she watched TV with so long ago in childhood. She knew that the man who had come to see her was
once, and was still, the boy who was her brother.

Jesus looked at Legion that way. He saw him, not as he
was, but as he could be again, whole and restored to life.
Jesus saw him as God created him, before the demons had
come. So after Christ had instructed the demons to go, he
asked the man his name, giving him a chance to speak, to
give the name by which he was known, but the response

came from still more demons. "We are called Legion!" They cried. "For we are many in this one man."

We all have our voices. Our legions. Don't we? When decisions are upon us, when we weigh our own choices, we hear voices in our own minds, do we not? When we ponder? When we pray? When we're searching for an answer? Isn't one of the dilemmas of every life how to sort out the myriad voices we all hear? Are we so different from this man? But the man who greeted Jesus *was* possessed of something different. Unlike a healthy person's spirit, where many options might be considered and weighed, the man who greeted Jesus was crippled by the voices within him. To the rest of his world he seemed a menace possessed of chaos and confusion.

When the world listens to us, do we sound as Christ would hear us, faithful and committed, yet loving and supportive of one another?

But who, then, are we in this gospel, beloved? Who, then, are we, as a people? As a church? Here we gather at this conference, to discuss, to debate, to share, and, yes, to struggle often with each other, we who are many. Are we one? Are we the one Body of Christ? Christ's own people? Or are we Legion? When the world watches us, and it *does* watch us like a thirsty person watches someone drink a cool glass of water. When the world watches us, do we appear as Christ sees us, whole and blessed? When the world listens to us, do we sound as Christ would hear us, faithful and committed, yet loving and supportive of one another? Are we the one beloved body of Christ our Lord? Or do we appear as the demoniac in the graveyard? Filled with a thousand conflicting voices? Filled with anger? Filled with rage?

Are we clothed in our right mind, or do we bruise ourselves and do one another harm as we thrash about under the load of conflicting passions that assail us? Do we reach out our hand to Jesus crying, "Heal us Lord! Heal us!"? Or do we answer when he calls us, by our own true names, and say, "We are Legion." When the world hears us talking, does it hear the Savior's voice, full of mercy, full of love, or does it hear the voice of a Legion—two thousand angry egos, each trying to overpower the others? We must be so very careful, beloved sisters and brothers, because the hungry, thirsty world is listening and watching.

But there is a hopeful promise here for us. When we find ourselves trapped, as was this man, Jesus stands among the tombstones where we're hiding, bruised and shaken. He hears us as we raise our many voices to each other. He is with us in this hall, and will hear our every word. Let us beg him now to touch us so our exile among the dead can be ended. When Christ touched the man who was Legion, he was restored to his right mind. And his many voices were healed and harmonized into a beautiful voice with only one word to share. "Go back and tell your friends," the Savior told the man now healed, "Go back and tell your friends of what the Lord has done for you, and what mercy has been shown you." Once possessed of a thousand voices. Now a single message remained. "Tell the world what God has done for you, and what mercy has been shown you."

Beloved, Christ would silence no one! All are precious to him here. Christ would stifle no one's voice for through our voices comes the Spirit! Those who know me know I would hear everyone's voice who in conviction and faith offers an opinion or a plea before this body. I am not preaching unity at any cost. But, at some point, unity is a precious thing. Without it we will have lost the miracle that makes us strong. Without it we will have lost each other, and I would not lose one of you—no, not even one. Nor would I have any of your eloquent voices stilled.

But once Christ's healing hand has touched us, once our conversations are over and the Holy Spirit has led us, once his command to go into all the world has sent us forth from here, our mission beyond these walls is sacred! We are to spare the world our squabbles! We are to spare the world our deliberations! Before them we are to support and care for one another. We are to submit, no matter the radical nature of that submission, which is more radical for some than for others, we are to submit to one another, and to the will of the Body. The Body of Christ. Some of us will never know how painful, how unbelievably self-sacrificial it can be for others of us to submit to one another in the love of Christ and for the sake of the Body. For some of us, the pain is beyond the call of Christ, and they must leave us to bloom in another garden where Christ will plant them. I know about this, because once I left a garden in which I had been planted. The exquisitly beautiful garden of the Roman Catholic Church. I had to leave there because Christ called me to be his priest. So believe me, I understand that at some point submission becomes incompatible with the will of Christ.

But the message of our gospel this morning is this. Simply this. Once our struggles to decide are over. Once our decisions have been made. Once each voice has been heard and weighed, we must allow the hand of Jesus to touch us, heal our hurts, and give us one voice with which we are then sent out to tell the world one thing! One thing! One simple holy thing! We are to tell the world what God has done for us and what mercy has been shown us. Nothing else can give life to the world that needs Christ! Nothing else can heal our world but the mercy of God! Not our doing! Not our striving! Not our contests with each other! Only Jesus! Only the Savior, whose mercy makes us one! To the world that watches us, listens to us, strains to understand us, let us only speak of this! Only this one thing, beloved. Speak of the mercy Christ has shown us for it is great. It is great.

Christ has shown me this, and it is a great miracle, and a great mercy. No matter what our differences may be. No matter what conversations may arise here. No matter what the

> *I am not preaching unity at any cost. But, at some point, unity is a precious thing. Without it we will have lost the miracle that makes us strong.*

march of time, and public life, and the current age has done to change us or our world, you all are still to me as you have always been, dearest brothers, beloved sisters. We are just as Christ has made us—his own children. His own friends. Just as Christ looked past the demons and saw a man, whole and healthy, we can look now on each other, and see each other for who we are: we can look past all divisions to see a brother's face, a sister's face, the face of our beloved, the face of Jesus Christ.

Christ will take us by the wrist, in this place, at this moment, and lead us to a table He himself has prepared. He will pull us toward each other, and in his leading hand is healing! He will heal our deepest wounds and reveal us at this table to be only as he sees us! Brothers and sisters, His very Body. His voice to the world of God's great mercy. This is the table He has prepared with his own bleeding hands. This is the table he has set, to bring us home to one another, to make us whole, to set us free. Who would break the bonds with which he has bound us? To himself and to each other? Who would refuse to share this supper?

But beware all who come here! Look around at those who are with you. Can you see them? Are they not all here? The ones with whom you agree? The ones with whom you know you will disagree? The ones whose faces are a different color? The ones whose ideas of God and yours are so very different? There are Democrats here. There are Republicans here. There is at least one socialist here. There are gay people here. There are *all* of these here, because we are here, but whoever comes to the table of Christ must agree to be a sister or a brother to all the others! Mind you, we don't have to agree on all things to come to the table together. Whoever comes to the table of Christ must come in truth first, but we must also come in love and in peace. For whoever comes to the table of Christ becomes Christ's Body and Christ's Body is not divided, because it possesses his heart, and his soul, and his capacity to love and to forgive. In essence, to come to this table is to come to Christ and accept Christ's will, and adopt Christ's message, and to place the desires of Christ above our own desires, whatever they may be. To come to this table is to acknowledge your family, your brother, your sister, and renew your sacred covenant to serve the Lord and one another.

But be not afraid, there is a great blessing here, regardless of the cost, for to come to this table is to be healed by God, clothed in glory, and restored. Once we have come, there will be no more strangers here, regardless of the years, regardless of our differences. Once we have come, we will be as we should be, brothers and sisters, the Body of Christ. Christ's touch will make us whole, so that we will have one word among us, one word and one word only—in the blending of our many voices, Legion will give way to Jesus, and we will

Mind you, we don't have to agree on all things to come to the table together. Whoever comes to the table of Christ must come in truth first, but we must also come in love and in peace.

arise to speak only of God's mercy and what great things have been done for us. If you will be healed. Come to the table. If you will own one another, brother and sister, come. But beware, if you do come, the claim of Christ is on you. To be His Body. To speak His word. To share His mercy with one another and with the world.

Remarks Before the American Muslim Council[4]

Samuel R. Berger

*U.S. National Security Advisor, 1996– ; born October 28,
1945, in Sharon, Connecticut; B.A., Cornell University,
1967; J.D., Harvard Law School, 1971; early career highlights include posts as legislative aide to Senator Harold E.
Hughes of Iowa and Congressman Joseph Resnick of New
York, speechwriter for George McGovern, legislative aide to
New York City Mayor John V. Lindsay; Deputy Director of
policy planning, Department of State, 1977–1980; Hogan &
Hartson law firm; senior foreign policy advisor, 1993–1996.*

Editors' introduction: In a speech before the American
Muslim Council, Samuel L. Berger stated that American
Muslims form an important bridge between the United
States and the Muslim world. "You understand the immediate impact of our policy abroad. Your support for what
we do—or at least your clear understanding of our thinking—strengthens our policy and increases its likelihood of
success." Kosovo is of particular importance, "Because
there are so many other people in other places struggling
to learn its lesson. That depriving a people of their
humanity based on their religion or ethnicity cannot be
permitted to succeed if we are to enter a new century less
bloody than the one we are leaving."

Samuel R. Berger's speech: I'm delighted to speak before
the American Muslim Council, and to discuss with you
our vital relationship with the Muslim world—a relationship that has received too little attention among foreign
policy elites.

I'm proud to speak with you today for a few reasons. First,
as a general rule, I think it's important for the President's foreign policy advisers to meet representatives of ethnic and
religious groups in the United States.

You understand the immediate impact of our policy abroad.
Your support for what we do—or at least your clear understanding of our thinking—strengthens our policy and
increases its likelihood of success. One of the most positive
forces for a principled, purposeful American foreign policy is
the engagement of Americans with roots overseas.

I am also proud to speak to you because American Muslims have a critically important role to play as a bridge
between the United States and the Muslim world.

---

4. Delivered in Washington, D.C., on May 7, 1999. Reprinted with
permission.

Our relationship with the Islamic community is vital to almost everything we are trying to do, from Kosovo to the Middle East to Asia. We have come a long way toward deepening the relationship but we have a long way still ahead.

From the time President Clinton took the oath of office, this Administration has reached out to the Muslim community worldwide. The President's respect for Islam proceeds from a basic grasp of two facts.

One, Muslims constitute a quarter of the world's population; it is self-evident you will play an important role in shaping the world of the next century. Two, Muslims are rapidly redefining our own nation. Islam is the fastest growing religion in the United States, practiced by some six million Americans, in over 1,200 mosques and Islamic centers.

The President and First Lady have sought to learn more about Islam and the Muslim world in a variety of ways. They have traveled extensively to Muslim nations, from Indonesia to Central Asia to Africa, seeking to strengthen our bonds and work as partners. Last October's Wye Agreement came about in no small measure because of the President's insistence that Palestinians, whether Muslim or Christian, be treated as full and equal partners. In November, he proposed sending $400 million over three years to the Palestinian people as part of the Wye Supplemental.

In December, he delivered a historic address in Gaza to members of the Palestinian National Council. And just last week, he wrote to Chairman Arafat to reaffirm our support for the aspirations of the Palestinian people to determine their own future on their own land.

We have also committed to bolster Jordan's economy as it undergoes a transition to a new leader and bolstered our relations with countries like Egypt, or Saudi Arabia, or Kuwait.

Here at home, the President and First Lady have met with and reached out to members of the American Muslim community. The First Lady inaugurated what I hope will become a long tradition at the White House by celebrating the end of Ramadan with Muslims. And, just this week, the President appointed Laila Al-Marayati, a Muslim, as a member of the United States Commission on International Religious Freedom.

Importantly, the President has made a conscious effort to dispel the old stereotypes of Islam, both in his aggressive search for peace in the Middle East and in his public statements.

Last September, he gave the keynote speech at the opening of the United Nations General Assembly. The thrust of the speech concerned terrorism—a problem many Americans mistakenly link to Islam. The President stated what has always been our position, that we abhor terrorism and its pursuit of innocent victims. But he went to great lengths to

Our relationship with the Islamic community is vital to almost everything we are trying to do, from Kosovo to the Middle East to Asia.

say that "there is no contradiction between Islam and America."

Perhaps most clearly, Bosnia and Kosovo have refuted the claim that Islam and the West are locked in a clash of civilizations. What Kosovo proves, beyond a doubt, is that Western and Islamic nations can unite to fight evil and protect innocent people—no matter what their background. There is no clash of civilizations—just a clash of values between those who seek a future of peace and prosperity and those who maintain power by resorting to violence and hatred.

We are not fighting for Muslims against Orthodox Christians in Kosovo—we are fighting against the notion that, at the end of the 20th century, people can be singled out for destruction and expulsion because of their faith or heritage.

We are not fighting for Muslims against Orthodox Christians in Kosovo—we are fighting against the notion that, at the end of the 20th century, people can be singled out for destruction and expulsion because of their faith or heritage. Two days ago, at Spangdahlem Air Base in Germany, the President said that kind of policy makes life unbearable and civilization impossible. That is why we have opposed violence against the Kurds and Marsh Arabs in Iraq, against Muslims in Bosnia, against Serbs in Krajina, and now against Albanians in Kosovo.

I heard some heart-rending stories yesterday at a Kosovar refugee center in Germany. Women raped. Men rounded up to be killed and burned. Perhaps the most eloquent statement came from a young man who took the microphone, paused for a long time to compose himself, and then sat back down in tears. "I cannot talk about Kosovo," he said sadly.

These emotionally battered survivors reaffirm our determination to restore decent lives to a people whose only crime is that they want to enjoy their culture and their faith. We will not rest until the Serb forces have withdrawn from Kosovo, the refugees have returned home, and an international security force is in place to protect ethnic Serbs and Albanians alike. Nineteen allies, from across Europe and North America, with different political cultures and different relationships to the Balkans, are in complete agreement. We must do right by the people of Kosovo if we are to do right by the generation before us who fought fascism and the generation of our children who deserve a different future.

The Kosovo conflict has been agonizing for all parties involved, though we should remember it took four years to build an allied consensus in Bosnia, and only after 250,000 people had died. And in confronting this issue the United States has worked closely with Islamic nations to address the urgent needs of the Kosovar refugees. The contributions have come from all over—including generous shipments of food, medicine, and supplies from Egypt, Jordan, Kuwait, Saudi Arabia, the United Arab Emirates, Qatar, Iran, Pakistan, Bangladesh, and Turkey—which has taken in more refugees than any non-frontline state. That generosity has stirred the world.

It's undeniable that stereotypes still endure. Images of America as anti-Muslim and anti-Arab still pervade the Muslim world; images of Islam as a hotbed of fanaticism and terrorism remain here. There has been plenty of misunderstanding and miscommunication on both sides.

Now we must make an effort to overcome such prejudices and forge common cause for the things we all care about in the future: peace, self-respect, and cooperation. That is the wave of the future. It must include people from the entire world, irrespective of religion, nationality, or ethnic origin.

Many Islamic nations continue to doubt our intentions. But the old labels of hegemony and Great Satan will not stick. The United States believes that governments and economies work better when individuals are allowed to make political and economic decisions for themselves—but this is not an ideological straitjacket we are seeking to impose on others. Rather, we are eager to help Muslim nations test that belief for themselves, and on their own terms.

As you know all too well, many Americans are naive about Islam. They think it is monolithic and uniform, or confined to the Middle East, or absent from the United States—of course, none of these are true. The same woman who might be arrested for wearing a head scarf in Turkey might be arrested for refusing to wear a veil in Afghanistan. Malaysia, Pakistan, Uzbekistan, Algeria, and Senegal are worlds apart from each other. Even neighbors are very different: Jordan and Syria, Syria and Iraq, Iraq and Iran. Simplistic images lead to simplistic policies; we need to deal with the world as it is.

To consider the nations of Islam, in all their diversity, is to contemplate the future of the world. It is a future that could go in several directions. We can see enormous potential for Muslim nations across the world. Despite huge challenges and ongoing violence, Indonesia has a chance to embrace democracy and economic reform this summer.

Nigeria, a nation roughly half Muslim (48%), is also preparing for a historic transition. Morocco is making remarkable progress toward pluralism and democracy. In Iran, we see and hear the rising voices of reform. In Jordan, King Abdullah, who will fill his father's large shoes well, has acted quickly to strengthen his nation's economy and improve its ties to the rest of the world. I look forward to his visit here on May 18.

But there are also reasons to be worried. The nuclear tension between Pakistan and India began with religious rivalry. Central Asia is a volatile realm of competing political and economic interests. In Algeria, violence continues to take its deadly toll. There are unspeakable penalties imposed upon women in Afghanistan. And there are still too many countries in the Muslim world—stretching from Mauritania to Malaysia—with pockets of desperate poverty. Let's face it:

To consider the nations of Islam, in all their diversity, is to contemplate the future of the world.

another century of poverty will breed another century of hatred.

A key source of tension between the United States and the Muslim world is the ongoing situation with Iraqi sanctions. Everyone believes that the Iraqi people deserve a chance to lead better lives. But those sanctions remain in place for a specific reason—they have deprived Saddam Hussein of $120 billion of oil revenue he would use to rebuild his arsenal and attack his neighbors. He certainly would not use it to help the people he has gassed, terrorized, and suppressed since coming to power. We were prepared to move forward with oil-for-food as early as 1991, but Saddam would not countenance the idea until forced to do so in 1996. We want to do whatever is necessary to meet the humanitarian needs of the Iraqi people, and we are willing to increase oil-for-food accordingly.

We have never sought to hurt innocent people—we have only tried to stop Saddam from inflicting more unnecessary pain on them.

The way these troubled places define their future, for better or worse, will determine much of the character of the next century. If we work hard to nurture the positive developments, hand in hand with our Muslim partners, and if we give problems the consideration they deserve, we can crush the clash-of-civilizations theory once and for all.

In the process, we will help ourselves, and we will relearn a crucial lesson of our own history; people of different faiths have to coexist, even if they do not like everything about each other.

That is one of the reasons Kosovo is so important. Because there are so many other people in other places struggling to learn its lesson. That depriving a people of their humanity based on their religion or ethnicity cannot be permitted to succeed if we are to enter a new century less bloody than the one we are leaving.

Islam, like all great religions, places a high value on the sense that each person is part of a larger community. That we are uplifted by our kindness to people we do not know. That we are ennobled by our respect for each other, no matter how dissimilar we appear on the surface.

One of the most unforgettable moments of an unforgettable year was the funeral of King Hussein last winter. People of all nations came to pay respect, from East and West, Muslim and non-Muslim, royalty and commoners.

It was a remarkable spectacle—a mass of humanity, joined in bereavement for an extraordinary life that stood for our ability to overcome the boundaries that divide us.

That day marked the end of an era stretching back across nine presidencies—an era of great progress, but also of too much tension between the world's Muslims and the United States.

A new era is beginning, marked not only by a change in a calendar—not only by new ways to communicate—but by a confluence of events that has brought Muslim nations and the United States together for the same good reasons in Kosovo. Together we are protecting the right of a people to inhabit not only their homes, but their interpretation of the house of God as well.

We must seize this opportunity to build upon our history. The President has often noted the paradox that our supremely modern global civilization is still bedeviled by ancient animosities. Nothing mankind has conceived of is more profound than our soaring capacity to imagine a divine being—and nothing has done more to divide us than religion.

Millennium or no millennium, the time has come to face up to our oldest problem.

The Church in Cuba[5]

Bernard Cardinal Law

Archbishop, Archdiocese of Boston, 1984– ; born Torreon, Mexico, 1931; graduated Charlotte Amalie High School, St. Thomas, Virgin Islands; M.A., Harvard College, 1953; St. Joseph Seminary, St. Benedict, LA, 1953–55; Pontifical College Josephinum, Worthington, OH, 1955–61; ordained to Priesthood, Diocese of Natchez-Jackson, MS, 1961; Assistant Pastor, St. Paul Church, Vicksburg, MS, 1961–63; editor, Mississippi (Register) Today, Natchez-Jackson, Diocesan Newspaper, 1963–68; director, Natchez-Jackson Diocesan Family Life Bureau, 1963–68; executive director, Bishops' Committee for Ecumenical and Interreligious Affairs, Washington, D.C., 1968–71; Vicar General, Diocese of Natchez-Jackson, MS, 1971–73; Bishop of the Diocese of Springfield-Cape Girardeau, MO, 1973–84; College of Cardinals, 1985; chairman, Pro-Life Committee, National Conference of Catholic Bishops.

Editors' introduction: His Eminence Bernard Cardinal Law gave this address as part of the Inter-American Dialogue, to some 90 persons attending a conference at the American Academy of Arts and Sciences facility, co-sponsored by the Weatherhead Center for International Affairs and the David Rockefeller Center for Latin American Studies, Harvard University. The Boston Catholic Television Center broadcast the speech. In referring to the Pope's recent visit to Cuba, His Eminence noted that "the Cuban government could not have been more obliging and welcoming." He opposed the United States' embargo against Cuba.

Bernard Cardinal Law's speech: In preparing these remarks, I reviewed my correspondence file from persons who accompanied me to Cuba for the Pope's visit. Our direct flight from Boston to Havana might have established a record in itself! Every letter expressed appreciation for the opportunity to participate in a historic and profoundly moving event. Almost to a person there was the expressed desire to be of assistance to the Church in Cuba and to the Cuban people.

These pilgrims to Cuba included bishops, priests and sisters, and Catholic laity as well as Protestants and Jews. There were business leaders, bankers, doctors and a Health Care System President. There were heads of social service agencies and representatives of foundations. There were lawyers and judges, Congressmen, presidents of colleges, a law

---

5. Delivered in Somerville, Massachusetts, on March 13, 1988, at 12:30 p.m. Reprinted with permission.

school dean, and a university professor, and the editor of a national magazine. We were a wondrously diverse group, but we found unity in our conviction that the time is now for a change in U.S. policy towards Cuba.

Since returning from the Papal Visit, I have often been asked if I thought that change might now come to Cuba. The question misses the point that change has already come. An earlier barometer of change focused on the departure of Fidel Castro as the threshold for any substantive change. The events of the past year clearly demonstrate that that barometer simply does not work. The toothpaste is out of the tube, and Fidel Castro squeezed the tube.

Any blueprint for a change in policy which demands a change in leadership in another country is too rigid a starting point and depending on the means willing to be used to achieve that departure, could lack a moral claim. This is not to condone a dismal record on human rights. Religious freedom is certainly not yet fully developed in Cuba. The fact remains, however, that dramatic change has occurred within the past twelve months in the area of religious liberty. These changes could not have occurred without the active approval of President Castro. He has been a promoter, not an obstacle to what is now happening in Cuba.

It is not the visit alone, stunning though it was, which chronicles change. Events leading up to the visit must also be acknowledged. Some in Cuba with whom I have spoken place great emphasis on the private audience accorded Fidel Castro by Pope John Paul II. One must also note the mixed commission of government and Church to plan for the Papal visit which marks a sea change in that relationship. The Church was able to engage in a door-to-door nationwide mission in preparation for the Pope's visit. Religious processions were allowed, as were some outside religious celebrations. The exclusion of the Church from the use of public media was, at least in a modest way, but nonetheless establishing a precedent, lifted with the pre visit nationally televised address by the Archbishop of Havana, Jaime Cardinal Ortega.

Quite before the time of planning for the visit, the Church was allowed a new expression of social services through Caritas Cuba. While its work is still narrowly circumscribed, a principle of public, organized social service by the Catholic Church has been recognized. The backlog of visa requests by foreign clergy, religious and other Church workers has been broken as the number of visas has dramatically increased.

Change cannot be rooted in a precise paradigm for the future. If we are to measure change realistically, it must be measured against the past. The past that I know in terms of the Church in Cuba begins in 1984. Before then, there were confiscations of Church property, the closing of Catholic schools and other institutional works, the departure, and

Any blueprint for a change in policy which demands a change in leadership in another country is too rigid a starting point and depending on the means willing to be used to achieve that departure, could lack a moral claim.

some would argue the forced exile, of hundreds of Church personnel. There were the labor camps which number among their alumni the present Cardinal Archbishop of Havana. Pervading and justifying all this was an official version of history, employing a method with which we have become all too sadly accustomed in some current trends in the U.S. academy. It is the application of deconstruction to the study of the past in a way which serves an ideological end.

In an earlier visit to Cuba, I objected to President Castro concerning the severe intimidation of the omnipresent Committees of the Revolution. These watchdogs of Marxist orthodoxy saw as dangerously subversive the baptism of a child or the visit of a priest or the regular attendance at Mass. Castro's response, replete with Church history according to Marx, made the claim that the state did allow for religious freedom. The State was powerless, in his explanation, to counter the strong anti-Church sentiment of the people borne of what he described as the Church's oppressive and sinful past.

For the past fourteen years, I have been in continual contact with the Church in Cuba. I was present in the Nunciature in Havana the first time Castro met with Cuban bishops. There were no more than three substantive encounters of this kind before the Pope's visit. During the past fourteen years there have been sporadic efforts on the part of the Cuban government to marginalize the Church by suggesting that the bishops were "counter revolutionary," which in our terms would mean unpatriotic and subversive.

Against that all too schematic background, focus on Havana, Sunday, January 25, 1998. The Plaza of the Revolution has a new face: a heroic-sized painting on the facade of the national library portrays Jesus in the familiar style of the Sacred Heart. One million Cubans, with a sprinkling of foreign pilgrims, are ranged in front of the altar. Fidel Castro, in a business suit, is in the front row.

For me, one among the many moving moments stands out in a particularly vivid way. During the Havana Mass, the Holy Father commissioned representatives from various dioceses to go forth and present the message of the Church. He presented each with a Bible. The last person to approach the Pope was an older woman, quite frail, who was helped up the stairs by two young men. When she approached the Holy Father, she threw her arms around him. There they were, aging and frail, this elderly woman and the Pope, with their common witness to fidelity in the face of Communist oppression. As she was helped down the stairs, she was accompanied by the thunderous applause of thousands of Cubans.

I wondered what she thought. Must it not have been for her the unfolding of a miracle? What had it been for her these past years in a land governed by Marxism? What must have been her joy in this sea of Cubans, so many young and ecstatic in their celebration of faith? I could only think of Anna in the incident recorded by St. Luke. Anna was an old woman, a widow, who spent her days in prayer and fasting in the Temple. When Mary and Joseph brought the infant Jesus to present him to God in the Temple, Anna came to the scene at that moment. St. Luke says, "She gave thanks to God and talked about the child to all who looked forward to the deliverance of Jerusalem."

It must be said that the Cuban government could not have been more obliging and welcoming. The Masses of the Holy Father were televised live nationally.

As the Holy Father left Jose Marti Airport on January 25th, he said that in our day "no nation can live in isolation. The Cuban people therefore cannot be denied the contacts with other peoples necessary for economic, social and cultural development, especially when the imposed isolation strikes the population indiscriminately, making it ever more difficult for the weakest to enjoy the bare essentials of decent living, things such as food, health and education. All can and should take practical steps to bring about changes in this regard."

These are important words of the Pope which have meaning not only for the Catholic faithful but for all women and men of good will, including those who exercise leadership in government. Current U.S. policy towards Cuba was set during the missile crisis. A few things have happened since then, however, including the tearing down of the Berlin Wall and the unraveling of Communist hegemony in Eastern Europe. The visit of the Holy Father to Cuba in January of this year is one of those defining events. A policy driven by events of an earlier time does not meet the challenge of new possibilities which the Holy Father's visit opens up.

A policy driven by events of an earlier time does not meet the challenge of new possibilities which the Holy Father's visit opens up.

One of the strongest impediments to new policy initiatives is the pressure of partisan politics. Is it but the musings of an unrealistic cleric to suggest than an earlier pattern of a bipartisan foreign policy could serve us well again? To that end, I propose the establishment of a bipartisan National Commission on U.S./Cuban relations. Such a Commission, perhaps Presidential or conceivably organized by a non-governmental body, would have as its charge the development of policy initiatives which could build on the changes already perceived in Cuba since the Pope's visit. The work of this Commission should be completed within three to six months. It should not take longer than this because the Commission's work would be essentially a simple and straightforward task.

The Commission might be co-chaired by President Carter and President Bush or President Ford. It ought to include Senator Lugar, Representative Hamilton, a U.S. Bishop, Elizabeth Dole (head of the American Red Cross), two corporate CEO's, two prominent Cuban-Americans, someone from the field of medicine, and someone representing the concerns of the media.

Since the Holy Father's visit, there has been the release of more than 400 prisoners. While one political prisoner is one too many, this direct response to the Holy Father's visit cannot be dismissed. So very much more needs to be done to broaden the scope of human rights in Cuba. However, I am convinced that the best way to do this is to move the starting point of U.S. Policy from the missile crisis to the Papal visit. The Holy Father has amply demonstrated that a policy of positive engagement can achieve far more change within Cuba than can the embargo.

Cardinal Ortega has commented on the so-called Helms-Burton Act that "Any economic measure that aims to isolate a country and thus eliminates the possibility of development, thus threatening the survival of people is unacceptable."

There is no moral justification for the current embargo. In terms of effectiveness as an agent of change it has proven to be a complete failure.

It is impossible to reasonably support the embargo against Cuba while at the same time granting most-favored nation (MFN) status to the People's Republic of China, and while moving into closer relations with Vietnam. Both of these nations have a deplorable record on human rights in general and on religious liberty specifically. If openness is thought to further freedom in those nations where change is not so evident, how is that a different standard is applied to Cuba where there is evident change?

We should not wait for the report of a bipartisan commission to introduce some measures which would ameliorate human suffering in Cuba, which would foster cultural, religious and other interchanges, and which would therefore, encourage the new attitude of openness and change within Cuba. It is time for the U.S. to respond positively to the change that is occurring in Cuba.

There is no moral justification for the current embargo. In terms of effectiveness as an agent of change it has proven to be a complete failure. The most egregious aspects of the embargo, namely the prohibition of sale of food and medicine, must be lifted immediately. The two bills currently in Congress which would do this should be immediately passed. What is needed in Cuba is the ability to purchase food and medicine in the U.S. A singular focus on facilitating charitable donations of food and medicine is patently inadequate.

There are certain things that can be done tomorrow by the President of the United States.

The President should agree to license direct, humanitarian flights to Cuba.

The President could take immediate action to ease remittance restrictions, increase visiting privileges, and expand opportunities for U.S. citizens particularly Cuban-Americans, to visit Cuba by restoring direct flights. The right to travel is a Constitutional right. It should not be violated for outdated political reasons.

The President could restate that he will continue suspending the international trade bans of Helms-Burton indefinitely. This would help the people of Cuba and it would ease the concerns of our closets allies and trading partners.

The President should give serious critical attention to the legal opinion that concludes that the Executive Branch has the legal and constitutional right to grant a general license for medicines and for food. Such an action on the part of the President would, of course, effectively end the food and medicine embargo immediately.

The foreign policy initiatives of a President can be decisive. President Nixon went to China. President Carter brought Begin and Sadat to Camp David. President Reagan met Gorbachev in Iceland to ease nuclear tensions and President Bush followed up by reducing our nuclear weapons. President Clinton has the possibility of charting a new relationship between the United States and Cuba.

Let me end by recounting an incident during the Pope's visit. One of the pilgrims traveling with us took a walk along the waterfront. He was alone, it was raining, and the pavement was slippery. He stumbled and fell, with a resultant large cut in the head. Some passersby stopped their car and took him to the emergency room of the nearest hospital. The care he received was both professionally competent and compassionate. However, he was struck by the fact that the only medicine he could observe on the shelf in the treatment room was some alcohol. When the doctor arrived to stitch his wound, he first reached into a pocket of his white coat, removed a light bulb, and screwed it into the empty socket so that he could see more easily. It is not just a bulb that is missing. There is often a lack of power with devastating consequences, especially in surgery. The lack of medicines— more quickly and cheaply attainable from the U.S.—severely restricts the treatment that can be provided. Even more basically, the effects of the lack of sufficient food threaten the most vulnerable members of the population, the old and the young.

I would submit that the people of Cuba deserve better than that from us. I would submit that it adds no honor to our country to deprive a people of those necessities which should never be used as bargaining chips.

Change is occurring in Cuba. The question is, do we have the political will and moral courage to change?

VI. Communication, Education, and the Arts

Leading the Way Out of the Credibility Crisis[1]

Sandra Mims Rowe

Editor of The Oregonian, *Portland; graduated East Carolina University, Greenville, N.C., 1970; completed program for Management Development, Harvard University's Graduate School of Business, 1990; reporter, assistant city editor, features editor, managing editor, executive editor, and vice president, the* Virginian-Pilot *and the* Ledger-Star, *Norfolk and Virginia Beach, Virginia, 1962–93; at the* Virginian-Pilot *and the* Ledger-Star, *won the* Pulitzer Prize *for general news reporting, 1985; under her leadership,* The Oregonian *won the Pulitzer Prize for explanatory reporting, 1999;* past president, American Society of Newspaper Editors; *member of the Pulitzer Prize Board, 1994– .*

Editors' introducton: Editor Sandra Mims Rowe addressed some 400 editors and journalists from daily newspapers around the United States, newspaper management, and guests attending the American Society of Newspaper Editors annual convention. Concluding that journalists should not "out-TV television," Rowe advised newspapers "to play down—not play up—the trivial, the perverse, the bizarre." The speech was carried by C-Span, published in *American Editor* (May 1998), widely quoted in other journalism-related publications, and studied in journalism classrooms.

Sandra Mims Rowe's speech: "I am not the editor of a newspaper," Mark Twain said. "And I shall always try to do right and be good, so that God will not make me one."

Well, my friends, we must have royally fouled up. For here we are, editors leading newsrooms in a time of frighteningly low respect for the newspapers we hold dear.

I am here to talk to you about editors and their responsibility for the credibility of newspapers when many readers have concluded we have none. We don't trust you, they shout. You can't even get little things right, so you must really blow it on the big things. You're arrogant. You don't respect the privacy of others. You're too negative. You're too liberal. You don't write about things important to me.

---

1.   Delivered in Washington, D.C., on April 1, 1998. Reprinted with permission of Sandra Mims Rowe.

Faced with the litany of criticism—sadly, particularly shrill right now—some journalists believe this is a grim time for newspapers.

It needn't be. We haven't yet done our best work.

If this is a time characterized by a continuing cultural coarseness, it is also a time when newspapers can demonstrate excellence and satisfy an unsated thirst for quality.

If this is the most cynical of times, a time with trust for no one—not politicians, government itself, big business, and certainly not the media—then it also is a time when things that matter to readers cry out for the attention of reporters and editors.

And if this is a time when the destructiveness and tawdriness of mass media hang like a curse over even the best-intentioned newspaper editors, it is also a time when changing values and new media players should prompt us to seek higher ground.

In many newsrooms standards are unclear or, given recent evidence, wildly inconsistent.

We have climbed steep hills in years past. Newspapers are better written and edited than ever before. Newspapers are delivered on time now—in many markets hitting the doorsteps long before dawn. Our color registers. Our ink doesn't smear as much. We confess error, chat up readers, design our pages, and sharpen our headlines.

Yet newspaper circulation falls, or at least stalls. What will heal—or help—us? The answer lies in more work—this time on the hardest problems, ourselves and the character of our newspapers. To get more credibility, we first must stop squandering what we have.

In many newsrooms standards are unclear or, given recent evidence, wildly inconsistent. Editors routinely talk about the gap between the journalistic values they hold most dear and those they think guide the reporters they work beside. They worry whether they can hire people with the skill and breadth and understanding to do the job. Reporters say they don't get the journalistic support they need from their bosses. They wonder whether their editors have sold out journalistic values for business ones. They long for the inspiration provided by leaders with abiding passion for the gritty world of journalism.

If newsroom values are out of whack or reporters and editors are out of touch with each other and with their communities, whose responsibility is that?

It is ours.

Our challenges are not limited to our newsrooms. In some companies the talk has shifted to financial and marketing imperatives to such an extent that journalists have concluded their owners are blindly driven by Wall Street, unconcerned about the quality of journalism. There are happily some newspaper companies that continue to invest generously in their newsrooms and in the professional development of newsroom staffs. But, as profits have hovered near all-time records, many companies have not invested in journalistic training significantly enough to demonstrate their commitment to the highest standards. Nor have beginning salaries at most papers become competitive with those in other professions. It is now left to editors to provide the leadership within their companies to demonstrate the true relationship between quality journalism and long-term success in the marketplace.

But if editors are too weary for the fight, too weighed down with their own faded ideals, who will raise high the journalistic flag within today's media giants?

We must.

And while editors wage these battles within their companies, they witness a growing chasm between journalists' perceptions of how professionally we fulfill our responsibilities and the public's.

In a January Pew Research Center report, 63 percent of respondents believe news stories are often inaccurate, up from 56 percent just a year ago.

Two thirds of those surveyed said coverage of the personal and ethical behavior of politicians is excessive, and 65 percent said the press gets in the way of society solving its problems. Editors will either confront the massive challenges in their newsrooms and their companies and in the public's view of our work, or continue the hand-wringing and self-flagellation, and do nothing.

Leaders will choose action.

Leadership is a wondrous thing and in short supply in all endeavors, no less so in newspapers.

I am reminded of Margaret Thatcher's advice to George Bush during the early days of the Persian Gulf crisis. "Remember, George," she said, "this is no time to go wobbly."

Editors, this is no time to go wobbly. We show leadership by clearly and forcefully articulating standards.

What are our standards, for instance, on the use of anonymous sources? In the face of intense competitive pressure and in hot pursuit of story, the salient standard in the early Clinton–Lewinsky coverage appears to have been that someone said it, therefore we write it; the wire service sent it, therefore we print it.

That is not leadership. It is a sorry squandering of the credibility we have. Newspaper editors are the primary journalistic standard bearers in each community. We all inherited the best practices and highest ideals of our craft and the courage of those who preceded us. We have debts that have to be paid not just with proper grammar and usage, but with decisions that show respect for our communities and our profession.

Editors will either confront the massive challenges in their newsrooms and their companies and in the public's view of our work, or continue the hand-wringing and self- flagellation, and do nothing.

Other media that do not share newspaper standards are recasting the definition of news. But we do not have to be pulled along.

Commercial television, a kaleidoscope of hype and irrelevancy, first creates then exploits fame. TV news, dumbed down to such an extent its patron saints despair, seeks emotion more than enlightenment. We can't out-TV television. We should not try.

The newest news dispenser, the runaway Internet, makes a journalist out of anybody who has a modem. It values speed and sensationalism above accuracy. New media will not adopt our standards. We are foolish to treat them as if they have. Let Matt Drudge be Matt Drudge, but let's not pretend he operates from a base of sound journalistic standards. The high road is there if we will just take it. If newspaper journalism and journalists long for greater respect, then newspaper editors must supply the discipline to play down—not play up—the trivial, the perverse, the bizarre.

Think back to the O.J. criminal trial. In the papers I checked there were between 75 and 100 O.J. stories on Page 1 during those nine months. That's two or three a week on Page 1. What if most newspaper editors had decided not to play up that trial to such an extent? What if we had said let other media go gaga, we're going to move most of these stories inside the paper? Instead we could have displayed an additional significant, interesting local story on the front page. Would newspapers have been worse off for that decision? I don't think so. One editor, one day at a time, could have made this call.

And this individual decision-making by individual editors—reinforcing the highest journalistic standards—is the only way out of the muck for us.

The notion that readers have created the demand for lowest-common-denominator journalism is false. We are doing that ourselves. We can and must stop.

As we apply our own highest standards we could also further our credibility by better communicating them to readers.

Readers are in the dark about journalists' goals and decision-making. Explaining ourselves does not have to be self-serving. It can and should be respectful.

Several editor-written columns I see—notably those by Jerry Ceppos in San Jose and Rich Oppel in Austin—respectfully anticipate readers' concerns and give insight into newsrooms. They don't make excuses. They're not filled with promotional fluff. They communicate standards and help demystify the institution.

In early February, Ceppos wrote a column explaining to readers how the *San Jose Mercury News* would determine what was worth printing in the Clinton–Lewinsky mess. In the column, he gave readers a foundation other than the lowest common denominator on which to judge his newspaper's decisions. By sharing those standards with readers, he also differentiated his newspaper from other media. Without saying so directly, he made clear the *Mercury News* stands for quality.

As Ceppos himself would tell you, the walk through the fires of hell he and his editors endured last year in the wake of the "Dark Alliance" series has had a way of clarifying his focus on the subject of credibility and the leader's responsibility for it. In the Clinton–Lewinsky mess, had each of us discussed our standards—for language, for explicit sexual references, for use and identification of sources—in our newsrooms and shared them with readers, we could have made better critical judgments on the reams of reports we were receiving from the wire services.

Addressing credibility further requires that we finally face up to our readers' complaints of "bias." Two thirds of the public believe the press tends to favor one side when dealing with social and political issues. We refuse to come to grips with this criticism because we believe we are doing God's work and we simply can't imagine why we are damned rather than cheered for our efforts.

In our defensiveness, we never get to the core of the issue, which is point of view more than partisan political bias.

Journalists think stories are not biased if they are balanced, if they reflect views on both sides of an issue or have obligatory quotes from two sides in a conflict. But opinion rears its head in ways that are broader and more fundamental than including both sides in a controversy.

Readers see our point of view in the way we approach and define certain stories. We too easily accept conventional wisdom. We are disinclined to challenge the underlying premises that drive us.

If we are perceived as writing more about and understanding better the arguments of those who demand more money for education, but not looking as deeply at the arguments calling for more efficiency in school spending, we are seen as biased. If we write as though it is government's responsibility to fix all social or institutional problems, we are seen as biased. If we use anecdotal leads to humanize the tragic circumstances of criminals rather than victims, we are seen as biased. If we report on extremes—the polar opposites—when our readers live mostly in the middle, we are seen as biased.

We can't just keep digging in. We should willingly examine our practices, consider how readers view us and open substantive conversations in our newsrooms about the demands of excellence.

We practice journalism in a period of rising expectations. People simply expect more in all things. We must respond. People fortunately still expect maturity and judgment from newspapers. That is why they are disappointed when they don't think they see it. They expect that editors will apply

We can't just keep digging in. We should willingly examine our practices, consider how readers view us and open substantive conversations in our newsrooms about the demands of excellence.

principled and consistently high standards. They don't expect us to be guided by situational ethics, to speak high-mindedly then to pursue every hiccup as if it were The Truth. They don't expect us to fill our columns with speculation, hearsay and opinion, rather than fact. This is the good news: people expect more of newspapers than they do of other media. In today's littered media marketplace, newspapers have an unexploited opportunity to differentiate ourselves in substance and in quality.

Quality journalism requires significant investment. If we buy a top-quality car or piece of furniture or clothing, we expect that the manufacturer has invested heavily in attention to detail and the proficiency of employees.

In newsrooms, the lack of adequate resources to teach and guide newspaper staffs and to pay them sufficiently to keep the brightest young people in journalism directly affects our credibility.

With readers today much more knowledgeable about many subjects than in the past, and with the huge array of sources for that information at their fingertips, journalists must have more than a superficial grasp of complex material.

What once was typical for journalists—a tendency to have broad-ranging interests but superficial knowledge—is a liability in today's media-savvy world.

What once was typical for journalists—a tendency to have broad-ranging interests but superficial knowledge—is a liability in today's media-savvy world. Our audience won't accept our reporting as authoritative unless we are able to write authoritatively. Superficial understanding doesn't cut it.

Other industries know that, in a competitive environment, teaching more advanced skills is the key to survival. High-tech firms average more than $900 per employee a year on training, and the average of all companies is $500. If newspaper spending on training equaled that of high-tech firms, a newspaper staff of 100 would invest $90,000 annually in training.

Unfortunately, newspapers spend considerably less on training than the average business. But our people already know that. A 1993 Freedom Forum study showed that 93 percent of American journalists wanted regular training but that only 14 percent of American newspapers provided it. The report concluded that the lack of opportunity for professional development is one reason newspapers are losing some of their best talent.

Professional-level training is desperately needed in journalistic skills, ethical decision-making, and in the dozens of specialty subjects we presume to report on for our readers.

Newspapers have the profits to invest whatever is needed to make newsrooms centers of learning that combine the intellectual rigor of university life with the energy and drive for action in the best newsrooms. Surely owners must understand that, no matter how fine a college education reporters have when hired, we must not rely on learning by osmosis once they enter newsrooms. Editors should wage an unrelenting campaign to get more training and teaching in newsrooms.

When I embarked on this quest for greater attention to the cause of improving newspaper credibility, a friend suggested that I was really talking about character.

Credibility means accuracy and reliability and trust which, to be sure, would be a great prize. But pursuit of that prize might be easier, he suggested, if we adopted the larger goal of journalistic character.

Credibility can be measured more or less. Character is felt and ties directly to the whole nature of content rather than just to its accuracy. Character as the criterion involves how we choose stories, how we play them, how we perceive our priorities and readers' interests and needs.

Regarding that, nothing I know of offers deeper insight than the words of the late Charles Kuralt. In a speech 15 years ago, Kuralt pleaded with us to turn at least part of our attention away from the pursuit of the entertainer, the politician, and the criminal and toward "the decent and honest and sometimes noble lives of our fellow citizens—and to the worlds of work within our communities—the worlds of law, medicine, education, science, business, and the arts."

If we would do that, Kuralt said, we may do more than merely inform people. "We may help educate them occasionally. We may help broaden their vision and elevate their spirits. We may accept the responsibility we have to be better than we are, broader than we are, calmer and more reflective than we are."

Kuralt wanted to know about people and what they did; his love was language and his art—storytelling. He was fascinated by the grain of the wood, and ignored the dirt in the cracks. He celebrated a world of joy, loss, trial, and achievement. He traveled the country honoring ideas and lives of all sort.

He knew that journalism was not just fact-gathering and blathering, but at its heart was storytelling.

It is the love of storytelling and a passion for ideas and for people that makes the labor of newspapering a privilege.

So, you might logically ask, if wise journalists with passion for craft and excellence have been unable to effectively tackle the credibility problem in simpler times, what makes us think we have the determination or ability to do anything about it today? Just this: I believe there is a growing consensus among editors that we have recently directed extraordinary time and attention to the very real concerns about market share and corporate mission statements and quarterly budget revisions. We have gained knowledge from that and no doubt benefited. But we have been diverted from the place where our passion is most needed: in our newsrooms. We can change that.

We must stand unflinchingly for what we believe—with owners and publishers no less than in our newsrooms. We cannot be reluctant to confront the most difficult issues on either side of our house. It is a time for inspired and courageous leadership.

ASNE hopes to help you provide leadership in newsrooms through the Journalism Credibility Project. This four-year project—with funding from McCormick Tribune Foundation and the commitment of the next four presidents of ASNE—is designed to help us understand the factors that impact credibility and build on the credibility we have.

Credibility is not theoretical, philosophical, or remote from our work. It is at the heart of our professional lives.

Credibility is not about selling more newspapers. It is about building the quality and integrity of our news.

It is not about finding some new journalistic fad or silver bullet to solve our problems. It is about thoroughly understanding, clearly articulating, and relentlessly applying the highest professional and ethical standards.

It is not about finding some new journalistic fad or silver bullet to solve our problems. It is about thoroughly understanding, clearly articulating, and relentlessly applying the highest professional and ethical standards.

It is not even about what we have the right to do; obviously, we have the right to print just about anything we want. It is about doing the right thing.

Our central responsibility as editors is to make the believability—a combination of accuracy, authority, skill, judgment, and respectfulness—of our newspapers *the* central concern of our newsrooms. Ahead of profits. Ahead of what corporate thinks of us. At the front of the line—in time, commitment, and passion.

We do this in part by being open, not defensive, about our weaknesses. We talk about them. We examine our successes and failures, in meetings, in memos, in the middle of the newsroom floor where we can be overheard by all. We do this by nurturing editors who are alive with passion for craft and for coaching reporters and photographers—flesh-and-blood editors who aren't reluctant to state their responsibilities to their newsrooms and who honor their hopes and ideals, editors who understand that everything they do, everything they print contributes to their newspaper's character and credibility with the public.

That is all the prize that editing a newspaper has ever had to offer. It is a great deal indeed.

Thank you.

From the Vast Wasteland to the Vast Broadband[2]

William E. Kennard

Chairman, Federal Communications Commission (FCC), 1997– ; native of Los Angeles, CA; graduated Phi Beta Kappa, Stanford University, 1978; law degree, Yale Law School, 1981; Assistant General Counsel and Legal Fellow, National Association of Broadcasters; FCC's Advisory Committee on Minority Ownership in Broadcasting, 1980s; as partner and member of board of directors of Verner, Lipfert, Bernhard, McPherson and Hand law firm, Washington, D.C., involved in broad range of communications issues; General Counsel, FCC; Treasurer, Secretary, and Assistant Secretary of the Federal Communications Bar Association; first African American to chair the FCC; author of several articles on communications law topics.

Editors' introduction: Chairman William E. Kennard delivered this speech to members of the National Association of Broadcasters. Kennard envisioned "the most exciting era in the history of television."

William E. Kennard's speech: Thank you, Eddie, for that kind introduction.

It's good to be back here again at the NAB convention. I've been chairman now for about a year and a half. It's been quite an exciting time, and lots of fun.

As chairman of the FCC, I find it interesting the way people are always trying to interpret what you do. People are always trying to put you in one box or another.

Last year, a group of pirate broadcasters held a demonstration outside the FCC. They marched down the street with a huge caricature of me as the puppet, Pinocchio. And they had a caricature of the NAB as a big monster pulling all of my strings. And a big sign said, "Kennardio: the Puppet of the NAB."

Now, that's a group that is really in touch with what is going on in Washington these days.

I must say, though, Eddie, that puppet looked better than the monster.

Well, that was kind of fun. The *Washington Post* wrote a big story about it.

A few weeks ago, the *Washington Post* had an article about the very first television transmission. It was 72 years ago. And this transmission wasn't a baseball game or a play. It was a phone call, a conversation between Herbert Hoover,

---

2.   Delivered on April 20, 1999. Reprinted with permission of William
E. Kennard.

who was then the Secretary of Commerce, and Walter Gifford, the president of AT&T. AT&T actually developed and arranged the transmission.

The call was between Washington, D.C., and Bell Labs in New Jersey. And after the call Hoover told reporters, "I am glad to welcome television as the latest product of scientific discovery. It promises that, where the voice has led the way over the telephone wires, the eye will ultimately follow."

Two things struck me about this debut of television in America. First, it was not a passive show; it was interactive. And second, it happened over telephone wires. Call it early convergence.

So here we are, on the eve of the next century, and we find ourselves back where we started. The "eye" is again following the voice. Millions of Americans are going on-line and using copper-wire technology to download images and to listen to music from radio stations around the country. And they're using streaming video to watch everything from the Senate floor to the floor of the New York Stock Exchange.

It's all about broadband—and I mean that in the broadest sense of the word.

In 1961, FCC Chairman Newt Minow proclaimed that television was a "vast wasteland." Today, almost four decades later, I survey the television landscape and see the limitless potential of broadband. Television is making the journey from the vast wasteland to the vast broadband. It is entering the most exciting era in the history of television, an era that will empower television audiences like never before. TV will empower viewers to reach into their television sets and paint their own landscapes: landscapes of entertainment, information, education, and discovery.

Now, some people are saying that the broadband future will be the death knell of television.

They say, Look what happened just a couple weeks ago. Yahoo! and Broadcast.com—two companies that didn't even exist 10 years ago—announced a merger that will form a company with a combined market capitalization of over $40 billion—that's one third bigger than CBS.

These Internet media companies are taking steps to jump from the PC to the TV platform. That's why some say that these companies with their popularity, their technology, and —for now—their market multiples could, in the long run, end up putting all of you out of business.

So, once again, some are writing the obituary of the broadcast industry. We've heard this before, haven't we? People telling broadcasters that you are yesterday's news. Counting you out of the future.

In fact, sometimes you counted yourselves out—telling the FCC to put the brakes on cable television and direct broadcast satellites and satellite radio—because you believed that

Television is making the journey from the vast wasteland to the vast broadband. It is entering the most exciting era in the history of television, an era that will empower television audiences like never before.

all of these technologies would do you in. That they would kill free, over-the-air-broadcasting.

It didn't happen. And the broadband Internet companies won't kill broadcasting either.

Let's take a closer look at the merger between Yahoo! and Broadcast.com.

Broadcast.com started by taking content from traditional television and radio stations and using streaming technologies to transmit that content over the Internet. Broadcast.com built a business around the idea that people would want rich media content on an interactive, individually selected basis.

But more than that, Broadcast.com—like many of today's Internet companies—took a risk on a future that is not yet here. The key to streaming video or even audio isn't content —there's plenty of that. Hey, they'll broadcast anything— even this speech! In fact, they're webcasting this as I speak.

No, for streaming media companies the key is the distribution system. You need lots of bandwidth; you need really big pipes. And as you know, most Americans don't have that bandwidth yet. Even so, the tremendous promise of interactive, customized multimedia made overnight billionaires of Broadcast.com's founders.

Their risk paid off, for now. But what the Broadcast.coms of the world still need to come up with are better ways to deliver their content.

So they'll experiment with IP Multicasting, better compression techniques, different approaches to caching, or with whole new distribution pipes like satellite. But, in the end, what they're really trying to do is come up with a good point-to-multipoint model. And that's just another word for broadcasting.

So Broadcast.com, and RealNetworks, and Spinner.com aren't just Internet companies, they're also broadcasters. In the coming world of convergence, both Internet companies and broadcasters have the opportunity to capture a huge new market.

And you, the broadcasters, have the advantage in this competition. And not just because of your experience or that you are still the most watched medium today.

No, your advantage isn't just content, it's distribution. Broadcasters have a big pipe that everybody needs—and unlike cable companies and phone companies, you don't have to invest in physical connections into every home. Eventually you'll need to develop a backchannel so your viewers can have a truly interactive experience, but you'll have many options to do that. What's most important is that you already have a 20 megabit-per-second digital pipe into almost every home in America.

If there's one thing that's clear from everything I've seen at this terrific show, it's that DTV is not just about TV as we

In the coming world of convergence, both Internet companies and broadcasters have the opportunity to capture a huge new market.

know it. It's also about data. Data is the "killer app" of digital TV. Just as the jet airplane revolutionized travel in the sky, when the broadcast airwaves go digital, it will revolutionize television in this country. I am convinced of that.

With the launch of John Glenn into space last year, the first digital broadcasts began. From stations in big cities to stations in smaller markets—like WKOW in Madison and WBNS in Columbus—you are undertaking the transition to digital ahead of schedule. And I applaud you for this foresight. You should all be proud.

And I also hope to see continued progress on compatibility standards. I believe that in this area the role of the FCC is to facilitate, not regulate. That is why as a first step, the FCC staff will host a Technical Roundtable on May 20 to discuss the progress of industry efforts.

Already, I'm encouraged by this weekend's announcement by NCTA and CEMA of a digital cable-ready interface standard. I look forward to learning more about this agreement, but, above all, I look forward to working together to make sure that consumers enjoy a smooth transition to the digital age.

And I'm confident that the future for broadcasters in the digital age is bright. By the end of 2001, over 20 million PCs will be shipped that are equipped for ATSC-compliant tuner cards. With this, short video clips can be broadcast to our desktops and cached on users' PCs or set-top boxes. Time shifting made easy.

And the potential applications are limitless.

As convergence reshapes old industry boundaries, I have two goals that will not change: promoting competition and promoting opportunity.

When you tally up the assets needed in the broadband world, broadcasters win hands down. You have plenty of spectrum, tremendous reach with established brands, the ability to produce great local content, established networks, and relationships with local and national advertisers.

I believe that you will use those assets to do great things in the broadband business. And that you will continue to provide great service to our nation. With this opportunity comes a special set of responsibilities.

Some are fundamental to the safety of our nation—like the emergency broadcast system—and some are fundamental to the strength of our society.

Foremost among them is ensuring that the airwaves foster a robust competitive environment, where we have a diversity of content and opportunity.

As convergence reshapes old industry boundaries, I have two goals that will not change: promoting competition and promoting opportunity.

While the onrush of technology makes convergence inevitable, let me be clear: convergence is not synonymous with consolidation. Convergence means more choices. It's new media companies, like Yahoo!, coming to TV screens. It's established media, like you in this audience, assuming leading roles on the Internet. It does not mean new industries controlled by a handful of giant conglomerates.

Another fundamental responsibility is to our children. Congress directed that broadcasters offer our children programming that will educate and uplift them.

And we must ensure that there always will be opportunities for employment. Opportunities for a young college student to get an internship at a local TV station and a foot in the door into your industry. I got an opportunity like that and it's one of the reasons I am here before you today.

When I spoke here last year, I challenged you to work with me to promote opportunity and diversity in the broadcast industry.

Some of the leaders in this industry and in the NAB have come forward with energy and commitment and some creative new ideas. I commend Mel Karmazin and Lowry Mays for their leadership, for rising to the challenge.

I am encouraged by their efforts and I hope these efforts will lead to meaningful new ways to create more opportunity in broadcasting for all Americans. The airwaves are a wonderful resource and we must seek ways to use them more efficiently, to create more outlets for expression and more opportunity in our country.

That's why I want to work with you, not against you, to find a way to make low-power radio work. Low-power radio has the potential to create outlets for an array of new voices like churches, community groups, and colleges. It can give voice to those ideas not always heard, but which many yearn to hear.

Now, I know many of you are very concerned about this. In fact, some people are saying that I want to write the obituary for radio.

Well, I want to be very clear about two things. One, this FCC is committed to preserving the technical integrity of FM radio. And two, this FCC is committed to a digital future for radio. Low-power radio will not change that.

And, frankly, it is not helpful to hear only rhetoric that "the sky is falling" even before the rule-making comments have been filed. It's not helpful and it only serves to undermine the credibility of your arguments in the end.

Broadcasters will rise to the challenges and opportunities created in the digital world, just as you have risen to challenges in the past.

Think about it. Ten years ago, it was the Big Three. Today the Big Three are not three competing companies, but three competing industries—broadcast, cable, and Internet—all racing ahead into the digital future.

And your competitors will be doing so with business plans that do not rely solely on a model of mass-market advertising. They're using subscriptions, shares of e-commerce sales, and other new media incentives to boost the bottom line.

Low-power radio has the potential to create outlets for an array of new voices like churches, community groups, and colleges. It can give voice to those ideas not always heard, but which many yearn to hear.

Just as business plans must change for this new world, so must the regulatory structure.

Some say that we should eliminate all of our ownership rules. Just get rid of them all. Eliminate all the local rules on radio and television as well as the network audience cap.

I don't think that's the right answer. This is not the time to completely deregulate broadcast ownership. Our ownership rules reflect core values of competition and diversity.

But, at the same time, we can't keep broadcasters in the dark ages of black-and-white-era rules. With the changing realities of today's marketplace, you need the flexibility to seize the opportunities and open the frontiers of the Information Age.

That's why I want you to join with me in crafting commonsense ownership relief. What do I mean by commonsense? I mean that we need to bring all of our ownership proceedings to a conclusion. We need to bring more certainty to the marketplace. And we need to revise our rules to give broadcasters more flexibility in an increasingly competitive world, without undermining our rightful reverence for outlet diversity.

What do I mean by flexibility? I mean that consolidation that preserves voices is not bad. And common ownership that provides new voices is good.

My challenge is to work with you to find the right balance.

Your challenge is to seize the opportunities of the broadband future.

You know, the entrepreneurial fervor of companies like Broadcast.com, Yahoo!, Amazon, and all these Internet companies takes us back to an earlier time in your business. The same spirit that drove these men and women drove men like Sarnoff and Paley. It drove the early TV pioneers to use technology in ways never tried. It gave them the courage to break out of the old molds and deliver images to America's homes in ways never seen. Their work unleashed an industry with more power and influence in our culture than anything ever seen before.

The transforming power of digital technology will do this again. I am convinced that television's broadband future is *vast*—and will be richer than anything imagined today.

This will happen. And broadcasters will help make it happen.

Thank you.

Changing the American High School to Fit Modern Times[3]

Richard W. Riley

U.S. Secretary of Education, 1993– ; born January 2, 1933, Greenville County, SC; Bachelor's degree, Furman University, 1954; U.S. Navy, 1954–1956; L.L.B., University of South Carolina Law School; South Carolina House of Representatives, 1963–1977; Governor of South Carolina, 1979–1987; partner, Nelson, Mullins, Riley and Scarborough.

Editors' introduction: Speaking before the National Press Club in Washington, D.C., Richard W. Riley explained, "Congress needs to pass school modernization legislation, fulfill its promise to reduce class size, and provide the American people with a budget that makes education a high priority." He expressed disappointment with current Congressional inaction on school modernization legislation.

Richard W. Riley's speech: Good afternoon. Over the last five years, I have had the opportunity to come to the National Press Club to make my annual back-to-school speech on a variety of topics. Last year, I used the occasion to make a set of policy recommendations about improving teacher quality. I am pleased to report back to you that we are seeing some progress on this central issue when it comes to improving American education.

Last year, Congress passed our $75 million teacher quality legislation and put down a first installment to meet the President's challenge to reduce class size by supporting 100,000 new teachers in the early grades—teachers who have a special skill in teaching reading.

I also challenged America's higher education community to give the education of America's future teachers a much higher priority. I am pleased that over 100 college and university presidents are gathering in Washington today and tomorrow to join me at a "University Presidents' Summit on Teacher Quality." Some of these leaders are in our audience today.

Why Have This National Conversation?

Today, I want to start a national dialogue on the American high school and make a set of recommendations to get that conversation going. There are several reasons why we need to put the spotlight on these high-school years of learning.

The first is simply demographics. The Baby Boom Echo generation—53 million strong in 1999—is getting older and

---

3. Delivered before the National Press Club Washington, D.C., on September 15, 1999.

the pressure point is going to be more and more the American high school. In the next ten years, we will educate an additional 1.3 million high-school students.

Let us also recognize that how we learn and work has changed dramatically. We are in a new era, driven by science and technology, and our schools need to give young people both the capacity to do college-level work and the essential skills to prosper in our new economy.

A second reason is what young people are telling us themselves. Several weeks ago, I released a poll of over 1,000 high-school students—the Shell Poll. This poll told us that the great majority of America's high-school students are optimistic, ambitious and have very good values. They want to go to college. They are thinking seriously about the future. But teenagers will tell you that growing up isn't easy. They told us in the poll that it is "tough" being a teenager and that they are looking for help. They feel increased pressure to go to college and get good grades. While the majority of students gave their high schools good marks, they also told us that they were bored and that many of them were willing just to get by.

Many of our young people have strong ambitions but no sense of direction about how to start achieving those ambitions. The poll also told us that about 20 percent of our nation's high-school students—that's about 2.7 million teenagers—are being challenged by a host of problems, such as drugs and alcohol, staying in school, or a troubled family life.

We need to listen hard to what our young people are telling us. Teenagers by their nature are passionate, creative, open to new ideas, and full of energy to discover the world around them. We need to find new ways to capture all of this positive energy, and we need to make sure that teenagers are part of the solution.

Finally, tragedies like Columbine have made all of us take a second look at the American teenage experience. Why are we losing some of our young people? What can we do in our high schools to make sure that every young person feels connected? For all these reasons and others, I believe that now is the right time to challenge ourselves to do some creative thinking about the future of the American high school.

Stuck in a Time Warp

Many experts have noted that the American high school is one of the most enduring and unchanging institutions in our society. Even as the world is changed all around them, the majority of our nation's high schools seem to be caught in a time warp from long ago. In his well-known book *Horace's Compromise*, published in 1984, Ted Sizer took a searching look at the American high school. He wrote, "As one visits communities one is gradually struck by how similar the structure and articulated purpose of the American high

We are in a new era, driven by science and technology, and our schools need to give young people both the capacity to do college-level work and the essential skills to prosper in our new economy.

school are . . . the framework of grades, schedules, calendar, courses of study, even rituals, is astonishingly uniform and has been so for as least 40 years."

Little has happened in the last 15 years to make Ted Sizer change his observation. Now, I am not somebody who believes in change simply for change's sake. Yet, there is something out of sync here in 1999, if we continue to accept the unspoken assumption that too often defined the American high school of 50 years ago.

Fifty years ago, one third of the students were being prepared for college, one third drifted through high school but eventually got decent jobs, and one third were tagged as low achievers and expected to drop out.

Years ago this assumption could prevail because we lived in an industrial era. Muscle power mattered as much as brain power when it came to making a living. In the South, where I come from, you could leave high school as early as tenth grade and make a decent living in a cotton mill. But those times are over and the old factory model of thinking needs to be left behind as well. Yet today, we still seem to be using America's high schools as "sorting machines," tagging and labeling young people as successful, run of the mill, or low achievers.

The American high school needs a purpose that is more than just helping students get through it.

We need all of our young people learning to high standards in what Alan Greenspan has called the new "economy of ideas." This is why I continue to challenge the unspoken assumption in American education that we expect some young people to drop out, fail out, or lose out, and that there is nothing we can do about it. One fact I find especially troubling is the high Hispanic drop-out rate. Reforming our high schools must engage these Hispanic young people to stay in school.

So what are we to do about the American high school?

Leon Botstein, the president of Bard College and a passionate champion of America's young people, has suggested in his book *Jefferson's Children* that the American high school is "obsolete." He goes on to argue that at the very least young people need to be finishing high school by age 16 and assuming a new set of responsibilities to increase their sense of adulthood.

While I disagree with Leon Botstein's premise that high schools are obsolete, there is merit in his assertion that the "weakest part of America's educational system is located at the juncture of adolescence and schooling." Leon Botstein goes on to make the salient point that our high schools, with their rigid structures, can deaden the curiosity of our young people precisely when they are most curious.

It seems to me that we need to go in a new direction. The American high school needs a purpose that is more than just helping students get through it. Yes, many of our high schools do a very fine job of preparing young people for college. At the other extreme, some high schools are little more than a way station for young people who already know that life is very unfair.

Some of you may have read the article a few days ago in the paper about a Jesse Jackson-led tour of two high schools in Chicago that exemplified these extremes.

One school—Neuqua High School in Naperville—is a $62 million suburban high school on a 50-acre campus. The other—Harper High School in center-city Chicago—has a science lab with no running water and a drop-out rate of about 33 percent. This gives me the opportunity to express some frustration.

All of our efforts to improve American education not only require new thinking but also new investments. For three years now, President Clinton has been asking the Congress to help this nation modernize and build more schools. We need to build 6,000 new schools to keep up with rising enrollment in the next ten years. Yet, the Republican-dominated Congress has done nothing to address this pressing issue. I remain perplexed by this partisan brick wall.

Congress needs to pass school modernization legislation, fulfill its promise to reduce class size, and provide the American people with a budget that makes education a high priority. We are not even near that now, and I remain disappointed by the current congressional inaction.

While record numbers of high-school seniors are going on to college, we still are not doing a very good job of preparing them to stay in college.

There are other reasons why we need to go in a new direction to improve the American high school. While record numbers of high-school seniors are going on to college, we still are not doing a very good job of preparing them to stay in college. Almost half of entering college freshmen drop out by the end of their second year.

And close to 30 percent of all students entering a four-year college have to take remedial courses. That's not good enough in my book. I think colleges and universities should be putting school districts on notice when they continually send them students who have to take remedial classes. So where can we improve?

Improving Academic Rigor

First, we need to accelerate learning. For six years now, I have been talking continuously about ending the tyranny of low expectations. This can only happen if our nation's high schools end the practice of putting some students into low-achieving or dead-end courses that tell these young people that we have just about given up on them.

High schools justly take great pride when their graduates go on to the best colleges and universities. But we can't place all of our focus only on the gains at the top. We need to have an unwavering focus on academic achievement, combined with a "no excuses" attitude for those at the bottom.

If a student is struggling, the answer has to be an intense intervention effort—some combination of tutoring, after-school, Saturday schooling, and summer school—to help that student meet high standards.

I encourage local school districts to make the extra effort to test all of their eighth graders prior to entering high school to make sure that their reading and math skills are up to date.

If a child needs to improve his or her skills, do it during the summer before the student starts taking geometry and biology.

This leads me to, once again, urge high schools to encourage their students to take the tough core academic courses. Research tells us that the single most important factor in making sure a student gets admitted to college and completes the college degree is the academic intensity of the student's high school curriculum. Taking the tough courses counts much more than test scores or class rank. This is especially true for minority students. Right now just over half of all high school students are taking the core academic courses. Let's set a goal of 75 percent by 2005.

I believe that every high school in America should be offering advanced placement (AP) or other advanced courses in the core subjects within the next two years, and a fuller range of AP courses within the next three to five years. Today, only 49 percent of our high schools offer AP courses and only 10 percent of our students take these demanding courses.

I remain deeply concerned that we continue to shortchange many of our young people, particularly our minority youth, by not even giving them the opportunity to stretch their minds.

This year, we have asked the Congress for $20 million to expand AP opportunities. Distance learning and the Internet are surely two ways to get more AP courses to our nation's rural schools.

I encourage many more states to create high school exit exams where students demonstrate what they know and are able to do. About half of the states in the country have exit exams in place or in development. Years ago, I opposed high stakes exit exams because minority students really had less chance to succeed in the days immediately following integration.

Today, I believe high school exit exams can help stimulate new efforts to raise up minority achievement, if we give every student the individual support needed to pass the exam.

Like other lawyers, I went to law school and then got ready to take the bar exam. Like most graduates of a law school, I discovered that the bar review helped me in many ways to integrate what I had learned in law school.

I believe that similar types of review courses could be established to help high school seniors achieve two goals: to help students prepare for high-school exit exams, and to help them integrate what they have learned for a senior-year portfolio.

Let me suggest one other way to raise standards. I believe that in this new economy every high school student should be close to fluent in a foreign language when he or she graduates. We should begin teaching foreign languages in our elementary schools, and then in middle schools and high schools. English is a beautiful language and every American student must be a master of it. English is surely a world language. But learning a foreign language exposes young people to new cultures and new horizons, and helps them understand English better.

Now, all this push to get young people to learn more is going to provoke the question: when are they going to have time to do it? Between sports, the band, or other extracurricular activities, between work, going to school and just hanging out, something has to give. Let me suggest the answer. We need to stop letting teenagers work more than 20 hours a week during the school year.

Helping young people develop a work ethic is an important part of growing up. The research, however, is quite clear. Students who work too much put earnings over learning and are too tired to study. Parents need to set limits on how much time young people spend working.

Building a Foundation for Change

Now, an important point. The effort to raise standards can't be done overnight, and we shouldn't assume that the current structure of the school day is the best and only way to get the job done.

If we just add another layer of requirements on to a rigid school structure that already gives teachers little time to plan or interact with their students, then we will have missed the boat entirely.

You need to build a foundation and give teachers and principals the resources, the time, and the flexibility to find the right way to help all of the young people. If we just add another layer of requirements on to a rigid school structure that already gives teachers little time to plan or interact with their students, then we will have missed the boat entirely.

Teachers are the heart and soul of our schools, and we have to do a better job of listening to them. And principals have to be close to magicians to balance day-to-day demands while redesigning their schools for the future.

So we need to support creative principals and teachers who see themselves as architects for a new type of high school that is more flexible, open, demanding, and challenging.

This is why this Administration is asking the Congress for new support to reform America's high schools. We are seeking in our proposed Elementary and Secondary Education Act Reauthorization substantial new budget authority to help 5,000 high schools improve or redesign themselves. And we have created a network of high schools on the cutting edge of reform. These new American high schools are setting a new standard of excellence for all students.

Start with Good Teaching

Building a new foundation for America's high schools has to begin and end with good teaching. This is why 100 college presidents have graciously come to Washington for this important summit on improving teacher education. We simply have to elevate the task of preparing the next generation of teachers to the highest level of university leadership.

High school teachers, and for that matter all teachers, have to be given the opportunity to raise their professional standards. They have to be masters of their field whether it is history, physics, technology, or music.

This intense effort to give future teachers the tools they need is only the beginning. As one principal wrote me, 98 percent of her students are "digital children." New teachers simply have to be masters in knowing how to teach using technology and, frankly, we're not there yet.

Another high school principal made this important point which I support. She said that her dream would be to have her students in class nine months of the year, but have her teachers working an extra month to six weeks to plan the curriculum, to understand how to teach to new high standards, and to learn new teaching skills. It seems to me that the high school of the future is simply going to have to go in this direction.

This requires teachers to have a central role in redefining how they teach. If we ask teachers to do the extra work to raise achievement levels, I believe we should pay them for the effort. You can't get good teachers on the cheap.

If we ask teachers to do the extra work to raise achievement levels, I believe we should pay them for the effort. You can't get good teachers on the cheap.

Helping Young People Build Connections

I also believe that we need to find ways to create small, supportive learning environments that give students a sense of connection. That's hard to do when we are building high schools the size of shopping malls. Size matters.

The National Association of Secondary School Principals in their important study, Breaking Ranks, makes the key point that students learn best in schools with about 600 students. While we may not be able to change the size of every high school building, there are many ways that we can make young people feel more connected.

We can create schools-within-schools, academic houses, and make sure that every high school student has an advisor for all four years that the student can count on all the time. At Central Park East High School in New York City, the morning homeroom has been turned into a student advisory period. The students get focused about what they are doing and relate it to their lives.

Certainly we need many more counselors and mentors in our high schools and not just to help young people get ready for college. Growing up is "tough," teenagers tell us, and they are looking for guidance and support. Given the recent violent tragedies, I support the new efforts in the Congress to increase funding both for counselors and mental health counselors.

Two Key Transitions: Ninth and Twelfth Grades

Two very important transition points take place in the American adolescent experience: when young people first enter high school, and when they graduate. These transitions really amount to rites of passage, as they come at key moments in adolescent development. We need to see them in a new light.

The typical eighth grader, for example, leaves a much smaller elementary or middle school, and suddenly finds himself in a very big and at times impersonal high school. The transition can, at times, be overwhelming. The result is that some students become low achievers, some drop out, and some decide that they are not college material.

And suicide prevention experts tell us that ninth grade is the most troubling year. So this first transition deserves our attention. Several recommendations come to mind.

Schools can create a smoother transition in a number of ways, such as freshmen academies, regular contact with the same group of teachers and advisors, and transition courses that address new challenges from study skills to understanding other cultures. The key is to create smaller and more personalized learning environments for these young people.

Parents need to stay very involved with their children when they enter high school. This is so important and goes against the common assumption that parents should give their teenagers more independence. The truth of the matter is that teenagers want to grow and have new experiences; at the same time, they want to know that their parents are there for them. Parents need to realize that they are still the most important source of support and guidance for teenagers. Sometimes it is hard to break through.

My message to parents is to stay involved. Slow down your lives. I hear a real concern from parents about their children being bombarded by a multitude of messages—some of them harmful—from television, movies, the Internet, and even from their children's best friends.

Young people can be very tough on each other at a time when relationships are so important to them. They create cliques, groups, and select out those they do not want. Our high schools have to push back against this tendency, and students are telling us that this is where they need the most support. Community groups and faith communities can also play a positive role in helping schools meet this challenge. The message should be very clear—every teenager matters.

This is why I believe that schools should set a real goal that every student has some adult to turn to for advice and support. It may be a counselor, a mentor, a coach, or a teacher. But the key is to make sure that every teenager has that sense of security about knowing whom to turn to when he or she is struggling.

The freshman year is also a crucial year for getting young people on the right track in terms of taking the right courses and getting them thinking about going on to college. This is why I want to recommend highly something that Gene Bottoms is doing as part of his "High School That Works" initiative that is supported by the Southern Regional Education Board.

Freshmen who participate in this program, which is now in more than 500 high schools across the South, sit down with their parents and a high school advisor and sketch out a six-year plan. The young people get the message that they have new and higher horizons, and that going to high school has a larger purpose.

Creating New Pathways to Learning and Adulthood

We can also do more to create new pathways to learning and to adulthood. In a world exploding with knowledge, with teenagers hooked on the Internet as never before, the traditional seven-periods-a-day way of learning may not be the best or the only way to educate our young people.

New pathways to learning and adulthood mean new connections to colleges and universities, new connections with other institutions in the community, whether it is a hospital, a bank, a zoo, or a museum. Close to 230,000 high school students, for example, are now taking college-level courses across the country. Tech Prep courses and School-to-Work programs, for example, are great ways to link highschool students to community colleges.

High schools of the future need to see themselves as the starting place where young people launch themselves into other learning experiences, and then come back to their high school to integrate what they have learned.

I also encourage schools to do some creative thinking about the senior year experience. Some high school seniors start "checking out" once they have filled out their last college application or received an early acceptance notice from college. The young people tell us in a very direct way that they want to move on.

Senior year should be a well-thought-out transition into adulthood with students being given increasing responsibility. They should be given many more opportunities to be out in the community in structured internships, apprenticeships, or service-learning opportunities. By treating these young men and women as adults, we send a powerful message that we expect adult behavior from them as well.

Conclusion

I end now with this thought. Believe in our young people. I say that again—believe in our young people. Please help me give them a message of hope, promise, and possibilities. I am

In a world exploding with knowledge, with teenagers hooked on the Internet as never before, the traditional seven-periods-a-day way of learning may not be the best or the only way to educate our young people.

tired and weary of the worn-out nostalgia and pessimism that seems to haunt American thinking when it comes to our young people.

Let us reject the twin belief that once there was a time in American education when all things were better, and the negative assumption that this generation of young people can't quite cut it. Our young people don't buy that and neither do I.

Surely, in this time of peace and prosperity, in this great nation—the world's best democracy and hope—we can send a more positive message than that to our nation's young people.

I believe in America's young people. They are optimistic and ambitious and they are looking for direction. If you don't know a highschool student, go out and meet one.

The high school student you meet will be full of possibilities and bored at the same time; extraordinarily creative and, at times, absolutely clueless. High school students will be full of themselves, and scared to death about what people are thinking about them. They are our children and grandchildren. And in a few years, when all of us are in our rocking chairs, they will be our leaders.

Let's give them hope and promise for the coming times, and let's create high schools that are exciting, exploring, creative, and challenging, high schools that spark all of our young people to see the full value of their God-given potential.

Thank you.

Lifting Up Our World[4]

Myles Brand

President and professor of philosophy, Indiana University, 1994– ; born New York, NY, 1942; B.S., Rensselaer Polytechnic Institute, Troy, NY; Ph.D., University of Rochester, 1967; Provost and Vice President for Academic Affairs, Ohio State University, 1986–89; faculty and administrative positions, University of Arizona, University of Illinois at Chicago, and the University of Pittsburgh; President, University of Oregon, 1989–94; Chairman of the American Association of Universities; author of 57 books, articles, and book chapters on philosophy; author of numerous articles and addresses on issues in higher education.

Editors' introduction: President Myles Brand gave the keynote address at an annual meeting sponsored by the Buchanan Counseling Center at Clarian Health Partners Hospital. Brand spoke to some 500 community members, administrators, physicians, and persons associated with the Buchanan Counseling Center in the banquet room. The speech followed dinner and an awards ceremony for local businesses who have family-friendly policies, and was warmly received. President Brand discussed how a "search for moral values . . . affects the way we educate our young people and operate our businesses."

Myles Brand's speech: Thank you for that generous introduction. I wish my father were present tonight to hear those words and that my mother were here to believe them. I know that they would enjoy this evening as much as I have. Their hearts would be warmed, as mine has been, by your celebration of sound values and by the fine work of the Buchanan Counseling Center. I'm delighted to be here, and I am very happy to be able to talk with you this evening.

Tonight I'd like to talk about the search for moral values in our contemporary society and about how that search affects the way we educate our young people and operate our businesses.

The great Greek philosopher Heraclitus once said nothing endures like change. That is especially true of twentieth-century America. Historians have observed that, in the past century, more Americans have experienced greater change in a shorter period of time than in any other era in our history.

We've moved from an agricultural to an industrial to a knowledge-based economy. We've achieved a level of affluence that even royalty did not enjoy in past ages. While at

We've moved from an agricultural to an industrial to a knowledge-based economy.

---

4.   Delivered in Indianapolis, Indiana, on November 19, 1998, at 9:30 p.m.
Reprinted with permission of Myles Brand.

the same time, vast populations in our own country and around the globe have sunken deeper into poverty and deprivation.

We've traveled our galaxy and traversed the geography of the atom. We've consumed more natural resources than were used by all people throughout history prior to this century. And we've redefined gender roles more basically than they have been reshaped in any corresponding period in the past twenty centuries.

Transformations of such great magnitude and consequence bring about abundant creativity and invention, as new technological advances and new forms of coping with life emerge. But they also create a cultural climate of discontinuity and anxiety as familiar ways and long-held principles lose their force. I know that I am preaching to the choir when I say that seismic shifts such as these have real impact on human bonds, on the way we educate our young people, and the way we structure and run our businesses. Our former president Jimmy Carter once said that we must adapt to changing times while holding fast to unchanging principles. As a college president, I spend a lot of time thinking about how we can best educate our young people to do just that. What truths or principles *should* they live by—what values *ought* they hold on to as they face the new millennium?

A lot of attention is given these days to the apathy of our youth. I was interested to read in the newspaper a couple of weeks ago about the conference of Nobel Peace laureates that took place at the University of Virginia. The conference was convened to illustrate how each individual can make a difference. The gathering included seven of the world's greatest advocates for peace—among them were His Holiness the Dalai Lama of Tibet, Archbishop Desmond Tutu of South Africa, and Rigoberta Menchu Tum of Guatemala, who defends the rights of indigenous peoples.

It was the largest gathering of Nobel Peace laureates that's ever occurred, and it reflected the peace prize winners' commitment to work together to influence a broad range of human rights issues. Archbishop Tutu asked the crowd of students—many of whom had camped out all night to get tickets for the event—for help in realizing his dream of a world that is more caring and compassionate, a world where people matter more than profits.

How do we educate our young people to do that?

I think we do it not by giving our youth answers—answers that they think are outdated in our contemporary society—but by giving them the tools to ask the right questions. As a professional philosopher, I have dedicated my life to the belief that asking the right questions is as important as finding the right answers.

But before I talk with you about that, I would like to share with you a story about my own questioning.

A couple of years ago, I received a remarkable phone call from IU's Dean of International Programs. He told me that the Dalai Lama would be visiting Indiana University in a few weeks. And then he added, "You will have the opportunity to spend some time with him."

My first thought was that this was wonderful news. Students, faculty and staff, as well as the entire Bloomington community, would have the chance to hear from one of the world's great spiritual leaders. And I would be able to meet with him one-on-one. I thought this was an incredible, once-in-a-lifetime opportunity.

But then I had second thoughts. What would I ask the Dalai Lama?

Here was my one chance to ask this wise man one question. I certainly did not want to waste the opportunity. I began to imagine what it would be like to be nearing the end of my life and realize that I had asked the Dalai Lama the wrong question!

I spent the next several weeks thinking about the meeting. In my mind, I reviewed the issues that had occupied the great Western philosophers for 2,500 years. I did not want to ask the Dalai Lama to adjudicate differences between Plato and Aristotle, or Leibniz and Hume, nor did I want to waste my question on some technical matter of interest only to contemporary philosophers. I already knew the standard answers and responses to all these issues. No, I wanted to ask him a question about the human condition, a question whose answer would help me better understand the world in which we live.

Those weeks were agonizing. I queried my friends and colleagues. I affirmed, then rejected, idea after idea. I wanted to identify a question whose answer would not illicit a doctrinaire response, but rather required both worldly and other-worldly knowledge.

Finally, I settled on what I would ask and had only to await his arrival. Then the moment came. I followed the Dalai Lama into a small anteroom in the Indiana Memorial Union, where he sat in a comfortable chair. Dressed in his customary saffron robes, he exuded a warm and welcoming manner.

After a few pleasantries, including an exchange of ceremonial silk shawls, I reiterated how much we appreciated his visit to the IU campus. Then I said, "May I ask you a question?" He nodded approvingly.

My question was this: "Is the world becoming a more peaceful place?" He thought a moment, and then replied, "Last week I met with the Queen Mother of England, and it was my turn to ask a question. I had time for only one, so I asked her, 'Is the world becoming a more peaceful place?'"

Well, I was comforted to know that at least I had come up with a reasonable question.

As he sat with me, the Dalai Lama's first response to my question was, "Yes and no." And then he amplified his theme. The communications and information revolution is making the world a much safer place, he said. We know almost instantly what is occurring in the most distant regions. He said he believed that this ability to watch events as they are occurring will make it difficult, if not impossible, for the momentum to build toward another world war.

But he noted that violence and irresponsibility are part of the human condition and he could see no end to the personal injuries and meanness that individuals inflict on each other. In the many months that have followed our meeting, I have had occasion to reflect on the Dalai Lama's answer, which struck me as both idealistic and realistic. He was optimistic about our future, but also aware of the nature of the world in which we live.

Universities are uniquely well suited to lift up our society by giving people the tools they need to become moral and productive citizens.

Technology has been credited with many things, not all of them good. But his point that it leads not only to an understanding of those distant from ourselves, but also enables the world to observe whatever serious threats might be evolving, makes good sense. Unfortunately, his point that the world can never be an entirely peaceful place because of wanton violent acts rings true, too.

So now my question is, How do we educate our young people to create peace in violent world? How do we teach them to respect others? As I think about this question I am reminded of the words of Harriet Beecher Stowe, whom Abraham Lincoln called the little woman who helped to end slavery. Stowe once wrote that "every human being has some handle by which he or she may be lifted; and the great work of life, as far as our relations with each other are concerned, is to lift each one by his or her proper handle."

That is the challenge not only of business and of family counseling, but also of contemporary education. It is the challenge for Indiana University. I believe that handle by which we may be lifted is moral reasoning. Universities are uniquely well suited to lift up our society by giving people the tools they need to become moral and productive citizens. Indiana University takes that job seriously, and, I believe, does it exceptionally well.

Moral reasoning is not memorizing and reciting dictums, but rather it is reasoning from first principles. Two types of such principles about the rightness of action are consequentialist (e.g., utilitarianism) and deontological (the intentions with which one acts). There is a difference between happy accidents and good acts gone awry. Thinking through alternatives and making judgments about particular cases is moral reasoning.

As I think about the university's role in teaching moral reasoning, I am reminded of something I read last year that illustrates this point. Author Earl Shorris felt compelled to

write a book about poverty in America. The book he produced was published just last year. It's called *New American
Blues: A Journey Through Poverty to Democracy*. Shorris
embarked on this project by talking with the poor to see how
their ideas fit with what he had learned about poverty. He
interviewed more than six hundred people over the course of
three years. But it was the words of a young, street-tough
black woman named Niecie, who was incarcerated in a
women's prison, that finally directed the course of his
project.

In reply to Earl Shorris's question, "Why do you think people are poor?" this young woman, who was a graduate of the
crack houses and streets of Harlem, spoke not about lack of
jobs or money, but about moral poverty. She told the author
that if he wants to make a difference, he needs to begin with
the children. Niecie said, "You got to teach the moral life of
downtown to the children. And the way you do that is by
taking them downtown to plays, museums, concerts, lec-
tures, where they can *learn* the moral life of downtown."

By the "moral life of downtown," Niecie meant the humanities. This young woman, who had earned her high-school
diploma in a prison library and had begun to pursue a college degree there, was telling Shorris that the humanities—
the study of human constructs and concerns—provided a
moral alternative to the street.

An odd idea to say the least. How could visits to a museum
help a poor teenager raise himself out of poverty? How could
Plato or Shakespeare lead anyone out of a life of violence
and deprivation? It would seem that job training or political
organizing was the way out of poverty. But Niecie was saying that no one could step out of the soul-constricting circumstances of poverty without first learning to reflect on his
or her place in society. Of course, this perspective follows the
development of politics in ancient Greece, where reflection
on art, literature, drama, and philosophy taught citizens how
best to live their lives.

Challenged by this young prisoner's theory, Shorris went to
the Clemente Family Guidance Center in lower Manhattan,
which provides counseling to some of the city's poorest citizens. He proposed a year-long, college-level course in the
humanities to be held in Clemente's conference room. He
recruited faculty with the level of knowledge and prestige of
professors that the most talented students might encounter
at Harvard, Yale, Princeton. And then he recruited students.
The students had to be between 18 and 35. They had to have
an income of less than 150% of the official poverty threshold. And they had to be able to read a tabloid newspaper.

Fifty prospective students showed up for thirty available
slots. Of the thirty who were admitted, the oldest was a Lat-
ina mother of five who said she regularly answered her door
with a butcher knife in her hand. The next eldest was a

recovering addict. Both of them were in their thirties. The rest of the students were in their twenties. Shorris began the course by telling them they had been cheated because rich people learned the humanities and they didn't. He told them that the humanities are a foundation for getting along in the world, for thinking, for learning how to reflect on society instead of just reacting to whatever force is turned against you. He told them that study of the humanities will make them rich, not in money, but in life.

Between October and May, the students learned about and discussed art, literature, history, mathematics, science, and philosophy. They worked on three metal tables set up in the family guidance center's conference room. Of the thirty who began the course, sixteen finished it, and fourteen earned credit from Bard College. A year after graduation, ten of the graduates were either attending four-year colleges or going to nursing school. The others were attending community colleges or working full time—all but one. She had been fired from her job in a fast food restaurant for trying to start a union. What did they get out of the course? This might best be illustrated by a call Shorris received halfway through the course. The call was from a student named David, who was generally good-natured, but had a quick temper and a history of violent behavior. Throughout the course, David had been a good student who had made interesting connections between the humanities and daily life. When he called his teacher to say that he'd had a little problem at work, Shorris felt sure David was calling from jail.

David described a situation with a co-worker who had teased him about his sex life until he wanted to punch her. When Shorris asked what had happened, David said he asked himself what Socrates would do and then reasoned that his co-worker's envy of his active social life was not his problem after all. The power of moral reasoning gave David a handle on the situation—a handle that helped him lift himself up.

That brand of reasoning is the topic of a fascinating book describing the ways philosophy can help us develop ethical, community-friendly businesses and corporations like Smock Fansler Construction and Duke Realty. The book, which is written by Tom Morris, a former philosophy professor at Notre Dame, is called *If Aristotle Ran General Motors*. Tom Morris reasons that if Aristotle ran General Motors, there are a few things he would get straight right off the bat.

If Aristotle ran General Motors, he would rely on the ancient verities that continue to have crucial meaning for our times. He would create businesses that reflect and nurture the four dimensions of human experience—Truth, Beauty, Goodness, and Unity.

Not only is truth the best basis for productive relationships, no firmer foundation for excellence can be built. There are

If Aristotle ran General Motors, he would rely on the ancient verities that continue to have crucial meaning for our times.

three kinds of excellence both for individuals and for corporations.

There is the zero-sum game version of excellence, the top-dog model, in which someone only wins if everyone else loses. This model is problematic if all the thinking it promotes is adversarial and individualistic in nature. It is better to develop a less destructively competitive conception of excellence.

The second kind of excellence is best expressed by an old Hindu proverb: "There is nothing noble in being superior to another person. The true nobility is in being superior to your previous self." This comparative growth model of excellence is a much healthier model of competition, but it too has problems. It tends to be unduly self-centered and thus can blind us to opportunities that would help us more fully develop our potentialities for excellence.

Those opportunities can best be exploited within a *collaborative partnership conception of excellence*. And this is a model businesses across the country are adopting. Personal excellence is always to one extent or another relational. Corporate excellence is even more so. Our families, our friends, our mentors, and our colleagues inspire us to be the best we can be.

More than any other form of excellence, collaboration is founded on a premise of truthful relations and mutual respect. It requires leaders to become learners and followers to become teachers. Collaborative thinking requires the guidance of good competitive and comparative thinking, but it takes this thinking further.

If truth is the basis of the most productive conceptions of corporate excellence, where does beauty fit into best business practices? It's very simply a matter of appreciation. Environments and business practices that let employees know they are appreciated and that their need for aesthetically pleasing surroundings is respected go a long way toward enhancing productivity and performance. This is a principle we rely on heavily at IU.

The campus environment has great potential for stimulating the interest and imagination of our staff, students, and faculty. And that in itself soothes the soul, calms the spirit, and is an education in its own right. Our beloved chancellor, Dr. Herman B. Wells, repeatedly stressed his conviction that exposure to beauty, nature, and the arts is a central part of a complete education. He has often said that the environment on a university campus should provide an aesthetic and educational dimension. He believed that, wherever the eye rested, it should see something beautiful, something uplifting.

I couldn't agree more.

At IU, we also try to cultivate a family atmosphere—even though our family is a big one that includes some 92,000 stu-

> *The campus environment has great potential for stimulating the interest and imagination of our staff, students, and faculty. And that in itself soothes the soul, calms the spirit, and is an education in its own right.*

dents, 9,800 staff, and 4,600 faculty members. Creating organizations based on values that make for strong friendships and durable family ties makes real sense, especially in our mobile society where the workplace serves as a kind of extended family. One might add to the common ingredients of business success, such as leadership, empowerment, quality, service, and teamwork, qualities that describe ideal friendship or family life, such as appreciation, trust, forgiveness, communication, and, yes, love. The IU family embraces these values because we know that these are the qualities that encourage people to become deeply rooted in the values of an organization. They provide the soil in which we can grow to our fullest potential—the soil that cultivates sustainable excellence. As Tom Morris notes, they create a canvas for real human artistry.

And what of goodness, where does it fit into the life of the corporation and its employees? The naturalist philosopher Henry David Thoreau once said that goodness is the only investment that never fails. Nevertheless, there's a pervasive attitude in the business community that ethics and values are all about restraint and denial, not about active and productive investments. What are the moral rules that dominate modern business practices? The most cynical would argue that the dominant ethic is do whatever you need to do to succeed as long as you don't get caught. But that rule of conduct undercuts the very purpose of ethics, which is to preserve the ability of spiritually healthy and intellectually vital people to work together in harmonious relationships. That sort of relationship requires both wisdom and virtue.

Kant's categorical imperative, which commands us to treat other people as ends, rather than as means, is the best bedrock ethic for business practice. It is remarkably like the golden rule. I find it fascinating that nearly every culture and religion has a version of this all-encompassing ethic.

I am reminded of the story of the ancient Rabbi who was challenged to speak all of the wisdom he knew while standing on one foot. He took up the challenge and recited something very like the golden rule. For a Taoist, the ultimate ethos for relationships sounds like this: "View your neighbor's grain as your own grain, and your neighbor's loss as your own loss." For a Muslim, it sounds like this: "Let none of you treat his brother in a way he himself would not like to be treated. No one of you is a believer until he loves for his brother what he loves for himself."

All of these formulations have the same effect. They help us cultivate a moral imagination; they help us reflect on the consequences of our actions. In the words of the great old bluesman Brownie McGhee, "If there's one thing/ that I know for sure/ it is that you're going to reap/ just what it is that you sow."

And finally, unity has a valuable place in any successful corporation that chooses to treat its employees as whole people or in any culture that chooses to educate its young people for life, not just for work. We must create corporations—and educational institutions—that enhance individuality but also inspire us to work toward a common purpose, that enlarge our sense of personal and corporate dignity, but at the same time remind us of our humility.

An old bit of Hasidic wisdom expresses this idea perfectly. It says, "A person should always wear a garment with two pockets. In one pocket, there should be a note which reads, 'I am but dust and ashes.' In the other pocket, there should be a paper which says, 'for me the world was created.'"

If we can create organizations, both in business and in education, based on this magical combination of human values, organizations that speak both to our nobility and our humility, we can't go wrong. Such organizations will indeed make the world a better place, a place populated by caring, respectful people, not those prone to violence.

Thank you.

The Nancy Hanks Lecture on Arts and Public Policy[5]

Wendy Wasserstein

Playwright and contributing editor, New Woman; *born in Brooklyn and raised in Manhattan; B.A., Mount Holyoke College; M.F.A., Yale School of Drama; formerly contributing editor,* New York Woman *magazine and* Harper's Bazaar; *taught at Columbia University and New York University; authored plays* The Sisters Rosensweig; Uncommon Women and Others; Isn't It Romantic; Miami; Drive, She Said; The Heidi Chronicles; An American Daughter; The Object of My Affection; *published* Bachelor Girls; The Heidi Chronicles and Other Plays; The Sisters Rosensweig; *and* Pamela's First Musical; *for* The Heidi Chronicles, *1989, awarded Pulitzer Prize, New York Drama Critics Circle Prize, the Drama Desk Award, the Outer Critics Circle Award, the Susan Smith Blackburn Prize, and the Tony Award; serves on Very Special Arts Playwright Discovery Artists Selection Committee, Council of the Dramatists Guild, Board of the British American Arts Association, the MacDowell Colony Board, Theatre Development Fund's President's Council; spokesperson for Kid's Night on Broadway; honorary doctorate, Mount Holyoke College.*

Editors' introduction: Ms. Wendy Wasserstein gave the 1999 Nancy Hanks Lecture in the Eisenhower Theater of The John F. Kennedy Center for the Performing Arts, sponsored by Philip Morris Companies Inc., and presented by Americans for the Arts, the national organization dedicated to building a better America through the arts. Nancy Hanks, for whom the lecture series is named, served as president of Americans for the Arts, 1968 to 1969, and chair of the National Endowment for the Arts, 1969 to 1977. The Lecture honors Nancy Hanks' memory and provides an opportunity for public discourse at the highest level on the importance of the arts and culture to our nation's well-being. In her speech, Wasserstein maintained that "the arts reflect profoundly the most democratic credo, the belief in an individual vision or voice," that "to limit the arts is in fact elitist."

Wendy Wasserstein's speech: Thank you. It's truly an honor to be here today. I've always wanted to be in *Full Moon,* and this is the only way I figured out how to do it. So in two hours, I'll be on that moon with the great Bill Irwin.

---

5.   Delivered in Washington, D.C., on March 15, 1999, at 6:30 p.m. Reprinted by permission of Wendy Wasserstein.

The other night at a New York dinner party at Liz Robbins' house, the arts lobbyist, I sat next to Jim Robinson, the chairman of *Scholastic Magazine*, who said to me, "I hear you're giving the Nancy Hanks lecture." He went on to tell me that Nancy Hanks was on his board and what an extraordinary woman she was. He said, "She single-handedly changed arts funding in this country, and she also taught me a very important lesson. She told me you have to know when to ask for help." So for the extraordinary Nancy Hanks, and her legacy, I hope tonight can offer some deep appreciation and a little help from a friend.

When I look back on my own childhood, I would say in many ways the arts saved my life. Well, if not saved then gave it all the shape and a purpose. I'm often asked how I started writing plays. I can assure you that my nice Jewish parents never said to me, "Wendy, darling, please, please go into the not-for-profit theater. Whatever you do, we want you to have a life that is as financially insecure as possible. Please date actors. Rely on the kindness of critics and for heaven's sake, have no responsible health insurance."

Well this was definitely not the message sent to me. However, when I was young, my parents did send me to dancing school for the usual ballet and tap dancing lessons in the hope that I would become well-rounded. I've always thought that my well-roundedness went directly to my hips.

Actually my dancing school was the June Taylor School of Dance, home of the Jackie Gleason dancers. I've often told friends that I'm not the only person I know whose seminal influences were June Taylor and Robert Brustein. After dancing school, my parents always took me, in their words, "to take in a play." We saw a very eclectic mix of Broadway and off-Broadway. I will never forget sitting in the front row of Edward Albee's *Seascape*, with my parents, Morris and Lola.

It was also during a performance of *No Time For Sergeants*, when I was ten, that I began asking myself why aren't there any girls, who seem to be like me, on stage? Frankly, that was when I formed an esthetic. For children, theater opens possibilities for the imagination. All you need are people and a light switch.

At about the same time my parents took me to the theater, my older sister, Sandra, began bringing me to the New York City Ballet. We gasped at Edward Villela and Jacques D'Amboise in the *Apollo* and *Stars and Stripes*. For me, the epitome of feminine grace was not the Hollywood idols of that time, like Sandra Dee, but the glorious ballerinas I saw on the City Center stage.

Whereas adolescent life was completely chaotic, in the ballet, passion and exuberance were brilliantly contained. In fact, I still find one of the greatest solaces in life going to the ballet. In a world of spin, image makers and manipulated perceptions, the discipline and artistry of dance reminds me

For children, theater opens possibilities for the imagination. All you need are people and a light switch.

that there is a form of human achievement that is unarguably and profoundly true.

I believe it is impossible to separate the arts from education. As a child, I was diagnosed as someone with a reading problem at an early age. Words in books flew around the room for me. And I always thought I later wrote plays because there were no footnotes and no one could see my spelling or punctuation.

But at my elementary school there was a dancing teacher who took us to Prospect Park with a drum and called out colors as we danced. Of course, in retrospect, it sounds like a Brooklyn version of *Summerhill*, but for me it was an outlet of exuberance and creativity. We also put on plays at our school. Mini-versions of Shakespeare. I'll never forget Caesar appearing in his mother's butterfly, Martex sheets. And I can still play Mendelssohn's score for *A Midsummer's Night Dream* on a triangle, though I'm not often asked to.

Most of the students from those early productions did not become playwrights or actors. But we did learn that there was a form of work in which people come together to create an entity in which they all deeply care about. We also learned discipline. If you rehearsed and studied your lines, ultimately you'd have a better time.

Arts for children is not simply icing on the cake. It is a way of including everyone in a joint and joyous venture. Moreover, for those children with imaginations, it's a way to build confidence in their uniqueness.

I am often asked how my first play was done. Frankly, my mother, Lola, was walking down the street and ran into Louise Roberts, the former secretary at the June Taylor School of Dance. Louise asked my mother, "How's Wendy?" Lola began hyperventilating, "Wendy isn't going to law school, she's not marrying a lawyer, and now she's writing plays!"

I think to soothe my mother's spirits, Louise told her that she now was in charge of a new not-for-profit dancing school called the Clark Center which was across the hall from Playwrights Horizons at the Y on Eighth Avenue and 52nd Street. She said she would give Bob Moss, the artistic director of that theater, my play. I have been associated with the theater now for twenty-five years.

I am telling you that story not to go on and on about my mother, which I could do at length, but to underline that my generation of playwrights has been nurtured by the not-for-profit system. I remember when Playwrights Horizons moved from the Y to 42nd Street and the former Maidman Playhouse. In fact, the Sex Institute of Technology was still upstairs.

We had a gala opening when Joan Mondale came to christen Theater Row. Not-for-profit arts institutions are often pioneers in urban revival. The new 42nd Street, the Disney-restored theaters and E walks would not be there today if

Arts for children is not simply icing on the cake. It is a way of including everyone in a joint and joyous venture. Moreover, for those children with imaginations, it's a way to build confidence in their uniqueness.

arts organizations, sponsored by the Endowments, local arts councils, and artistic directors, like Andre Bishop, had not taken the initiative to change the urban landscape.

Of course, standing before you today, I know I am preaching to the converted. I don't have to convince you of the importance of theater, dance or any of the performing arts, or that new plays in this country are nurtured in the not-for-profit system from Washington State, Seattle Rep, to this stage right here at the Kennedy Center.

You know that one of the few continuing national communities are those established every time an audience attends a live theatrical event. We laugh together, cry together, and listen together. You also know that, in a country obsessed with the millennium, the true character of a nation is defined by its cultural life. If we all know this, why are the arts in this country prone to slipping under a narrow definition, "Elitist?"

A few years ago, I came to Washington to lobby for individual grants to authors with a group called Poets and Writers. I came with the actors Melanie Griffith, Joanne Woodward, and the author, Walter Mosley. At that time, Jane Alexander, who had been on Broadway in my play *The Sisters Rosensweig*, was the chairwoman of the National Endowment for the Arts. At that point, the then-Speaker of the House had refused to meet with her. At a breakfast that morning, the Speaker arrived and told Miss Griffith if his novel was ever made into a film, he had two parts for her.

During coffee, I was asked to talk about my NEA grant. I mentioned that I had won a $12,000 grant in 1984 that aided me in completing my play, *The Heidi Chronicles*, and, in my mind, that was a small investment for a play that ran on Broadway for two years, toured the country for two years, and kept many people employed and many inner cities lively. The Speaker looked up at me and said, "You know Arthur Murray never needed a grant to write a play."

Now from my years of dancing school, I know who Arthur Murray is. I even know his autobiography is called *Put a Little Fun in Your Life—Try Dancing*. But I was quiet. I knew we needed the funding. On my way out, the Speaker turned to me and said, "I'm terribly sorry, I meant Arthur Miller." I replied, "Yes, and he did have a grant. It was called the WPA."

It's a good story and by the way, we did save those grants. But it's not as relevant as the congressman I met that day who told me, sure, his daughter loved her ballet class but that didn't mean the government should fund it. The arts, he said, were extracurricular. Furthermore, they were no longer the popular culture. This is far more disturbing than the Murray/Miller controversy.

Not-for-profit arts in America are a $37 billion dollar industry. Individually we read statistics that opera is thriving, and museum exhibits have given Jackson Pollock and Van Gogh rock star status. So if everything is on the upswing, why is there still a lingering fear that the arts remain not a priority but a national extracurricular activity?

I remember the year I won a Guggenheim grant for playwriting. I felt enormous pride as if I had received a mandate to continue to work. But when I called my father and told him I had won an $18,000 grant, he said to me, "No daughter of mine is going on welfare!"

How much do we really value our artists? Are we giving them a message that to be successful is to find approval in the commercial arena?

It's another funny story. But the truth is that, for a grant with the distinguished reputation of a Guggenheim, it is a very small amount of money when you consider what a first year lawyer or marketing researcher is paid in our country. It reflects a question of priorities. How much do we really value our artists? Are we giving them a message that to be successful is to find approval in the commercial arena? Has the word "elitist" crept in because the American public has been skewed to believe that artists don't work for a living? The arts, for all their strength, remain valuable. We are a constant source of hot buttons and politicizations. At the slightest whiff of controversy, we are forced to fear that all funding will disappear. Anyone who speaks out about the NEA will be asked inevitably about Maplethorpe, Karen Finley, and now, I'm sure, sub-commandante Marcos.

The point is, if there was a clear-cut commitment to the arts, then we actually could have a dialogue. Arts administrators are constantly forced to second-guess censors. Arts are by their nature controversial. Except in a society of socialist realists. Furthermore, our hot buttons seem to be about books and plays that those who hold the most adamant opinions have never seen. Bill Ivy, backstage, just told me the tide is turning. He had just met with 37 Congress people. Well, let's hope this is just the beginning of a big-time, permanent comeback.

The arts reflect profoundly the most democratic credo, the belief in an individual vision or voice. Our popular culture on the other hand, be it Hollywood or television, is based on a common denominator. When a movie previews, an audience votes on note cards if they did or didn't like the ending. A producer will reshoot a film in the hopes that he can fulfill the audience's expectation and sell more tickets. On the other hand, I remember distinctly an evening during a preview performance of *The Heidi Chronicles* when Joan Allen asked me if I minded if she said an "a" instead of a "the" in a certain line. There is nowhere that respects the integrity of creation more than the arts.

At the O'Neill Theater Center conference every summer, Lloyd Richards would begin by saying the conference was devoted to the playwright and to each one of us finding his or her distinctive voice. The arts' belief in human potential gives each of us—both the audience and the creator—pride in our society's ability to nurture individuals.

Is it elitist not to search for a common denominator? Is it elitist to believe in an individual's ability to craft his or her talent? At another dinner recently, the eminent sociologist Robert Mentor said to me, "Why is it that individual excellence is celebrated in sports but questioned in the arts?" Why is it that we sit in awe of the basketball superstar Michael Jordan and of course, Michael Jordan, the chairman of this board, but we believe that artists with similar outstanding talents should not be funded?

Why can't we celebrate the excellence of our artists without the undertow of elitism? There is no reason for our arts culture to be siphoned off to a marginal position from our national culture. No one wants to see Xeroxes every night but no one wants to see *Lethal Weapon IV* every night either. The truth is the national culture is a texture of both. But that will become more and more one-sided unless we make the arts a part of the next generation of Americans' lives.

I believe I became an artist because I had the good fortune of being taken to plays when I was young. Coming of age at a time when women's voices were suddenly being heard was further incentive to create.

The habit of the arts as a source of inspiration starts young. It is the job of all of us here to make them accessible to young Americans. It is also, I believe, the responsibility of all American artists to somehow contribute beyond their own work to the future of their art form.

Because the theater meant so much to me in my youth, I started a program at the Theater Development Fund this year to take New York City high school students to plays. My theory was I would put them in touch with my world, and I would see if it had any relevancy to them. I wanted students who were bright but had no previous interest in the theater, getting an agent, or meeting Drew Barrymore.

We chose eight DeWitt Clinton High School seniors, a mostly low-income high school in the Bronx. DeWitt Clinton, by the way, is the alma mater of Arthur Gelb from the *New York Times*, Neil Simon, and Ralph Lauren. This is the next generation. Our goal was to see eight plays, have post-play discussions, and for them to keep a journal.

The first play we saw was *On the Town*. Afterwards, we went out for pizza. They loved the music. They thought it was really modern. I told them who Leonard Bernstein was. As we talked, they told me they liked it a lot. I explained Betty Comden and Adolph Green were New Yorkers who had written this show when they were each twenty-four. At the end of our afternoon, I asked them if they would recommend the show to friends, and they said to me, "No, it's not cool to go to plays."

Not cool to go to plays is all of our issue. Of course it's not cool to go to plays if the price is $60 a ticket. No high school student from a low-income or middle-income family could recommend that. But it's also not cool if you're told in advance that it had nothing to do with your world. A bright boy in my group told me his friends made fun of him when he signed up to be in our pilot project. "What do you want to do that for?" What's not cool is when the arts are perceived as something that's "good" for you like gym or remedial math. In fact, I'd say over the past twenty years the image of gym has wildly improved while the image of the arts has dimmed.

The arts are the soul of a nation. They are also a culture's reflection of itself. In the arts, the students from DeWitt Clinton could find the power to express themselves and the world they hope to create. For both the not-for-profit sector and the profit entertainment industry, it is for all our benefit to have a generation of Americans who will each individually question ethics, morality, character, humor, and what beauty really is.

For every congressman who would say the arts are elitist, I would answer museums, plays and dance are not responsible for violence in elementary schools or hopelessness in adolescence. If the American family is changing and socio-religious structure is changing, one sure way to find identity, commitment, and joy is through the arts.

There has never been a time when there has been more information about weekend grosses, how much money movie stars are getting for their next picture, or what Gwyneth Paltrow did or didn't eat last night. But these are not the ideas that form the conscience of a nation.

I next took my DeWitt Clinton seniors to see the musical *Parade* based on the book by Alfred Uhry about the lynching of Leo Frank in Atlanta. Afterwards, we sat backstage at Lincoln Center as the stage manager, Roy Harris, explained to them the mechanics of the scenery. We talked about the play, its theme of anti-Semitism, and the entire issue of prejudice and race. They told me they had no idea that it was possible to lynch a white man in Atlanta. They told me it gave them a new perspective on their world.

When I told them that Hollywood filmmakers who determine which audiences will go to which film would never assume that they would like *Parade*, they told me, "They don't know anything about us! They think they do, but they don't."

The arts give a generation the ability to define its own time. It seems to me, on a very grassroots level, the future survival of the arts in this country may have something to do with the artists, playwrights, and dancers opening their worlds to the next generation. If painters could take eight DeWitt Clinton students to a museum for a year, if a dancer could take stu-

For both the not-for-profit sector and the profit entertainment industry, it is for all our benefit to have a generation of Americans who will each individually question ethics, morality, character, humor, and what beauty really is.

dents in Chicago to performances, if a musician could take sophomores to concerts in Atlanta, we might, on a fundamental level, rebuild a constituency and eliminate the curse word of "elitism."

There is nothing more inspiring for students than to meet an artist who has managed to make a life of creation. Whether the students become playwrights or merely learn to love their work and think for themselves. And, frankly, there's nothing more inspirational for an artist than being in touch with the future.

Recently I read an article about a playwright's work which said the author writes well but writes wrong. The arts, our culture's form of self-expression, seems to consistently get bogged down in issues of what is right and wrong, correct and incorrect, for us to do and say. There seems to be an impossible agenda on all sides that the arts must live up to. Perhaps it is finally time to celebrate excellence, to celebrate craft, discipline, ideas, and creation.

Not only am I a recipient of a NEA grant, but I have also been the chairperson of two NEA panels. The panel system works. Extraordinary plays have emerged from grants made to those authors. Maybe it's time we stop constantly turning inwardly fearful and, instead, figure out a way to move stronger into the future. The entire budget for grants to individual authors could not buy a Hollywood producer's summer share.

We are not dealing with an obvious national mandate, and it's time we did. A national campaign, co-sponsored by a partnership of the entertainment industry and the not-for-profit arts agencies, could vastly improve the image of the arts. The world of movies, television, graphic design, and high technology is all fed by those of us who developed a specific voice or craft in the not-for-profit arena. If the profit world is so enthused by our achievements, isn't it time they give back to initiators?

Once, when advocating arts in the school, a funder asked me how could I possibly believe the arts were more important than health or science? For a moment I felt like Marie Antoinette demanding, "Let them eat ballet." But frankly I don't believe the arts are extracurricular. A society is defined by its culture and that culture begins in early education. We must respect the potential of our children as opposed to deciding that only a few deserve to experience the joy of creation. The decision to limit the arts is in fact elitist.

Finally, there must be a more creative form of subsidy. Recently I was at a dinner for the Guggenheim Foundation in which Vartan Gregorian and the novelist Michael Cunningham both said that receiving that grant changed their lives. In other words, incentive goes a long way. If this society won't support its artists, or can't support its artists, at least

A national campaign, co-sponsored by a partnership of the entertainment industry and the not-for-profit arts agencies, could vastly improve the image of the arts.

we could signal to them our hopes for their work and our support.

Being an artist is an unbearably lonely job. Having an incentive for continuing work is one way to keep a community, if not fully subsidized, then, at least, recognized. In a world of polls and positioning, the arts remain the true arenas in which an individual can fearlessly look at the world and say, "Here's where we're going." The arts, our benchmark, and popular culture are separating. It's our challenge to bring them back together again.

The task of all of us here tonight is to give the next generation of artists and Americans a chance to find and define the character of this nation. In a country so profoundly dedicated to the individual vision and freedom of interpretation, the potential is magnificent. The arts remain the soul of this country and, with all of our support and the legacy of Nancy Hanks, it will be the source of an inspired vision for the next century.

Thank you very much.

Cumulative Speaker Index: 1990-1999

A cumulative speaker index to the volumes of *Representative American Speeches* for the years 1937-1938 through 1959-1960 appears in the 1959-1960 volume; for the years 1960-1961 through 1969-1970, see the 1969-1970 volume; for the years 1970-1971 through 1979-1980, see the 1979-1980 volume; and for the years 1980-1981 through 1989-1990, see the 1989-1990 volume.

Index